A HISTORY
OF THE MISHNAIC LAW
OF DAMAGES

PART TWO

STUDIES IN JUDAISM IN LATE ANTIQUITY

EDITED BY

JACOB NEUSNER

VOLUME THIRTY-FIVE

A HISTORY
OF THE MISHNAIC LAW
OF DAMAGES

PART TWO

A HISTORY OF THE MISHNAIC LAW OF DAMAGES

BY

JACOB NEUSNER

University Professor
The Ungerleider Distinguished Scholar of Judaic Studies
Brown University

PART TWO

BABA MESIA

TRANSLATION AND EXPLANATION

Eugene, Oregon

Wipf and Stock Publishers
199 W 8th Ave, Suite 3
Eugene, OR 97401

A History of the Mishnaic Law of Damages, Part 2
Baba Mesia
By Neusner, Jacob
Copyright©1983 by Neusner, Jacob
ISBN 13: 978-1-55635-366-6
ISBN 10: 1-55635-366-9
Publication date 3/20/2007
Previously published by E. J. Brill, 1983

For my brother
Judge Frederick D. Neusner
U.S. Department of Labor

TABLE OF CONTENTS

Preface IX
Abbreviations and Bibliography XV
Transliterations XXX

Introduction 1
    I. Baba Mesia Chapter One 16
    II. Baba Mesia Chapter Two 26
    III. Baba Mesia Chapter Three 41
    IV. Baba Mesia Chapter Four 53
    V. Baba Mesia Chapter Five 66
    VI. Baba Mesia Chapter Six 97
    VII. Baba Mesia Chapter Seven 109
    VIII. Baba Mesia Chapter Eight 121
    IX. Baba Mesia Chapter Nine 132
    X. Baba Mesia Chapter Ten 149

Index 156
Index to Biblical and Talmudic References 156
General Index 162

PREFACE

Baba Mesia stands at the head of the Mishnah's tractates, because it is exceptionally interesting and exhibits some of Mishnah's most disciplined and sustained formal constructions. Whole chapters adhere to a single syntactic pattern and express conceptions of unusual cogency and conceptual sophistication. Tosefta to this tractate for its part undertakes an unusually ambitious project of amplification and secondary expansion, as well as providing its usual supplementary information. Along with its companions, fore and aft, Baba Mesia forms the introductory curriculum for Mishnaic and Talmudic studies. The reason is not difficult to imagine. The framers of the curriculum choose for beginners those tractates which speak of commonplace things and express accessible and everyday principles.

My commentary in no way claims to command the heights of the historical exegesis of this tractate. It purports only to say what the tractate means in its original formulation, that is, what the people who make things up this way wish to say in their own day and to their own contemporaries. The character of this translation and explanation in detail expresses the purpose of the larger work of which it is part.

To present *a history of the Mishnaic law*, I have to give an account of the document itself, first of all to state what I believe Mishnah says, in a rendition, in English, as close to the formal and syntactical character of the Hebrew as English permits. This I do in the translation, which itself is a commentary in its word-choices, patterns, and its version of the division of sentences into stichs, of paragraphs into sentences, and of chapters into paragraphs. (But this last depends, for the convenience of the reader, on the printed text of Hanokh Albeck.) The translation makes no important contribution to the explanation of realia or the identification of various places, persons, and things, mentioned in the document. What it does contribute is the first translation of a rabbinic document to take full and faithful account of the rigidly formalized, public and anonymous character of Mishnaic language. I provide complete form-analytical translation of Mishnah and of Tosefta. The *explanation* is rather different from any of its predecessors, so different that it must be called "explanation." For if what have been done in the past are called commentaries, this cannot be represented as a commentary at all.

What I do not say invariably is more important than what I choose to discuss. By radically revising and abbreviating the established exegetical agendum, I believe I have made my richest contribution to the interpretation of Mishnah. This is in two aspects.

First, I have tried to force Mishnah to serve as its own commentary. I do so by relying heavily upon those formal and even substantive traits of the document which serve to provide a clear account of Mishnah's meaning and message. I pay careful attention to matters of form and formulation. We shall see time and again that principally through setting up a contrast, placing of a phrase, for emphasis, or other obvious linguistic and syntactical modes of highlighting its meaning, Mishnah serves as its own first, and therefore best, commentary. Second, I have revised what I believe to be the definition of those issues appropriate to, and even acceptable for, exegesis of Mishnah in particular, as a singular document of its period. This last point requires some amplification. There are two sides to the problem of explaining what Mishnah means. Both of them are generated by one absolutely false conception, or, more accurately, a single misleading analogy.

The first problem is the bringing to Mishnah of issues clearly extraneous to its original meaning. This set of comments plainly is needless because the issues are generated by later problems and questions. They are quite naturally addressed to Mishnah, however, by people who assume Mishnah speaks to them and therefore must address issues of importance to them. This ahistorical approach is possibly valid for the generating and unfolding of law. But it is not correct for the interpretation of what Mishnah as a concrete document meant to the particular people who made it up.

The second problem is corollary, namely, the placing of Mishnah's materials into the context of a whole legal system. When Mishnah is read in a larger framework than Mishnah, we are prevented from seeing Mishnah's materials as a coherent corpus on their own. This latter approach to Mishnah is absolutely opposite to our purpose. For I propose to state, and, later, historically to account for the unfolding of, the law of Mishnah *in particular*. If we assume that Mishnah constitutes a single document—and the internally harmonious formal and intellectual traits of Mishnah require that we make that assumption—then we have no choice but to honor the limits of the document when attempting to describe and interpret it.

Until now all commentators to Mishnah have taken only a limited interest in the shape and structure of Mishnah itself. It goes without saying, none has asked a historical-exegetical question ("What does this mean to the person who originally said it *and* who did not know what his successors would want to say about it?") to begin with. For their problem was a different one. It was dictated by a social and intellectual task quite separate from ours. They addressed themselves not to the exegesis and expression (let alone the worldview) of a given document. Nor could they imagine the notion that the laws in their hands formed discrete units of information. Quite the contrary, they began with the conception of a completely unitary legal system, expressed in discrete documents originating in diverse places and time, but nonetheless all together forming a timeless, seamless conceptual structure. Their task was defined by this rather platonic metaphor, namely, to relate each of the parts to the transcendent whole, and to force the whole to encompass all of the parts. It is not, as I originally thought, the ahistorical (or, anti-historical) and harmonistic purpose of the earlier exegetes which made their Mishnah-commentaries so intellectually prolix, indeed, indifferent and irrelevant to the text under discussion. That is a misunderstanding which it has taken me many years to recognize. It is, rather, that the earlier exegetes presuppose something much more profound, much less susceptible to articulation. This is, as I said, the construct, "Jewish law," or "*halakhah*." Of this construct, to them Mishnah constitutes an important component. In their mind the correct approach to Mishnah's interpretation is to relate its *halakhah* to other *halakhah*, that is, to "*the* law." This harmonistic, atomistic and yet encompassing approach is natural for people who keep the law and who take for granted their audience wants to know *the* law, even though not all of the law of a given document is practical and practiced. But the point of interest is clear, and it explains to them what is relevant and what is not. Since social context and intellectual framework define what is relevant, their essays—to us, total chaos—to them are orderly and reliable. But the fact remains that in a different world, their language of exegesis is gibberish, just as is ours to them.

When we realize this fact, we understand why it is that the distinctive, documentary character of Mishnah itself has attracted so little interest. Mishnah as such has failed to define the boundaries of an appropriate exegesis. The definitive canon awaiting explanation and extension is other. That is to say, Mishnah is part of that other canon, the law in general. The canon awaiting interpretation is shaped by Mishnah, only in so far as Mishnah presents its share of legal statement—of *the* law. Consequently Mishnah is read not from whole to part, as a sequence of divisions, tractates, and chapters.

This I am the first to do, as the formal character of my work makes clear. And this is the right way to approach the document. But by others Mishnah has been and is read essentially as a mass of individual sentences, tens of thousands of bits of legal information, all of them part of, and arrayed against, a larger construct, *the* law, and each of them to be placed into juxtaposition with other bits and pieces of *the* law. So, as I said, the notion of "the *halakhah*" obliterates the character of Mishnah as an autonomous document and at best allows Mishnah the status of an authoritative *source* of law.

The same treatment, of course, is accorded to Tosefta, the two Talmuds, the diverse legal exegetical compilations, Sifra and Sifré, for example, and to much else. The result is that at each point exegetes tend to tell us "everything about everything," so to speak. It is not because they are confused, even though the results are confusing. For despite the fact that their commentaries appear to be not merely allusive, but irrelevant to the text at hand, and even though they are rich in unprovoked questions, artificial dilemmas, and invented solutions, the reason is that the fundamental theory of the document requires precisely those procedures which are followed. If, to take a current and choice example, Saul Lieberman's *Tosefta Ki-Fshutah* ("a comprehensive commentary to the Tosefta") treats Tosefta as an excuse for long disquisitions on diverse philological and legal questions, the reason is that that is precisely how Lieberman thinks the work should be done. And the reason, I believe, is not merely the ahistorical character of the mind-set of the traditionalist, but, as indicated, because of the more profound conviction as to the character of the law and its diverse documentary expressions.

The result to date has been an account of immense philological and legal value. We are able to explain a great deal about the meaning and intention of the sentences of the law, as found (as it happens) in Mishnah and Tosefta (and the rest of rabbinical literature). We can link together diverse conceptions and rules appearing here, there, everywhere; they are formed into a single fabric, even (in the monumental codes of the law) a seamless one. We have what is besought, which is the power to draw upon, and apply to specific circumstances, the whole wisdom and weight of the law. That is to say, the established exegetical program has succeeded in doing precisely what it set out to do. The tasks originally defined by the conception of "*the* law" have been carried out.

The one thing we cannot say on the basis of the available commentaries, both "traditional" and "scientific" (both are wildly inappropriate terms!) is to state clearly what it is that Mishnah (to take our example) wishes to say, in *its* own setting, within the limits of *its* own redactional framework, upon the subjects chosen by *it*, and for purposes defined within the mind of those specific people, its authors, who flourished in one concrete social setting. Reading the document by itself, in its historical context and therefore outside of its atemporal, *halakhic* context, requires a different approach. That approach is represented, I firmly believe, in the pages of this book. It is given by this explanation.

So the need for these volumes of translation and explanation is dictated not solely by the concluding, systemic description and interpretation. That was my conception for *Holy Things* and *Women*, and, in retrospect, I think I was too apologetic. Nor is the issue of the work solely the *historical*—primary, original—meaning of the text in the minds of the people who so phrased their ideas and arranged their sentences as to give us these, and not some other, expressions of their ideas.

The decisive and determinative issues are simply, What is the Mishnah? What is its shape and structure? What is the agendum of its law? How is that agendum to be delineated and interpreted as a complete and exhaustive account of what Mishnah wishes to say? These questions are answered in this book and its fellows.

The answers I give here are to these questions, not to those many others already dealt with, with greater or less measure of success, in the established and received exegetical tradition. People who want to know what "the tradition" has to say are not apt to open these books and stay on to study them in any event. Other sorts of readers will find their way to these pages. I do not think they will find the methods and suppositions alien or the results unsatisfying. I began this project weighed down by humility before the intellectual achievements of others who have studied these same problems. I conclude it with greater understanding, and not less appreciation, of their work. But at the same time I see much more clearly that, so far as they claim to speak about Mishnah, they have not done what they promised. So far as I claim to present and briefly to explain what it is that Mishnah, in its limits, for its purposes, to its chosen audience, wishes to say, I do what I claim to do.

That fact accounts for the traits of the translation and the character of the explanation—its brevity, severe limitation of the exegetical agendum, and above all, its insistence upon Mishnah's form and formulary expression as definitive of Mishnah's meaning. This is not meant to excuse or apologize. I have worked on Mishnah since 1972, and the last of these books is apt to appear not much before 1984. Twelve years are a long time to devote to a single document, however complex, when one's interest is in only a limited aspect of said document. For, when all is said and done, my real interest remains focused upon the history and structure of nascent rabbinic Judaism. That means the main work is yet before me, not behind. These twelve years and forty-three books of mine, not to mention many more years of work and many more books of my doctoral students, all are meant only to prepare the way for a different sort of analysis entirely. This is an approach to Mishnah which is at once more historical, more religious-philosophical, and more religious-historical than has even been attempted. I do not know whether it will succeed.

It remains to thank a few among the many to whom much is owed. First of all, I owe thanks to the John Simon Guggenheim Memorial Foundation for awarding to me yet a second Guggenheim Fellowship for 1979-1980 to facilitate completion of my *History of the Mishnaic Law of Appointed Times* and *History of the Mishnaic Law of Damages*. This recognition of the interest of the scholarly world in the results of my work is much appreciated. It also is important to me. At the same time I owe thanks to

Brown University for a second extraordinary research leave, awarded in the same connection.

Second, I wish to thank Brown University for paying the costs of typing these manuscripts. Provost Maurice Glicksman and Associate Dean Frank Durand received without complaint a shower of typists' bills. In an age of exceedingly painful budgetary choices, they loyally and generously paid my typists and did so promptly and courteously. This everyday and humble expression of their belief in the worth of my project is just as precious to me as those research fellowships and honorary doctorates which have come my way.

Third, I should be remiss if I did not mention by name the junior colleagues who in my graduate seminar read their work and heard about mine, the graduate students of the period in which this part of the project was coming to completion: Leonard Gordon, Peter Haas, Martin Jaffee, and Alan Peck; and my former colleague, Richard Samuel Sarason, now at Hebrew Union College-Jewish Institute of Religion, Cincinnati. Since the work of all of these as well as of some of my former students is an integral part of this project, they in due course will make their own contributions as well.

Fourth, my colleagues in the Department of Religious Studies have provided a constructive and helpful framework for my teaching and scholarship. I must single out Professors Wendell S. Dietrich and Ernest S. Frerichs with thanks not only for exemplary collegiality but for friendship and love. Finally, after all these years, I have to mention and take note of the enthusiastic support of my children, Samuel Aaron, Eli Ephraim, Noam Mordecai Menahem, and Margalit Leah Berakhah, who were infants when the work began, and who approach maturity as it ends. I never hoped they would read these books, but I should want them to be proud of knowing that, when I was doing the work, they charmed and cheered my life. I could not have done this work without them—nor should I have wanted to. Let a veil of silence be drawn before the next, the best, for only silence can contain all that is felt, all that words cannot say, in homage to Suzanne Richter Neusner.

Since the three Babas contain whatever Mishnah has to offer as a code of law in any ordinary current sense, I dedicate each of the parts of the work to lawyers who have been important to my family and to me. This volume is dedicated to my brother, Judge Frederick D. Neusner, on the occasion of his appointment as an Administrative Law Judge of the U.S. Department of Labor and of his retirement as Assistant Attorney General of the State of Connecticut.

J.N.

Providence, Rhode Island
May 31, 1979.
5 Sivan 5739.
'Ereb Shabu'ot.

ABBREVIATIONS AND BIBLIOGRAPHY

Abrahams	= Israel Abrahams, "Sanhedrin," in J. Hastings, *Encyclopaedia of Religion and Ethics*, XI, 184-185.
AE	= *Tosafot* R. ʿAqiba Egger. From Mishnah, ed. Romm.
Ah.	= ʾAhilot
Albeck	= Ḥanokh Albeck, *Shishah sidré Mishnah. Seder Nez̧iqin* (Tel Aviv, 1952).
Albeck, *Acquisition*	= S. Albeck, "Acquisition," *Encyclopedia Judaica* 2:216-221.
Albeck, *Avot*	= S. Albeck, "Avot Nezikin," *Encyclopedia Judaica* 3:986-989.
Albeck, *Damages*	= S. Albeck, "Damages," *Encyclopedia Judaica* 5:1233-1236.
Albeck, *Debt*	= S. Albeck, "Assignment (of debt)," *Encyclopedia Judaica* 3:768-770.
Albeck, *Din*	= Shalom Albeck, *Diné ha-mamonot ba-Talmud* (Tel Aviv, 1976).
Albeck, *Gerama*	= S. Albeck, "Gerama and Garme," *Encyclopedia Judaica* 7:430-431.
Albeck, *Gift*	= S. Albeck, "Gift," *Encyclopedia Judaica* 7:560-563.
Albeck, *Lost*	= S. Albeck, "Lost Property," *Encyclopedia Judaica* 11:504-506.
Albeck, *Maritime*	= S. Albeck, "Maritime Law," *Encyclopedia Judaica* 11:996-997.
Albeck, *Ownership*	= S. Albeck, "Ownership," *Encyclopedia Judaica* 12:1531-1534.
Albeck, *Property*	= S. Albeck, "Property," *Encyclopedia Judaica* 13:1146-1149.
Albeck, *Sale*	= S. Albeck, "Sale," *Encyclopedia Judaica* 14:675-680.
Albeck, *Sanhedrin*	= Chanoh Albeck, "ha-Sanhedrin u-Nesiʾah," *Zion* 1942-43, 8:165-178.
Albeck, *Torts*	= S. Albeck, "Torts," *Encyclopedia Judaica* 15:1272-1277.
Albeck, *Yeush*	= S. Albeck, "Yeʾush," *Encyclopedia Judaica* 16:774-775.
Amram	= D. W. Amram, "Retaliation and Compensation," *Jewish Quarterly Review* 1911, NS 2:191-211.
Aptowitzer	= Victor Aptowitzer, *Die syrischen Rechtsbücher und das mosäisch-talmudische Recht* (Wien, 1909).
Aptowitzer, *Law*	= Victor Aptowitzer, "Observations on the Criminal Law of the Jews," *JQR* 1924-25, 15:77ff.
Ar.	= ʿArakhin
Auerbach, C.	= C. Auerbach, "The Talmud—a gateway to the common law," *Western Reserve Law Review* 1951 (June), 3:5-49.
Auerbach, L.	= L. Auerbach, *Das jüdische Obligationrecht nach den Quellen und mit besonderer Berücksichtigung des romischen und deutschen Rechts systematisch dargestellt* (Berlin, 1871).
A.Z.	= ʿAbodah Zarah
B.	= Babylonian Talmud
B.B.	= Babaʾ Batraʾ
B.M.	= Babaʾ Meṣiʿaʾ
B.Q.	= Babaʾ Qammaʾ
Babany	= Leon Babany, *Institutions Juridiques des Romains, comparées aux Institutions Juridiques des Hébreux* (Paris, 1926).
Bacher	= W. Bacher, "Sanhedrin," in J. Hastings, *A Dictionary of the Bible*, IV:397-402.
Baruk	= H. Baruk, "Le tsedek dans le droit hebraïque; l'organisation de la justice et l'examen des temoignages," *Hatikvah* 1969, 7:9-35.
Baumgarten	= J. M. Baumgarten, "The duodecimal courts of Qumran, Revelation, and the Sanhedrin," *Journal of Biblical Literature* 1976, 95:59-78.

Bayne	= D. C. Bayne, "Essay on the Hebrew Civil Code," *Cleveland-Marshal Law Review* 1954, 3:23-32.
Beaucamp	= E. Beaucamp, "La justice en Israel," *Populus Dei* ...; studi in onore del Card. A. Ottaviani (Rome, 1969), 201-235.
Ber.	= Berakhot
Berger	= Isaiah Berger, ed., *Analytical Index to the Jewish Quarterly Review*, 1889-1908 (N.Y., 1956).
Berkovits	= E. Berkovits, "The biblical meaning of justice," *Judaism* 1969, 18:188-209.
Berlin, 1968	= Charles Berlin, *Harvard University Library. Catalogue of Hebrew Books* (Cambridge, 1968), I-VI.
Berlin, 1972	= *Supplement* (Cambridge, 1972), I-III.
Berlin, 1971	= *Widener Library Shelflist, 39. Judaica* (Cambridge 1971).
Bert.	= ʿObadiah of Bertinoro. From Mishnah, ed. Romm.
Beṣ.	= Beṣah
Bickermann	= E. Bickermann, "ʿAl ha-Sanhedrin," *Zion* 1938, 3:356-66.
Bik.	= Bikkurim
Blackman	= Philip Blackman, *Mishnayoth*. Vol. IV. *Order Nezikin. Pointed Hebrew Text, Introductions, Translation*, Notes, Supplement, Appendix, Indexes (London, 1952).
Blau, J.	= J. Blau, "Lex Talionis," *Yearbook of the Central Conference of American Rabbis* 1916, 26:336-66.
Blau, L.	= Ludwig Blau, *Der Concursus Vitierum nach Talmudischen Recht* (Budapest, 1887).
Blau, *Papyrus*	= Ludwig Blau, "Die Strafklauseln der griechischen Papyrus Urkunden beleuchtet durch die aramäischen Papyri und durch den Talmud," *MGWJ* 1919, 63:138-155.
Blau, *Prosbol*	= Ludwig Blau, "Prosbol im Lichte der Griechischen Papyri und der Rechtsgeschichte," *Sonderabdruck aus Festschrift zum 50-jahrigen bestehen der Franz-Josef-Landesrabbinerschule* (Budapest, 1927), pp. 96-151.
Blidstein	= G. Blidstein, "Notes on *Hefker Bet-Din* in Talmudic and Medieval law," *Diné Israel* 1973, 4:35-49.
Blidstein, *Capital*	= G. J. Blidstein, "Capital punishment; the classic Jewish discussion," in *Understanding the Talmud*, selected by A. Corré (N.Y., 1975), pp. 313-324.
Blinzer	= J. Blinzer, "Das Synedrium von Jerusalem und die Strafprozessordnung der Mischna," *Zeitschrift für die neutestamentliche Wissenschaft* 1961, 52:54.
Blum	= F. Blum, *Le Synhedrin* (Strassbourg, 1889).
Bossowski	= Frank Bossowski, "Roman Law and Hebrew Private Law," *Bulletino dell' Instituto di Diritto Romano "Vittoria Scialoje,"* 1939, XLVI n.s. V: 354-363.
Brauner	= R. A. Brauner, "Some Aspects of offense and penalty in the Bible and the literature of the ancient Near East," *Gratz College Annual of Jewish Studies* 1974; 3:9-18.
Büchler	= Adolf Büchler, *Das Synedrion in Jerusalem und das grosse Beth-Din in der Quaderkammer des jerusalemischen Tempels* (Wien, 1902).
Burkill	= T. A. Burkill, "Competence of the Sanhedrin," *Vigiliae Christianae* 1956, 10:80-96.
Buss	= Martin Buss, "The distinction between civil and criminal law in ancient Israel," *Proceedings of the Sixth World Congress of Jewish Studies* 1977, 6, 1:51-62.
C	= W. H. Loewe, *The Mishnah of the Palestinian Talmud (Hammishnah ʿal pi ketab-yad Cambridge)* (Jerusalem, 1967).

ABBREVIATIONS AND BIBLIOGRAPHY

Carmichel	= C. M. Carmichael, "A singular method of codification of law in the Mishpatim," *Zeitschrift für die Alttestamentliche Wissenschaft* 1972, 84:19-25.
Cazelles	= H. Cazelles, "La transgression de la loi en tant que crime et délit," *Populus Dei . . ., studi in onore del Card. A. Ottaviani* (Rome, 1969), 521-528.
Chajes	= H. P. Chajes, "Les Juges juifs en Palestine, de l'an 70 à l'an 500," *Revue des études juives* 1899, 39:39-52.
Cohen	= B. Cohen, "An essay on possession in Jewish law," in *Understanding the Talmud*, selected by A. Corré (N.Y., 1975) pp. 325-329.
Cohen	= Boaz Cohen, "The relationship of Jewish to Roman Law," *Jewish Quarterly Review*, 1944, 34:267-280.
Cohen, *Arbitration*	= Boaz Cohen, "Arbitration in Jewish and Roman Law," *Revue Internationale des Droits de l'Antiquité* 1958, 5:165-223.
Cohen, *Peculium*	= Boaz Cohen, "Peculium in Jewish and Roman Law," *American Academy for Jewish Research. Proceedings*, 1951, 20:135-234.
Cohen, *Justification*	= M. A. Cohen, "Justification and excuse in the Judaic and common law: the exculpation of a defendant charged with homicide," *New York University Law Review* 1977, 52:599-628, 970-3.
Cohn	= H. H. Cohn, "The penology of the Talmud," *Israel Law Review* 1970, 5:53-74.
Cohn, *Admission*	= H. H. Cohn, "Admission," *Encyclopedia Judaica* 2:290-292.
Cohn, *Ancient*	= H. H. Cohn, "Ancient Jewish equity," in *Equity in the World's Legal Systems . . . dedicated to R. Cassin* (Brussels, 1973).
Cohn, *Bet*	= H. H. Cohn, "Bet Din and judges," *Encyclopedia Judaica* 4:719-727.
Cohn, *Confiscation*	= H. H. Cohn, "Confiscation, expropriation, forfeiture," *Encyclopedia Judaica* 5:880-882.
Cohn, *Evidence*	= H. H. Cohn, "Evidence," *Encyclopedia Judaica* 6:991-997.
Cohn, *Pleas*	= H. H. Cohn, "Pleas," *Encyclopedia Judaica* 13:631-636.
Cohn, *Practice*	= H. H. Cohn, "Practice and procedure," *Encyclopedia Judaica*, 13:952-962.
Cohn, *Witness*	= H. H. Cohn, "Witness," *Encyclopedia Judaica* 16:584-590.
Cohn, *Talion*	= H. H. Cohn, "Talion," *Encyclopedia Judaica* (Jerusalem, 1971) 15:742.
Cohn, *Usury*	= H. H. Cohn, "Usury," *Encyclopedia Judaica* 16:27-33.
Conflict	= "Conflict resolution and the legal culture: a study of the rabbinical court," *Osgoode Hall Law Journal* 1971 9:335.
Criticism	= "Criticism of the state in ancient Jewish tradition" *Ohio State Law Journal* 1970, 31:322.
Danby	= Herbert Danby, "The Bearing of the Rabbinical Criminal Code on the Jewish Trial Narratives in the Gospels," *The Journal of Theological Studies* 1919-20, 21:51-76.
Daube	= D. Daube, "Negligence in the Early Talmudic Law of Contract (Peshiʿah)," *Festschrift Fritz Schulz* (Weimar, 1951).
Daube, *Civil*	= David Daube, *The Civil Law of the Mishnah* (New Orleans, 1944). (Also in *Tulane Law Review* 1943-4, 18:351-407.)
Daube, *Codes*	= David Daube, "Codes and codas in the Pentateuch," *Juridical Review* 1941, 53:242-261.
Daube, *Collaboration*	= David Daube, *Collaboration with tyranny in Rabbinic law* (Riddell Memorial Lectures) (London, 1965).
Daube, *Direct*	= D. Daube, "Direct and Indirect Causation in Biblical Law," *Vetus Testamentum* 1961, 11:266ff.
Daube, *Law*	= D. Daube, "The law of witnesses in transferred operation (in rabbinic thought)," in *Gaster Festschrift. Journal of the Ancient Near Eastern Society*, pp. 91-93.

Daube, *Romans*	= D. Daube, "Derelicto, occupatio, and traditio: Romans and rabbis," *Law Quarterly Review* 1961; 77:382.
Daube, *Studies*	= D. Daube, *Studies in Biblical Law* (Cambridge, 1947).
Daube, *Suicide*	= David Daube, "Josephus on suicide and liability of depositee," *Juridical Review* 1964, 1964:212.
Dem.	= Demaʾi.
Dembitz	= L. N. Dembitz, "Is there Roman law in the Talmud?" *Hebrew Union College Journal* 1901, V:160-61.
D'Ercole	= G. D'Ercole, "The juridical structure of Israel from the time of her origin to the period of Hadrian." *Populus Dei ...*, *studi in onore del Card. A. Ottaviani* (Rome, 1969) 389-461.
Deut.	= Deuteronomy
Ed.	= ʿEduyot
EG	= *Hiddush'é Eliyyahu Migreiditz*. From Mishnah, ed. Romm (Vilna, 1887).
Ehrman	= A. Z. Ehrman, "Antichresis," *Encyclopedia Judaica* 3:59-60.
Eisenstadt	= S. Eisenstadt, *En Mishpat* (Jerusalem, 1931) pp. 378-382.
Elon, *Actions*	= M. Elon, "Limitation of actions," *Encyclopedia Judaica* 11:251-254.
Elon, *Arbitration*	= M. Elon, "Arbitration," *Encyclopedia Judaica* 3:294-300.
Elon, *Compromise*	= M. Elon, "Compromise," *Encyclopedia Judaica* 5:857-859.
Elon, *Contract*	= M. Elon, "Contract," *Encyclopedia Judaica* 5:923-933.
Elon, *Execution*	= M. Elon, "Execution," *Encyclopedia Judaica* 6:1007-1020.
Elon, *Gevul*	= M. Elon, "Hassagat Gevul," *Encyclopedia Judaica* 7:1460-1466.
Elon, *HaAnakah*	= M. Elon, "Haʿanakah," *Encyclopedia Judaica* 7:1003-1007.
Elon, *Law*	= M. Elon, "Law of Obligations," *Encyclopedia Judaica* 12:1310-1316.
Elon, *Lien*	= M. Elon, "Lien," *Encyclopedia Judaica* 11:227-232.
Elon, *Pledge*	= M. Elon, "Pledge," *Encyclopedia Judaica* 13:636-644.
Elon, *Suretyship*	= M. Elon, "Suretyship," *Encyclopedia Judaica* 15:524-529.
Elon and Levitats	= M. Elon and I. Levitats, "Hazakah," *Encyclopedia Judaica* 7:1516-1523.
Elon and Levitats, *Hekdesh*	= M. Elon and I. Levitats, "Hekdesh," *Encyclopedia Judaica* 8:279-287.
Englard	= E. Englard, "The law of torts in Israel; the problems of common law codification in a mixed legal system," *American Journal of Comparative Law* 1974, 22:302-329.
Enker	= A. Enker, "Self-incrimination in Jewish law," *Diné Israel* 1923, 4:107-124.
Epstein	= Isidore Epstein, *Social Legislation in the Talmud* (London, 1943).
Epstein, *Nusaḥ*	= Y. N. H. Epstein, *Mabo lenusaḥ hammishnah* (Tel Aviv, 1954).
Epstein, *Tan.*	= Y. N. H. Epstein, *Meboʾot lesifrut hattanaʾim. Mishnah tosefta, ummidrashé halakhah*. Ed. E. S. Melammed (Tel Aviv, 1957).
Erub.	= ʿErubin
Eschelbacher	= Max Eschelbacher, "Recht und Billigkeit in der Jurisprudence des Talmud," *Judaica* (Berlin, 1912) pp. 501-514.
Falk	= Z. W. Falk, "Forensic medicine in Jewish law," *Diné Israel* 1970, 1:20-30.
Falk, *Einfluss*	= Z. W. Falk, "Zum fremden Einfluss auf das jüdische Recht," *Revue Internationale des Droits de l'Antiquité* 1971, 18:11-23.
Falk, *Elements*	= Z. W. Falk, "Elements of the Jewish Law of Torts," *Studi in onore di Giuseppe Grosso* (Turin, 1968).
Falk, *Hand.*	= Z. W. Falk, "Zum jüdischen Handelsrecht," *Revue Internationale des Droits de l'Antiquité* 1969, 16:11-19.
Falk, *Introduction*	= Z. W. Falk, *Introduction to Jewish law of the Second Commonwealth* (Leiden, 1972).

Falk, *Law*	= Z. W. Falk, *Hebrew Law in Biblical Times. An Introduction* (Jerusalem, 1964).
Fassel	= Hirsch Bar Fassel, *Das mosaisch-rabbinische Civilrecht* ... (Wien, 1852).
Faur	= J. Faur, "Law and justice in rabbinic jurisprudence," in *Samuel K. Mirsky Memorial Volume* (Jerusalem, 1970) pp. 13-20.
Fees	= Karl Fees, *Die Juden in der Jurisprudenz* (Wien, 1931) 9:3-12.
Fensham	= F. C. Fensham, "Aspects of Family law in the Covenant Code in light of ancient Near Eastern parallels," *Diné Israel* 1970, 1:5-19.
Fensham, *Widow*	= F. C. Fensham, "Widow, Orphan and the Poor in Ancient Near Eastern Legal and Wisdom Literature," *Journal of Near Eastern Studies* 1962, 21:129-39.
Finkelstein	= J. J. Finkelstein, "The Goring Ox: Some Historical Perspectives on Deodands, Forfeitures, Wrongful Death and the Western Notion of Sovereignty," *Temple Law Quarterly* 1973, 46:169-290.
Finkelstein, *Eye*	= L. Finkelstein, "An Eye for an Eye," *The Menorah Journal* 1936, 24:207-18.
Finkelstein, *Sanhedrin*	= L. Finkelstein, "Ha-Nesiʾut v-ha-sanhedrin bʾyisraʾel," *Hatekufah* 1946, 30:705.
Flügel	= Maurice Fluegel, *Spirit of the Biblical Legislation, in parallel with Talmud, moralists, casuists, New Testament, ancient and modern law, especially the social and political institutions* (Baltimore, 1893).
Flügel, *Charity*	= Maurice Flügel, *The Humanity, Benevolence and Charity Legislation of the Pentateuch and the Talmud. In parallel with the laws of Hammurabi; the doctrines of Egypt, the Roman XII tables and modern codes* ... (Baltimore, 1908).
Fränkel	= Zechariah Fränkel, *Der Geschichtliche Beweis* (Berlin, 1846), pp. 57-62.
Gamoran	= H. Gamoran, "The biblical law against loans against loans on interest," *Journal of Near Eastern Studies* 1971, 30:127-134.
Gamoran, *Controls*	= H. Gamoran, "Talmudic controls on the purchase of futures," *Jewish Quarterly Review* 1974, 64:48-66.
Gamoran, *Usury*	= H. Gamoran, "Talmudic usury laws and business loans," *Journal for the Study of Judaism in the Persian, Hellenistic and Roman Period* 1976, 7:129-142.
Gassman	= B. Gassman, "Talmudic law and procedure," *Criminal Law Review* 1958, 5:36.
Gershfield	= Edward M. Gershfield, *Studies in Jewish jurisprudence* (N.Y., 1971).
Git.	= Giṭṭin
Goitein	= E. Goitein, *Das Vergeltungsprincip im biblischen und talmudischen strafrecht* (Halle, 1891).
Good	= E. M. Good, "Capital punishment and its alternatives in ancient Near Eastern Law," *Stanford Law Review* 1967, 19:947.
Goodenough	= Erwin R. Goodenough, *The Jurisprudence of the Jewish Courts in Egypt, legal administration by the Jews under the early Roman Empire as described by Philo Judaeus* (New Haven, 1929).
GRA	= Elijah ben Solomon Zalman ("Elijah Gaon" or "Vilne Gaon"), 1720-1797.
Greenberg	= M. Greenberg, "Some Postulates of Biblical Criminal Law," *Yeheẓkel Kaufmann Jubilee Volume* (Jerusalem, 1960).
Greenberg and Cohn	= M. Greenberg and H. H. Cohn, "Oath," *Encyclopedia Judaica* 12:1295-1302.
Greenberg, *Herem*	= M. Greenberg and H. H. Cohn, "Herem," *Encyclopedia Judaica* 8:344-355.
Greenwald	= L. Greenwald, *Letoledot hassanhedrin beyisraʾel.* (N.Y., 1950).

Grunbaum	= Grunbaum, "Die Sklaven nach rabbinischen Gesetze," *Jüdische Zeitschrift* 1872, 10:26-45.
Gulack	= Asher Gulack, *The Obligation and its Security* (Jerusalem, 1939). In Hebrew.
Gulak, *Parallelen*	= A. Gulak, "Ältere talmudische Parallelen zur Novelle 97 des Kaiser's Justinians," in *Zeitschrift für vergleichende Rechtswissenschaft* 47:241-255.
Gulak, *Ur.*	= Asher Gulak, *Das Urkundenwesen im Talmud im lichte der griechischaegyptischen papyri und des griechischen und römischen Rechts* (Jerusalem, 1935).
Guttmann	= A. Guttmann, "The role of equity in the history of the *Halakhah*," in *Justice, Justice shalt Thou Pursue*; papers presented for Julius Mark (N.Y., 1975), pp. 71-92.
HA	= Emanuel Hai Riqi. *Hon 'asher*. In QMH.
Hag.	= Hagigah
Hal.	= Hallah
Harris	= John S. Harris, *Lex Talionis and the Jewish Law of Mercy* (London, 1924).
Haut	= I. H. Haut, "Jewish law of warranties. Some comparative aspects," *Israel Law Review* 1975, 10:102-130.
Hayyot	= Yishaq Hayyot, *Zeraʿ yishaq*. Ed. H. Y. L. Deutsch (N.Y., 1960).
HD	= *Hasdé David. Tosefta Neziqin* (Repr. Jerusalem, 1971).
Heinemann	= J. Heinemann, "Early Halakhah in the Palestinian Targumim," *Studies in Jewish Legal History in Honour of David Daube*, ed. B. S. Jackson (London, 1974).
Hertz	= Joseph H. Hertz, "Ancient Semitic Codes and the Mosaic Legislation," *Journal of Comparative Legislation and International Law* 1928, Series 3, V. 10:207-221.
Herzog	= Isaac Herzog, "Din ha-Melek we-Din ha-Torah," *Talpioth* 1957, 7(1):4-32.
Herzog, *Main*	= Isaac Herzog, *Main Institutions of Jewish Law* (London, 1929).
Higger	= M. Higger, "Intention in Talmudic Law," in *Studies in Jewish Jurisprudence*, ed. by E. M. Gershfield (N Y , 1971), 235-293.
Hildesheimer	= Esriel E. Hildesheimer, *Das jüdische Gesellschaftsrecht* (Leipzig, 1930).
Hirsch	= Samson R. Hirsch, *Horebh, a philosophy of Jewish laws and observances* (Repr.: London, 1962).
Hölscher	= Gustav Hölscher, *Sanhedrin und Makkot* (Tübingen, 1910).
Hoenig	= Sidney Hoenig, "Sof ha-Sanhedrin ha-Gedolah bi-Yemé Bayit Sheni," *Horeb* 1936, 3:169-175.
Hoenig, *Attic*	= Sidney Hoenig, "Synedrion in the Attic Orators, the Ptolemaic Papyri and its adoption by Josephus, the Gospels and the Tannaim," *Jewish Quarterly Review* 1946, 37.
Hoenig, *Great*	= Sidney Hoenig, *The Great Sanhedrin* (Philadelphia, 1953).
Hoffmann	= David Hoffmann, "Bemerkungen zur Geschichte des Synhedrions," *Jahrbuch der judischliterarischen Gesellschaft* 1970, 5:225-244.
Hoffmann, *Ger.*	= David Hoffmann, *Der oberste Gerichtshof in der Stadt des Heiligthums* (Berlin, 1878).
Hoffmann, *Syn.*	= David Hoffmann, "Die Präsidentur im Synedrium," *Magazin für die Wissenschaft des Judenthums* 1878, 5:94-99.
Holy Things	= Jacob Neusner, *A History of the Mishnaic Law of Holy Things* (Leiden, 1979) I-VI.
Holzmeister	= U. Holzmeister, "Zur Frage der Blutgerichtsbarkeit des Synedriums," *Biblica* 1938, 19:43-59, 151-174.
Hor.	= Horayot

Horovitz	= J. Horovitz, "Auge um Auge, Zahn um Zahn," *Judaica, Festschrift zu Hermann Cohens siebzigsten Geburtstage* (Berlin, 1912), 609-58.
Horowitz	= George Horowitz, *The Spirit of Jewish Law* (N.Y., 1953).
Hul.	= Ḥullin
HY	= *Tosefta Ḥazon Yeḥezqel. Seder Neziqin. I. Baba Meṣia* (Jerusalem, 1971). By Yeḥezqel Abramsky.
Hyamson	= Moses Hyamson, "Some points of comparison and contrast in Jewish and Roman Law," *Jubilee Volume of Jews College* (London, 1906), pp. 153-170.
ID	= Nathan Lebam. *Imré daʿat*. In QMH.
Isaacs	= Nathan Isaacs, "*The law*" *and the law of change* (Philadelphia, 1917).
Israelstam	= *Aboth. Translated into English with Notes, Glossary, and Indices.* By J. Israelstam (London, 1948: Soncino Press).
Jackson	= B. S. Jackson, "The Fence-breaker and the 'actio de Pastu pecoris' in early Jewish law [B.K. 55b]" *Jewish Journal of Sociology* 1974, 25:123-126.
Jackson, *Essays*	= Bernard S. Jackson, *Essays in Jewish and Comparative Legal History* (Leiden, 1975).
Jackson, *Intention*	= B. S. Jackson, "Liability for mere intention in early Jewish law," *Hebrew Union College Annual* 1971, 42:197-225.
Jackson, *Theft*	= Bernard Jackson, *Theft in Early Jewish Law* (Oxford, 1972).
Jacob	= B. Jacob, *Auge um Auge* (Berlin, 1928).
Jelski	= Israel Jelski, *Die innere Einrichtung des grossen Synedrions zu Jerusalem und ihre Fortsetzung im späteren palästinensischen Lehrhause bis zur Zeit des R. Jehuda ha-Nasi* (Breslau, 1894).
Jirku	= A. Jirku, "Drei Fälle von Haftpflicht im altorientalischen Palästina-Syrien und Deuteronomium cap. 21," *Zeitschrift für alttestamentliche Wissenschaft* 1967, 79:359-60.
Jirku, *Recht*	= Anton Jirku, *Das weltliche Recht im alten Testament* (Gütersloh, 1927).
Johns	= Claude H. W. Johns, *The Relations between the Laws of Babylonia and the Laws of the Hebrew Peoples* (London, 1914).
JQR	= *Jewish Quarterly Review*.
Juster	= Jean Juster, *Les Juifs dans l'Empire Romain* (Paris, 1914).
Justification	= "Justification and excuse in the Judaic and common law: the exculpation of a defendant charged with homicide," *New York University Law Review* 1977, 52:599-628.
K	= Georg Beer, *Faksimile-Ausgabe des Mishnacodex Kaufmann A 50* (Repr.: Jerusalem, 1968).
Kaatz	= S. Kaatz, "Maimonides und das Talionsprinzip," *Jeschurun* 1926, 13:43-50.
Kahn	= Lehman Kahn, *La Sociologie selon la legislation juive appliquée à l'époque moderne* (Paris, 1905).
Karl	= Zevi Karl, "Bet Din ha-Gadol she-be-Lishkat ha-Gazit," *Bitzaron* 1953, 29:114-119.
Katsh	= Abraham I. Katsh, *Ginzé Mishnah. One Hundred and Fifty-Nine Fragments from the Cairo Geniza in the Saltykov-Shchedrin Library in Leningrad Appearing for the First Time with an Introduction, Notes and Variants* (Jerusalem, 1970).
Kel.	= Kelim
Ker.	= Keritot
Kil.	= Kilaʾyim
Kilian	= R. Kilian, "Apodiktisches und kasuistiches Recht; im Licht ägyptischer Analogien," *Biblische Zeitschrift* 1963, n.s. 7:185-202.
Kingsbury	= E. C. Kingsbury, "Law as compact; ancient Israel's contribution

	to the understanding of law," *Journal of Human Relations* 1967, 15:411-422.
Kirschenbaum	= A. Kirschenbaum, "Double jeopardy and entrapment in Jewish law," *Israel Yearbook on Human Rights* 1973, 3:202-222.
Kirschenbaum, *Mehila*	= A. Kirschenbaum, "Mehila," *Encyclopedia Judaica* 11:1232-1234.
Kirschenbaum, *Shibuda*	= A. Kirschenbaum, "Shiʿbuda de-Rabbi Nathan," *Encyclopedia Judaica* 14:1397-1398.
Kirzner	= *Baba Kamma. Translated into English with Notes, Glossary and Indices.* By E. W. Kirzner (London, 1948: Soncino Press).
KM	= *Kesef Mishneh.* Joseph Karo. Commentary to Maimonides, *Mishneh Torah.* Published in Venice, 1574-5. Text used: Standard version of Maimonides, *Mishneh Torah.*
Kook	= S. H. Kook, "Heʾarah be-ʿInyané Sanhedrin," *Sinai* 5700-1939-40, 3 (part 7):94-95.
Kottek	= H. Kottek, "Gesetz und Ueberlieferung bei den Juden Babyloniens in Vortalmudischer Zeit," *Juedisch-literarische Gesellschaft Jahrb.* 1909, 6:280-303.
Kuenen	= A. Kuenen, "Über die Zusammensetzung des Sanhedrin," *Gesammelte Abhandlung zur Biblischen Wissenschaft* (Freiburg im Breisgau-Leipzig, 1894).
Lamm	= N. Lamm, "The Fourth Amendment and its equivalent in the Halachah (The Question of Privacy)," *Judaism* 1967, 16:300-312.
Landman	= L. Landman, "Civil disobedience, the Jewish view," *Tradition* 1969, 10, 4:5-14.
Lazarus	= *Makkoth. Translated into English with Notes, Glossary, and Indices,* by H. M. Lazarus (London, 1948: Soncino Press).
Lebendiger	= I. Lebendiger, "The minor in Jewish law," in *Studies in Jewish Jurisprudence,* ed. by E. M. Gershfield (N.Y., 1971) 91-180.
Leiser	= B. M. Leiser, "Custom and Law in Talmudic Jurisprudence," *Judaism* 1971, 20:396-403.
Levinthal	= Israel H. Levinthal, *The Jewish Law of Agency with special reference to the Roman and common law* (N.Y., 1923).
Levy	= J. Levy, "Die Presidentur im Synedrium," *MGWJ* 1855, 4:266-274, 301-307, 339-358.
Levy, *Wörterbuch*	= Jacob Levy, *Wörterbuch über die Talmudim und Midraschim* (1924. Repr., Darmstadt, 1963) I-IV.
Lieberman, B. B.	= B. B. Lieberman, "Torts in Jewish law," in *Studies in Jewish Jurisprudence* II (N.Y., 1974) pp. 231-240.
Lieberman, S.	= Saul Lieberman, *Hellenism in Jewish Palestine* (N.Y., 1950) pp. 4-10.
Lieberman, *Legal*	= Saul Lieberman, "Roman Legal Institutions in Early Rabbinics and in the Acta Martyrdom," *JQR* 1944, 35:1-57.
Lieberman, *Pal.*	= Saul Lieberman, *Greek in Jewish Palestine* (N.Y., 1942).
Lieberman, *Third*	= Saul Lieberman, "Palestine in the Third and Fourth Centuries," *JQR* 1945-46, 36:392-370, 37 (1946-47):31-54.
Lieberman, *TR*	= Saul Lieberman, *Tosefeth Rishonim* (Jerusalem, 1938) II. *Seder Nashim, Nezikin, Kadashim.*
Lillie	= W. Lillie, "Towards a biblical doctrine of punishment," *Scottish Journal of Theology* 1968, 21:449-461.
Linfield	= Harry Sebee Linfield, *The Relation of Jewish to Babylonian Law* (Chicago, 1919).
Loewenstamm	= S. E. Loewenstamm, "Midah Keneged Midah," *Enzyklopedia Miqraʾit* IV (Jerusalem, 1962) cols. 84-46.
M	= *Babylonian Talmud Codex Munich* (95) (Repr. Jerusalem, 1971).
M.	= Mishnah

Ma.	= Ma'aserot.
MacCormack	= G. MacCormack, "Revenge and Compensation in Early Law," *American Journal of Comparative Law* 1973, 21:81ff.
Macholz	= G. C. Macholz, "Zur Geschichte der Justizorganisation in Juda," *Zeitschrift für alttestamentliche Wissenschaft* 1972, 84:314-340.
Macholz, *Stellung*	= G. C. Macholz, "Die Stellung des Königs in der israelitischen Gerichtsverfassung," *Zeitschrift für alttestamentliche Wissenschaft* 1972, 84:157-182.
Maimonides, *Asseverations*	= *The Code of Maimonides. Book Six. The Book of Asseverations.* Translated from the Hebrew by B. D. Klien (New Haven & London, 1962: Yale University Press).
Maimonides, *Civil Laws*	= *The Code of Maimonides. Book Thirteen. The Book of Civil Laws.* Translated from the Hebrew by Jacob J. Rabinowitz (New Haven and London, 1949: Yale University Press).
Maimonides, *Comm.*	= Moses b. Maimon, *Mishnah. Seder Neziqin.* Trans. by Yosef Kappaḥ (Second printing, Jerusalem, 1969).
Maimonides, *Judges*	= *The Code of Maimonides. Book Fourteen. The Book of Judges.* Translated from the Hebrew by Abraham M. Hershman (New Haven, 1949: Yale University Press).
Maine	= Henry Maine, *Ancient Law* (London, 1910).
Mak.	= Makkot
Makh.	= Makhshirin
Maloney	= R. P. Maloney, "Usury in Greek, Roman and rabbinic thought," *Traditio* 1971, 27:79-109.
Mantel	= Hugo Mantel, *Studies in the History of the Sanhedrin* (Cambridge, Mass., 1961).
Margolith	= R. Margolith, "The Requisites for Appointment to the Sanhedrin," (Hebrew) *Sinai* 1946-7, 10:16ff.
Marmorstein	= A. Marmorstein, "Ab Bet Din," *Encyclopaedia Judaica* I, pp. 104-109.
May	= M. May, "Jewish criminal law and legal procedure," *Journal of Criminal Law and Criminology* 1940, 31:438-47.
Mayer	= S. Mayer, *Die Rechte der Israeliten, Athener und Römer mit Rücksicht auf die neuen Gesetzungen, für juristen, Staatsmänner, Theologen, Philologen, und Geschichtsforscher in Parallelen dargestellt . . .* Vol. I. *Das offentliche Recht* (Leipzig, 1862). Vol. II. *Das privat Recht* (Leipzig, 1866). Vol. III. *Geschichte der Strafrechtes Vergleichende Darstellung der Strafrechtlichen Gesetze und Bestimmungen aller Kulturvölker von Moses Solon . . . bis zur Gegenwart* (Trier, 1876).
McKay	= J. W. McKay, "Ex. 23:1-3, 6-8; a decalogue for the administration of justice in the city gate," *Vetus Testamentum* 1971, 21:311-325.
Me.	= Me'ilah
Meg.	= Megillah
Melammed, *Midrash*	= E. Ṣ. Melammed, *Hayyaḥas sheben midrashé halakhah lammishnah velattosefta* (Jerusalem, 1967).
Melammed, *Talmud*	= E. Ṣ. Melammed, *Pirqé mabo lesifrut hattalmud* (Jerusalem, 1973).
Men.	= Menaḥot
Mendelsohn	= S. Mendelsohn, *The Criminal Jurisprudence of the Ancient Hebrews* (Baltimore, 1891).
Mendenhall	= G. E. Mendenhall, "Covenant forms in Israelite tradition," *Biblical Archaeologist* 1954, 17:50-76.
Mendenhall, *Law*	= G. E. Mendenhall, "Ancient oriental and Biblical Law," *Biblical Archaeologist* 1954, 17:26-46.

Menes	= Abram Menes, "Die vorexilischen Gesetze Israels im Zusammenhang seiner Kulturgeschichtlichen Entwicklung," *Zeitschrift für die alttestamentliche Wissenschaften, Beihefte*, 1928, 50:1-143.
MGWJ	= *Monatschrift für die Geschichte und Wissenschaft des Judenthums*.
Mikliszanski	= J. K. Mikliszanski, "The Law of Retaliation and the Pentateuch," *Journal of Biblical Literature* 1947, 66:295-303.
Miq.	= Miqva'ot
Mishcon and Cohen	= *'Abodah Zarah. Translated into English with Notes, Glossary, and Indices*. By A. Mishcon and A. Cohen (London, 1948: Soncino Press).
ML	= *Mishneh Lammelekh*. Commentary to Maimonides, *Mishneh Torah*. Judah Rosannes 1657-1727. For source, see KM
Morell	= S. Morell, "The Constitutional limits of communal government in Rabbinic law," *Jewish Social Studies* 1971, 33:87-119.
M.Q.	= Mo'ed Qaṭan
MS	= *Mele'khet Shelomo*. Shelomo bar Joshua Adeni, 1567-1625. From Mishnah, ed. Romm.
Müller	= David Henrich Müller, *Die Gesetze Hammurabis und ihr Verhältnis zur mosaischen Gesetzgebung sowie zu den XII Tafeln* (Wien, 1903).
N	= *Mishnah 'im perush HaRambam. Defus Risho'n Napoli* [5]555 [1492] (Jerusalem, 1970).
Napier	= B. D. Napier, "Community under law," *Interpretation* 1953, 7:404-17.
Naz.	= Nazir
Ned.	= Nedarim
Neg.	= Nega'im
Nid.	= Niddah
Norden	= J. Norden, *Auge um Auge — Zahn um Zahn* (Berlin, 1926).
Noth	= Martin Noth, *Die Gesetze im Pentateuch, ihre Voraussetzungen und ihr Sinn* (Halle, 1940).
Num.	= Numbers
NS	= Ṣevi Gutmacher, *Naḥalat ṣevi*. In QMH.
Oettli	= Samuel Oettli, *Das Gesetze Hammurabis und die Thora Israels* (Leipzig, 1903).
Oh.	= 'Ohalot
Or.	= 'Orlah
Ostersetzer	= G. Ostersetzer, "Parhedrin-Porertin," *Zion* 1939, 4:294-306.
P	= *Shishah sidré mishnah. Ketab yad Parma Derossi 138* (Repr.: Jerusalem, 1970).
Pa	= *Mishnah ketab yad Paris. Paris 338-339* (Repr.: Jerusalem, 1973).
Par.	= Parah
Parly	= Jean de Parly, *Code civil et penal du Judaïsme* (Paris, 1896).
Passamaneck	= S. Passamaneck and J. Myers, "Aspects of land use and commercial regulation in medieval rabbinic sources," *Revue Internationale des Droits de l'Antiquité* 1969, 16:31-71.
Passamaneck, Rabbis	= S. M. Passamaneck and L. M. Brown, "The rabbis; preventive law lawyers," *Israel Law Review* 1973, 8:538-549.
Passamaneck, Two	= S. M. Passamaneck, "Two Aspects of rabbinical maritime law," *Journal of Jewish Studies* 1971, 22:53-67.
Patrick	= D. Patrick, "Casuistic law governing primary rights and duties," *Journal of Biblical Literature* 1973, 92:180-184.
Paul	= S. M. Paul, *Studies in the Book of the Covenant in the Light of Cuneiform and Biblical Law* (Leiden, 1970).
Pes.	= Pesaḥim
Pfeiffer	= Adalbert Pfeiffer, *Die Stellung der israelitischen Gesetzgebung zu den wichtigsten Problemen des sozialen Lebens* (Freiberg, 1905).

ABBREVIATIONS AND BIBLIOGRAPHY XXV

Pharisees	=	J. Neusner, *The rabbinic traditions about the Pharisees before 70* (Leiden, 1971) I-III.
Phelps	=	L. Phelps, "Moses and his laws," *Kentucky State Bar Journal* 1944 (June), 8:19-24.
Phillips	=	Anthony Phillips, *Ancient Israel's Criminal Law. A New Approach to the Decalogue* (Oxford, 1970).
Phillips, *Interpretation*	=	A. Phillips, "Interpretation of 2 Samuel XII:5-6," *Vetus Testamentum* 1966, 16:242-4.
Ploeg	=	J. P. M. van der Ploeg, "Les judges en Israel," *Populus Dei . . ., studi in onore del Card. A. Ottaviani* (Rome, 1969).
Preiser	=	W. Preiser, "Zur rechtlichen Natur der altorientalischen 'Gesetze,'" *Festschrift für Karl Engisch* (Berlin, 1969) pp. 17-36.
Prenzel	=	Giesela Prenzel, *Über die Pacht im antiken hebräischen Recht* (Stuttgart, 1971).
Prevost	=	M. H. Prevost, "Opinions des 'tannaïm' et 'responsa' des jurisconsultes classiques romains," *Revue Internationale des Droits de l'Antiquité* 1970, 17:67-80.
Purities	=	J. Neusner, *A History of the Mishnaic Law of Purities*, (Leiden, 1974-1977) I-XXII.
QA	=	*Qorban Aharon*. Aaron Ibn Ḥayyim (d. 1632). *Qorban Aharon, Perush LaSefer Sifra* (Dessau, 1749).
Qehati	=	Pinḥas Qehati, *Seder Neziqin* (Jerusalem, 1976) I-II.
QH	=	Moshe Zakhuta, *Qol haramaz*. In QMH.
QMH	=	*Qebuṣat meforshé hammishnah* (Jerusalem, 1962).
QS	=	Ḥayyim Sofer, *Qol Sofer*. In QMH.
Rabad	=	Supercommentary to Maimonides, *Code*.
Rabad, *Sifra*	=	R. Abraham ben David, *Commentary to Sifra*. From *Sifra*, ed. Weiss.
Rabinowitz	=	Jacob J. Rabinowitz, *Jewish Law: its influence on the development of legal institutions* (N.Y., 1956).
Radin	=	Max Radin, "The jurisprudence of the Jewish courts in Egypt: Legal administration by the Jews under Early Roman Empire as described by Philo Judaeus," *Classical Philology* 1930, 25:294-297.
Rakover	=	N. Rakover, "Lease and hire," *Encyclopedia Judaica* 10:1528-1536.
Rakover, *Shalish*	=	N. Rakover, "Shalish," *Encyclopedia Judaica* 14:1267-1268.
Rakover, *Shom.*	=	N. Rakover, "Shomerim," *Encyclopedia Judaica* 14:1455-1458.
Rappaport	=	Ṣevi Hirsch Hakkohen Rappaport, *Torat Kohanim*, with the commentaries ʿEzrat Kohanim and Tosefet HaʿEzrah (Jerusalem, 1972).
Revital	=	S. Revital, "Partnership," *Encyclopedia Judaica* 13:149-155.
R.H.	=	Rosh Hashshanah
Ring	=	Emanuel Ring, *Israels Rechtsleben im Lichte der neuentdeckten assyrischen und hethitischen Gesetzesurkunden* (Stockholm, 1926).
Rosenberg	=	J. M. Rosenberg, "Law and Morality in Jewish jurisprudence," *Congress bi-Weekly* 1974, 41:7-9.
Rosmarin	=	Moshe Rosmarin, *Sefer Debar Moshe. ʿAl Massekhet Horayot, Massekhet Abot, Sugya de Qiyyum Shetarot* (Jerusalem, 1978).
Rosner	=	F. Rosner, "Definition of death in Jewish law," *Medica Judaica* 1970, 1:33-36.
Rost	=	L. Rost, "Die Gerichtshoheit im Heiligtum," *Archäologie und AT; Festschrift für K. Galling* (Tübingen, 1970) pp. 225-231.
Roth	=	C. Roth, "Constitution of the Jewish republic of 66-70," *Journal of Semitic Studies* 1964, 9:295-319.
Rothstein	=	Gustav Rothstein, *Altorientalische Texte als Begleitschoffe zur*

	biblischen Urgeschichte und altisraelitischen Gesetzgebung ausgewählt von Dr. Gustav Rothstein (Frankfurt, 1925).
Rubin, Recht	= Simon Rubin, *Das Talmudische Recht auf den verschieden Stufen seiner Entwicklung mit dem Römischen vergleichen und dargestellt*, I, Abteilung Personenrecht I. Buch Die Sklaverei. Ein Beitrag zur Lehre von dem Menschenrechte im Judentum (Vienna, 1920). Part II (Vienna, 1938).
Rubin	= S. Rubin, *Der Nasciturus als Rechtssubject aus Zeitschrift für vergleichende Rechtswissenschaft*, XX Band (Stuttgart, 1907).
Sachs	= S. Sachs, "Über die Zeit der Entstehung des Synhedrins," *Zeitschrift für die religiösen Interessen des Judenthums* 1945, 2:301-312.
San.	= Sanhedrin
Sandmel	= S. Sandmel, "Money-lending," *Encyclopedia Judaica* 12:244-256.
Schaeffer	= Henry Schaeffer, *The Social legislation of the primitive Semites* (New Haven, 1915).
Schreier	= S. Schreier, "Le-Toledot ha-Sanhedriyah ha-Gedolah bi-Yerushalayim," *ha-Shiloaḥ* 5675-1914-15, 31:404-415.
Segal	= *ʿEduyyoth. Translated into English with Notes, Glossary, and Indices* By M. H. Segal (London, 1948: Soncino Press).
Segert	= S. Segert, "Form and function of ancient Israelite, Greek and Roman legal sentences," in *Orient and Occident*; *essays presented to C. D. Gordon* (Kevelaer, 1973).
Sens	= Yaʿaqob David Ilan, *Tosafot Shens* (Bené Beraq, 1973).
Septimus	= B. Septimus, "Obligation and superogation in Halakha," *Yavneh Review* 1969, 7:30-39.
Shab.	= Shabbat
Shabu.	= Shabuʿot
Shachter and Freedman	= *Sanhedrin. Translated into English with Notes, Glossary, and Indices.* By Jacob Shachter and H. Freedman (London, 1948: The Soncino Press).
Shapiro	= A. Shapiro, "Rabbinical responsa and the regulation of competition," *American Journal of Economics and Sociology* 1970, 29:71-76.
Sheb.	= Shebiʿit
Sheq.	= Sheqalim
Shilo	= S. Shilo, "Loan," *Encyclopedia Judaica* 11:414-420.
SifraFink.	= *Sifra or Torat Kohanim. According to Codex Assemani LXVI.* With a Hebrew Introduction by Louis Finkelstein (N.Y., 1956).
SifraHillel	= *Sifra.* With the Commentary of *Hillel b. R. Eliaqim*. Ed. by Shachne Koleditzky (Jerusalem, 1961).
Sifra ed. Weiss	= *Sifra*, ed. Isaac Hirsch Weiss (Repr.: N.Y., 1947).
SifHillel	= *Sifre... ʿim Perush... Rabbenu Hillel bar Eliaqim.* Ed. Shachne Koleditzky (Jerusalem, 1958).
SifHorovitz	= *Siphre d'Be Rab. Fasciculus primus: Siphre ad Numeros adjecto Siphre Zutta.* Ed. H. S. Horovitz (Leipzig, 1917).
SifIshShalom	= *Sifre debe Rab. ʿIm Tosafot Meir ʿAyin.* Ed. Meir IshShalom (Friedman). (Vienna, 1864. Repr.: N.Y., 1948).
SifLieberman	= *Siphre Zutta (The Midrash of Lydda).* II. *The Talmud of Caesarea* (N.Y., 1968), ed. S. Lieberman.
SifNeṣiv	= *Sifre... ʿEmeq HaNeṣiv.* Naftali Ṣevi Yehudah Berlin (Jerusalem, 1960).
SifPardo	= *Sefer Sifre Debe Rab.* David Pardo (Salonika, 1799. Repr.: Jerusalem, 1970).
SifVolk	= *Sifre... ʿim hagahot... HaGRA veʿim perush Keter Kehunah.* Ṣevi Hirsch Hakkohen Volk. Ed. Yaʿaqob Hakkohen Volk (Jerusalem, 1954).

Sif Yasq	= *Sifre Zutta leSeder Bamidbar* ... *ʾAmbuhaʾ deSifre.* Yaʿaqob Zeʾeb Yaskobitz (Lodz, 1929. Repr.: Bené Beraq, 1967) I-II.
Silverstein	= A. J. Silverstein, "Consumer protection in Talmudic law," *Commercial Law Journal* 1974, 79:279-82.
Silverstein, *Right*	= A. J. Silverstein, "Right of appeal in Talmudic law," *Case-Western Reserve Journal of International Law* 1973 (Winter) 6:33-47.
Silverstein, *Liability*	= A. J. Silverstein, "Liability of the Physician in Jewish law," *Israel Law Review* 1975; 10:378-388.
Silverstone	= *Shebuʿoth. Translated into English with Notes, Glossary, and Indices.* By A. E. Silverstone (London, 1948: Soncino Press).
Simon and Slotki	= *Baba Bathra. Translated into English with Notes, Glossary, and Indices.* By Maurice Simon and Israel W. Slotki (London, 1948: The Soncino Press).
Simonis	= Henry S. Simonis, *Zum alten jüdischen Zivilrecht* (Berlin, 1922).
Simonis, *Some*	= Henry S. Simonis, *Some Aspects of the ancient Jewish Civil Law* (London, 1928).
Skweres	= D. E. Skweres, "Das Motiv der Strafgrunderfragung in biblischen und neuassyrischen Texten," *Biblische Zeitschrift* 1970, 14:181-197.
Slotki	= *Horayoth. Translated into English with Notes, Glossary, and Indices.* By Israel W. Slotki (London, 1948: Soncino Press).
Smith	= G. A. Smith, "The Jewish Constitution from Nehemiah to the Maccabees," *The Expositer* 1906 (7th series) Sept., 193-209.
Smith	= John M. P. Smith, *The Origin and History of Hebrew Law* (Chicago, 1931).
Solomon	= R. Solomon, *L'Esclavage en droit comparé juif et romain* (Paris, 1931).
Sot.	= Soṭah
Sperber	= D. Sperber, "On the transfer of property from Jew to non-Jew in Amoraic Palestine (200-400)," *Diné Israel* 1973, 4:17-34.
Sperber, *Flight*	= D. Sperber, "Flight and the Talmudic law of usucaption, a study in the social history of 3rd century Palestine," *Revue Internationale des Droits de l'Antiquité* 1972, 19:29-42.
Sperber, *Laesio*	= D. Sperber, "Laesio enormis and the Talmudic law of *onaʾah*, a study in the social history of 3rd century Palestine," *Israel Law Review* 1973, 8:254-274.
Suk.	= Sukkah
Sulzberger	= Mayer Sulzberger, *The Ancient Hebrew Law of Homicide* (Philadelphia, 1915).
Sulzberger, *Polity*	= Mayer Sulzberger, *The polity of the ancient Hebrews* (Philadelphia, 1912).
T.	= Tosefta
T	= *Sidré Mishnah. Neziqin, Qodoshim, Tohorot. Ketab yad Yerushalayim, 1336. Ketab Yad beniqud lefi messoret Teman.* (Repr.: Jerusalem, 1970). Introduction by S. Morag.
Ta.	= Taʿanit
Tem.	= Temurah
Ter.	= Terumot
Toh.	= Ṭohorot
TR	= See Saul Lieberman, *Tosefet Rishonim.*
Tucker	= G. M. Tucker, "Legal background of Genesis 23," *Journal of Biblical Literature* 1966, 85:77-84.
Tucker, *Witnesses*	= G. M. Tucker, "Witnesses and 'dates' in Israelite contracts," *Catholic Biblical Quarterly* 1966, 28:42-45.
T.Y.	= Ṭebul Yom
TYB	= *Tifeʾret Yisraʾel Boʿaz.* See TYY.

TYT	= *Tosafot Yom Tob*. Yom Tob Lipmann Heller, 1579-1654. From reprint of Mishnah, ed. Romm.
TYY	= *Tife'ret Yisra'el, Yakhin*. Israel ben Gedaliah Lipschütz, 1782-1860. (With supercommentary of Baruch Isaac Lipschütz = TYB.) From reprint of Mishnah, ed. Romm.
Unknown	= *Mishnah. Sedarim Zeraim, Moed, Nashim. Unknown Edition*. Printed in Pisaro or Constantinople. (Jerusalem, 1970).
Uqs.	= 'Uqṣin
Uziel	= B. Uziel, "Din u-Mishpat," *Sinai* 1945, IX:107ff.
V	= *Talmud Babli. Nidpas 'al yedé Daniel Bomberg bishenat 5282* [= 1522]. *Venezia* (Venice, 1522. Repr.: Jerusalem, 1971).
Van Selms	= A. Van Selms, "The Goring Ox in Babylonian and Biblical Law," *Archiv Orientalni* 1950, 18/4.
Vat 130	= *Manuscripts of the Babylonian Talmud. From the Collection of the Vatican Library*. (Jerusalem, 1972). Series A.
Vat 112	= *Manuscripts of the Babylonian Talmud. From the Collection of the Vatican Library* (Jerusalem, 1974). Series B.
Wahrhaftig	= S. Wahrhaftig, "Labor law," *Encyclopedia Judaica* 10:1325-1330.
De Ward	= E. F. De Ward, "Superstition and judgment, archaic methods of finding a verdict," *Zeitschrift für die alttestamentliche Wissenschaft* 1977, 89:1-20.
Waxman	= M. Waxman, "Civil and Criminal Procedure of Jewish Courts," *Students Annual of the Jewish Theological Seminary* (N.Y., 1914), pp. 259-309.
Webber	= G. J. Webber, "The principles of the Jewish law of property," *Studies in Jewish Jurisprudence* II (N.Y., 1974) pp. 1-12.
Weinberg	= M. Weinberg, "Die Organization der jüdischen Ortsgemeinden in der talmudischen Zeit," *MGWJ* 1896-97, 41:588-604, 639-660; 673-691.
Weingreen	= J. Weingreen, "The Deuteronomic legislator; a proto-rabbinic type," in *Proclamation and Presence: Old Testament Essays in Honour of G. H. Davies* (Richmond, Va., 1970) pp. 76-89.
Weis	= P. R. Weiss, *Mishnah Horayoth. Its History and Exposition* (Manchester, 1952: Manchester University Press).
Weisfeld	= Israel Harold Weisfeld, *Labor Legislation in the Talmud* (Chicago, 1946).
Weismann	= J. Weismann, "Talion und öffentliche Strafe im Mosaischen Rechte," *Festschrift für Adolf Wach I* (Leipzig, 1913) pp. 22-40.
Weiss-Halivni	= David Weiss-Halivni, "The role of the *mara d'atra* in Jewish law," *Proceedings of the Rabbinical Assembly* 1976, 38:124-129.
Williams	= G. R. Williams, "The purpose of penology in the mosaic law and today," *Bibliotheca Sacra* 1976, 529:42-55.
Wines	= E. C. Wines, *Commentaries on the laws of the ancient Hebrews, with an essay on civil society and government* (N.Y., 1853).
Wolfson	= H. A. Wolfson, "Synedrion in Greek Literature and Philo," *Jewish Quarterly Review* 1945-46, 36:303-306.
Women	= Jacob Neusner, *A History of the Mishnaic Law of Women* (Leiden, 1980f.) I-V.
Wagner	= V. Wagner, *Rechssätze in gebundener Sprache und Rechtssatzreihen im israelitischen Recht* (Berlin, 1972).
Y.	= Yerushalmi. Palestinian Talmud.
Y.T.	= Yom Ṭob
Yad.	= Yadayim
Yaron	= R. Yaron, "The goring ox in Near Eastern law," in *Jewish Law in Ancient and Modern Israel*, ed. by Haim Cohn (N.Y., 1971).

Yaron, *Introduction*	= Reuven Yaron, *Introduction to the law of the Aramaic papyri* (Oxford, 1961).
Yaron, *Laws*	= R. Yaron, *The Laws of Eshnunna* (Jerusalem, 1969).
Yaron, *Systems*	= R. Yaron, "Jewish Law and other Legal Systems in Antiquity," *Journal of Semitic Studies* 1959, 4:308ff.
Yeivin	= Israel Yeivin, *A Collection of Mishnaic Geniza Fragments with Babylonian Vocalization. With Description of the Manuscripts and Indices* (Jerusalem, 1974).
Yeb.	= Yebamot
Z	= M. S. Zuckermandel, *Tosephta. Based on Erfurt and Vienna Codices* (Repr.: Jerusalem, 1963).
Zab.	= Zabim
Zeb.	= Zebaḥim
Zeitlin	= S. Zeitlin, "Studies in talmudic jurisprudence; possession, pignus and hypothec," *JQR* 1969, 60:89-111.
Zeitlin, *Pol.*	= Solomon Zeitlin, "The Political Synedrion and the Religious Sanhedrin," *JQR* 1945 (Oct.) v. 36.
Zeitlin, *San.*	= Solomon Zeitlin, "ha-Sanhedrin bi-Yeme ha-Bayit ha-Sheni" *ha-Doar* 1941, 22, 7:109.
Zeitlin, *Syn.*	= Solomon Zeitlin, "Synedrion in the Judeo-Hellenistic Literature and Sanhedrin in the Tannaitic Literature," *Jewish Quarterly Review* 1946 (Jan.)
Zeitlin, *Title*	= Solomon Zeitlin, "The Titles High Priest and the Nasi of the Sanhedrin," *JQR* 1957-58, 48:1-5.
Zeitlin, *Greek*	= Solomon Zeitlin, "Synedrion in the Greek Literature, the Gospels and the Institute of the Sanhedrin," *JQR* 1946 (Oct.) 36.
Ziegler	= Ziegler, *Die Königsgleichnisse des Midrash beleuchtet durch die Kaiserzeit* (Breslau, 1903).
Zucrow	= Solomon Zucrow, *Adjustment of Law to Life in Rabbinic Literature* (Boston, 1928).
Zunz	= Leopold Zunz, "Etwas über die jüdische Literatur," in Zunz, *Gesammelte Schriften*, v. 1.
Zuri	= Jacob Samuel Zuri, *Shitat ha-taʿanot* (London, 1933).
ZY	= *Zeraʿ yiṣḥaq*. By Yiṣḥaq Ḥayyot (Brooklyn, 1960).

Mrs. Lee Haas served as bibliographical research assistant for this project.

TRANSLITERATIONS

א	=	ʾ	מ ם	=	M
ב	=	B	נ ן	=	N
ג	=	G	ס	=	S
ד	=	D	ע	=	ʿ
ה	=	H	פ ף	=	P
ו	=	W	צ ץ	=	Ṣ
ז	=	Z	ק	=	Q
ח	=	Ḥ	ר	=	R
ט	=	Ṭ	שׁ	=	Š
י	=	Y	שׂ	=	Ś
כ ך	=	K	ת	=	T
ל	=	L			

INTRODUCTION

Baba Qamma deals with the restoration of the normal, whole condition of one's property and person when these have been subjected to damages. It therefore focuses attention upon the compensation to be paid for damages done by another person's property or by another person. Baba Mesia takes up the issue of the preservation of the proper order of an orderly society. This tractate pays special attention to the issues which have gone before: property relationships. Having restored the wholeness and stasis of diminished property and injured persons, we now provide rules for the maintenance of that perfection which is the *status quo*.

The tractate begins where the foregoing one concludes, with matters of one's material possessions. Baba Qamma ends with attention to restoring what has been stolen, and, predictably, Baba Mesia commences (unit III) with the issue restoring what has *not* been stolen, but lost. It proceeds to deal in detail with one's responsibilities for the property of others.

Its second major interest—units IV and V below—is in equitable relationships between buyer and seller, on the one side, an employer and employee, on the other. At issue in the former is the equivalent of theft, namely, overcharging and usury, and of primary concern in the latter is the definition of what each party owes to the other. These are essentially two aspects of the same principle: a fair and complete balance between what the one gives and what the other gives. Usury, on the one side, or oppressive labor conditions (e.g., denying the right to nibble at the grain on which a worker is laboring), on the other, would upset that perfect order at which Mishnah aims.

The closing unit turns to a fresh matter, real estate, with special attention to relationships of partners in a given house and to relationships between landlord and tenant or tenant-farmer. Only when we come to Baba Batra shall we be able to characterize the fundamental concern of the law before us. It would appear from the materials contained within the limits of the present tractate that at issue, once more, is the maintenance of a perfect balance and an exact exchange: *just weights, just measures*, applied to these other areas of economic and social interchange.

The reader will find convenient a survey of the relevant biblical passages, the facts of which are utilized in important ways in our tractate. As we shall see, the people who frame the tractate in no way are interested in the logic of the order or structure of the biblical codes. They have their own ideas on how they wish to organize and lay out their law. To be sure, they refer constantly and faithfully to Scripture's facts. But they are remarkably uninterested in Scripture's order or redactional and formulary preferences. Following Albeck (pp. 53-55), we find these verses laid out in the sequence in which they prove important in this tractate.

Deut. 22:1-4

You shall not see your brother's ox or his sheep go astray, and withhold your help from them; you shall take them back to your brother. And if he is not near you, or if you do not know him, you shall bring it home to your house, and it shall be with you until your brother seeks it; then you shall restore it to him. And so you shall do with his ass; so you shall do with his garment; so you shall do with any lost thing of your brother's, which he loses and you find; you may not withhold your help. You shall not see your brother's ass or his ox fallen down by the way, and withhold your help from them; you shall help him to lift them up again.

Lev. 25:14

And if you sell to your neighbor or buy from your neighbor, you shall not wrong one another.

Lev. 25:17

You shall not wrong one another, but you shall fear your God; for I am the Lord your God.

Ex. 22:20

Whoever sacrifices to any god, save to the Lord only, shall be utterly destroyed.

Lev. 19:33

When a stranger sojourns with you in your land, you shall not do him wrong.

Ex. 22:23-24

If you do afflict them, and they cry out to me, I will surely hear their cry; and my wrath will burn, and I will kill you with the sword, and your wives shall become widows and your children fatherless.

Lev. 25:35-37

And if your brother becomes poor, and cannot maintain himself with you, you shall maintain him as a stranger and a sojourner he shall live with you. Take no interest from him or increase, but fear your God; that your brother may live beside you. You shall not lend him your money at interest, nor give him your food for profit.

Deut. 23:20-21

You shall not lend upon interest to your brother, interest on money, interest on victuals, interest on anything that is lent for interest. To a foreigner you may lend upon interest, but to your brother you shall not lend upon interest; that the Lord your God may bless you in all that you undertake in the land which you are entering to take possession of it.

Deut. 23:24-25

When you go into your neighbor's vineyard, you may eat your fill of grapes, as many as you wish, but you shall not put any in your vessel. When you go into your neighbor's standing grain, you may pluck the ears with your hand, but you shall not put a sickle to your neighbor's standing grain.

Ex. 7:15

If a man delivers to his neighbor money or goods to keep, and it is stolen out of the man's house, then, if the thief is found, he shall pay double. If the thief is not found, the owner of the house shall come near to God, to show whether or not he has put his hand to his neighbor's goods.

For every breach of trust, whether it is for ox, for ass, for sheep, for clothing, or for any kind of lost thing, of which one says, "This is it,' the case of both parties shall come before God; he whom God shall condemn shall pay double to his neighbor.

If a man delivers to his neighbor an ass or an ox or a sheep or any beast to keep, and it dies or is hurt or is driven away, without any one seeing it, an oath by the Lord shall be between them both to see whether he has not put his hand to his neighbor's property; and the owner shall accept the oath, and he shall not make restitution. But if it is stolen from him, he shall make restitution to its owner. If it is torn by beasts, let him bring it as evidence; he shall not make restitution for what has been torn.

If a man borrows anything of his neighbor, and it is hurt or dies, the owner not being with it, he shall make full restitution. If the owner was with it, he shall not make restitution; if it was hired, it came for its hire.

Lev. 19:13

You shall not oppress your neighbor or rob him. The wages of a hired servant shall not remain with you all night until the morning.

Deut. 24:14-15

You shall not oppress a hired servant who is poor and needy, whether he is one of your brethren or one of the sojourners who are in your land within your towns; you shall give him his hire on the day he earns it, before the sun goes down (for he is poor, and sets his heart upon it); lest he cry against you to the Lord, and it be sin in you.

Ex. 22:25-27

If you lend money to any of my people with you who is poor, you shall not be to him as a creditor, and you shall not exact interest from him. If ever you take your neighbor's garment in pledge, you shall restore it to him before the sun goes down; for that is his only covering, it is his mantle for his body; in what else shall he sleep? And if he cries to me, I will hear, for I am compassionate.

Deut. 24:10-13

> When you make your neighbor a loan of any sort, you shall not go into his house to fetch his pledge. You shall stand outside, and the man to whom you make the loan shall bring the pledge out to you. And if he is a poor man, you shall not sleep in his pledge; when the sun goes down, you shall restore to him the pledge that he may sleep in his cloak and bless you; and it shall be righteousness to you before the Lord your God.

Deut. 24:17-18

> You shall not pervert the justice due to the sojourner or to the fatherless, or take a widow's garment in pledge; but you shall remember that you were a slave in Egypt and the Lord your God redeemed you from there; therefore I command you to do this.

Deut. 24:6

> No man shall take a mill or an upper millstone in pledge; for he would be taking a life in pledge.

As we observed in Baba Qamma (Part I, pp. 2-4), we shall now see that the order and sequence of Mishnah's topics in no way are dictated by Scripture. Nor on the basis of the verses just now surveyed should we have been able to predict those subjects which will be given extended attention, e.g., issues of bailments, or those which will have been treated in a perfunctory way, e.g., disposition of a utensil given as a pledge for a loan. Mishnah takes over from Scripture a vast legacy of facts but makes these facts distinctively Mishnaic. We now turn to a survey of how the framers of Mishnah have laid out the topics at hand.

As we noticed, this tractate takes up where the preceding one leaves off. The one following, moreover, is so closely tied to this one that Tosefta to Baba Mesia treats in a single chapter Mishnah Baba Mesia Chapter Ten and Mishnah Baba Batra Chapter One. We shall see that the concluding unit of Baba Batra attends to damages done to property belonging to others, thus concluding the opening tractate's long essay on damages. Now we take up further matters of property, no longer having to do with issues of damages. As I see it, the tractate yields four units, each one of them continuing into its successor: responsibility for the possessions of others; commercial transactions; laws of labor and bailment; and real estate.

The third of the four is somewhat less clearly focused upon a single topic than the others, for it is put together in accord with a theory of redaction other than the prevailing one. Normally, Mishnah groups together in a single spot all of its rules on a given topic. But here, there is a sequence of two alternating subjects: relationships between worker and employer, then rules of rentals and bailments, then relationships between worker and employer, and, again, rules of bailments. If there were only a single go-around on the two distinct themes, we might suppose that there are flaws in the redactional work of the unit, or that another theory of redaction than the prevailing one has come into play. But as matters stand, the unit repeats its sequence of topics in two well-composed topical cycles. That seems to me to mean the sequence is deliberate. In any event, the tractate as a whole is continuous with its neighbors, fore and aft, and follows a reasonably logical sequence.

We shall now consider its organization in the context of its predecessor, just as, in Part III, at the end of the Babas, we shall see all together the whole sequence of topics.

Baba Qamma

I. *Damage by Chattels.* 1:1-6:6

A. *The fundamental rules of assessing damages when the cause is one's property, animate and inanimate.* 1:1-2:6

1:1 There are four generative causes of damages: ox, pit, crop-destroying beast, and fire. While they differ, they have in common the trait that they do damage and one is responsible for what they do.

1:2 In the case of anything of which I am liable to take care, I am deemed to render possible whatever damage it may do—whole or in part. Exceptions: property held by the cult, not held by Israelites, not actually owned, and what is located in the domain of the defendant (whose property has caused the damage).

1:3 Assessment of compensation for injury is in terms of ready cash, but it is paid in kind.

1:4 These five are deemed harmless (so that, if they do damage, the owner pays only half-damages, with liability limited to the value of the carcass of the ox which did the damage), and these five are deemed attested dangers (so that liability is unlimited by the value of the ox which did the damage). In general: a beast is not regarded as an attested danger in regard to butting, pushing, biting, lying down, or kicking. The tooth is an attested danger to eat whatever is suitable for eating, and the like.

2:1 *Exposition of M. 1:4:* How is *the leg* deemed an attested danger in regard to breaking something as it walks along?

2:2 *Exposition of M. 1:4:* How is *the tooth* deemed an attested danger in regard to eating what is suitable for eating?

2:3 The dog or goat which jumped from the top of the roof and broke utensils—the owner pays full damages, because they are attested dangers. If the dog took a cake which had a cinder attached and ate the cake and set fire to grain, for the cake the owner pays full damages, and for the standing grain, half. The former is what the dog is liable to do, the latter is unusual.

2:4 What sort of animal is deemed harmless, and what is one which is an attested danger? The procedure for declaring a beast an attested danger.

2:5 *Exposition of M. 1:4:* An ox which causes damage in the domain of the one who is injured is liable—how so? If it happened in public domain, the owner pays half damages, but if it was in the domain of the injured party, he pays full damages.

2:6 Man is perpetually deemed to be an attested danger, under all circumstances.

B. *Damages done in the public domain.* 3:1-7

3:1 He who leaves a jug in the public domain and someone else came and stumbled on it and broke it—the latter is exempt. If the jug did damage, the one who left it there is liable.

3:2-3 He who pours water into the public domain, and someone else was injured on it, is liable. Five-part construction makes the single point that one who creates a hazard in the public domain is liable for damages.

3:4 Two pot-sellers going along in single file, the first stumbled and fell and the second stumbled over the first—the first is liable to compensate the second for his injuries. He did not warn the other.

3:5 This one comes with his jar, and that with his beam—if the jar of this one was broken by the beam of that, the owner of the beam is exempt, for he had every right to walk along where he did, just as did the other.

3:6 Two going along in the public domain, one running, the other ambling, or both running, and they injured one another—both exempt. Both have every right to be there.

3:7 He who chops wood in private property and the chips injured someone in public domain, or contrariwise, is liable.

C. *Exercises and illustrations on the ox.* 3:8-4:4

3:8 The oxen generally deemed harmless which injured one another —the owner pays half-damages of the excess of the value of the injury done by the less injured to the more injured ox. If both were attested dangers, the owners pays full damages for the excess. Further exercises on the interplay between the one deemed harmless and the one which was an attested danger.

3:9 Meir and Judah on the interpretation and application of Ex. 21:35.

3:10 There is he who is liable for the deed of his ox and exempt on account of his own deed or exempt for the deed of his ox and liable on account of his own deed. The principles illustrated are that man inflicts humiliation, but oxen do not; that the rule of Ex. 21:26-7 applies to the owner, not to the beast; and that one is not liable for the death-penalty and for damages simultaneously.

3:11 A triplet which uses the facts of this unit to illustrate the proposition that the one who lays claim against his fellow bears the burden of proof.

4:1 An ox deemed harmless which gored four or five oxen, one after the other—[the owner] pays compensation to the last among them, next to the next-to-the last, and so on.

4:2 An ox which is an attested danger as to its own species, but not an attested danger as to what is not its own species—for that for which it is an attested danger, the owner pays full damages, and for that for which it is not an attested danger, he pays half-damages.

4:3 An ox of an Israelite which gored an ox belonging to the sanctuary —the owner is exempt, since Ex. 21:35 excludes oxen belonging to the sanctuary. The same is so for a gentile. Illustrated: M. 1:2.

4:4 An ox of a person of sound senses which gored an ox belonging to a deaf-mute, idiot, or minor—the owner is liable. But one belonging to a deaf-mute, idiot, or minor which gored an ox belonging to a person of sound senses—the former is exempt. Procedure for declaring an ox belonging to a deaf-mute, etc., to be attested danger.

D. *The ransom and the death-penalty for the ox.* 4:5-5:4

4:5 An ox which gored a man who died—if it was an attested danger, the owner pays the ransom price. If it was deemed harmless, he is exempt.

4:6 An ox which was rubbing itself against a wall, and the wall fell on a man—if it had intended to kill another beast and killed a man, etc., the ox is exempt.

4:7 An ox belonging to a woman, an estate, a guardian, etc.,—these oxen are liable to the death-penalty.

4:8 An ox which goes forth to be stoned and which the owner declared to be sanctified is not sanctified, and if the meat is properly slaughtered, it is nonetheless prohibited. But if this was before the court-process was complete, it is sanctified; the meat is permitted.

4:9 If one handed an ox to a bailee, the bailee takes the place of the owner.

5:1 An ox deemed harmless which gored a cow, and a newly-born calf was found dead beside her, so we do not know whether or not the ox killed the calf—the owner pays half-damages for the cow, and quarter-damages for the calf.

5:2-3 The potter who brought his pots into the courtyard of a householder without permission, and the beast of the householder broke them—the householder is exempt. If the beast was injured on them, the owner of the pots is liable. If the householder gave permission, however, he bears liability.

5:4 An ox intending to gore its fellow which hit a woman and caused a miscarriage—the owner of the ox is exempt from paying compensation for the offspring.

E. *Damages done by the pit* (M. 1:1). 5:5-7

5:5 He who digs a pit in private domain and opens it into public domain, or in public domain and opens it into private, or in private and opens it into private, is liable for damage done by pit.

5:6 A pit belonging to partners, and one passed it and did not cover it, and the second did likewise—the second is liable.

5:7 All the same are an ox and all other beasts so far as falling into a pit (and various other biblical references to an ox) are concerned. Why is an ox specified?

F. *Crop-destroying beast* (M. 1:1). 6:1-3

6:1-2 He who brings a flock into a fold and shut the gate properly, but the flock go out and did damages is exempt. If he did not shut the gate properly, he is liable.

6:3 He who stacks sheaves in the field of his fellow without permission and the beast of the owner of the field ate them—the owner of the field is exempt. (Cf. M. 5:2.)

G. *Damages done by fire* (M. 1:1). 6:4-6

    6:4 He who causes a fire to break out through the action of a deaf-mute, etc.

    6:5 He who sets fire to a stack of grain, in which utensils were located—Judah: The one who lit the fire pays compensation for whatever was in the stack which burned up. Sages: Only for the stack of wheat.

    6:6 A spark which flew out from under the hammer and did damage—the smith is liable.

II. *Damages done by persons. Theft.* 7:1-10:10

A. *Penalties for the theft of an ox or a sheep, in line with Ex. 22:14.* 7:1-7:7

    7:1 More encompassing is the rule covering payment for twofold restitution than the rule covering payment of fourfold or fivefold restitution.

    7:2 If one stole an ox or sheep on the evidence of two witnesses and was convicted of having slaughtered or sold it on the basis of their testimony, or on the basis of the testimony of two other witnesses, he pays fourfold or fivefold restitution. If he stole or sole an ox or sheep on the Sabbath, etc., he pays fourfold or fivefold restitution.

    7:3 If he stole an ox or sheep on the evidence of two witnesses and slaughtered or sold it on the basis of their testimony, and they turned out to be false witnesses, they pay full restitution.

    7:4 If one stole on the evidence of two and was accused of having slaughtered or sold the ox or sheep on the basis of only one witness, he pays twofold restitution but not fourfold or fivefold restitution.

    7:5 If one sold all but one hundredth part of the stolen ox or sheep, he pays twofold restitution but not fourfold or fivefold restitution.

    7:6 If the thief was dragging a sheep or ox but it died in the domain of the owner, he is exempt. If he lifted it up or removed it from the domain of the owner and then it died, he is liable.

    [7:7 They do not rear small cattle in the Land of Israel, but they do so in Syria and in the wastelands which are in the Land of Israel.]

B. *Penalties for assault.* 8:1-7

    8:1 He who inflicts injury on his fellow is liable for compensation on five counts: injury, pain, medical costs, loss of income, and indignity.

    8:2 Continuation of foregoing.

    8:3 He who hits his father or mother but did not make a wound, etc., is liable on all counts.

    8:4 A deaf-mute, idiot, and minor—meeting up with them is a bad thing. He who injures them is liable, but they who injured other people are exempt.

    8:5 He who hits his father or mother and did make a wound is exempt, because he is tried for his life.

    8:6 He who boxes the ear of his fellow pays a *sela*; if he smacked him, he pays two hundred *zuz*; with the back of his hand, four hundred *zuz*.

    8:7 Even though the defendant pays off the plaintiff, he still has to seek forgiveness. If one says, "Blind my eye," the one who does so still is liable.

C. *Penalties for damages to property. Restoring what is stolen.* 9:1-10:10

9:1   He who steals wood and made it into utensils pays compensation in accord with the value of the wood at the time of the theft.

9:2   If he stole a beast and it got old, he pays compensation in accord with the value at the time of the theft.

9:3   If he gave something to a craftsman to repair and the object was spoiled, the craftsman is liable to pay compensation.

9:4   He who hands over wool to a dyer and the dye in the cauldron burned the wool—the dyer pays the value of the wool.

9:5   He who stole something from his fellow worth a *perutah* and took an oath that he had stolen nothing and then wants to make restitution must take the object to him, even all the way to Media.

9:6   If the thief paid back the principal but not the added fifth, he need not do so. If he paid back the added fifth but not the principal, he needs to do so.

9:7   If he paid back the principal but swore falsely about the added fifth and then confessed, he has to pay back an added fifth on the added fifth.

9:8   If a person denied having a bailment and takes an oath falsely and then witnesses testify that the oath was false, he pays twofold restitution. Had he confessed on his own, he would have had to pay back the principal, an added fifth, and a guilt-offering.

9:9-10   He who steals from his father and takes an oath to him (that he did not do so), and then the father died pays back the principal and added fifth to the other sons or brothers.

9:11   He who steals from a proselyte and takes an oath to him and then the proselyte dies—lo, this one pays the principal and added fifth to the priests, in line with Num. 5:8.

9:12   If he had paid over the money to the men of the priestly watch on duty and then died, the heirs cannot retrieve the funds from the priests, since it is said + Num. 5:10.

10:1   He who steals food and gives it to his children—they are exempt from making restitution.

10:2   If tax-collectors took one's ass and gave him another, lo, it is his, because the original owners have given up hope of getting it back.

10:3   He who recognizes his utensils or books in someone else's possession and a report of theft had circulated—the purchaser takes an oath to him specifying how much he had paid the thief, then the original owner pays that price and retrieves his property.

10:4   If one suffered a loss to help someone else save his property, he can claim only wages, unless he had established a prior condition for compensation for his loss.

10:5   He who stole a field from his fellow, and bandits siezed it from him—if it is a blow from which the whole district suffered, he may say to the original victim, "Lo, there is yours before you."

10:6   He who stole or borrowed something from his fellow or with whom the latter deposited something in a settled area, may not return it to him in the wilderness.

10:7   He who says to his fellow, "I have stolen from you, and I don't know whether I returned the object or not," is liable to pay restitution.

10:8 He who steals a lamb from a flock and returned it and the lamb died or was stolen again is liable to make it up.

10:9 They do not purchase from herdsmen wool, milk or kids, since these are likely to have been stolen from the owner of the flock.

10:10 Shreds of wool which the laundryman pulls out belong to him. Those which the woolcomber pulls out belong to the householder.

Baba Mesia

III. *The disposition of other peoples' possessions.* 1:1-3:12

  A. *Conflicting claims on lost objects.* 1:1-4

1:1-2 Two lay hold of a cloak—both take an oath and they divide it. If one party concedes the claim to the other for part, only the other part, not conceded, is subject to an oath.

1:3-4 If one was riding on a beast and saw a lost object and said to his fellow, "Give it to me," but the other took it and said, "I take possession of it"—the latter has acquired possession of it.

  B. *Returning an object to the original owner.* 1:5-2:11

1:5 Things found by someone's dependents belong to him. Things not found by his dependents do not.

1:6-8 If one found bonds of indebtedness, he should (not) return them. Lists of commercial papers and documents not to be returned.

2:1-2 What lost items are the finder's, and which ones is he liable to proclaim (seeking the owner)?

2:3-4 If one found pigeons tied together behind a fence, he should not touch them. If there is evidence that an object belongs to someone, it should not be touched.

2:5 Exegesis of Deut. 22:2. Everything which has distinctive marks and which is subject to a claim must be returned to the owner.

2:6 And for how long is one liable to make proclamation of having found an object?

2:7 If a claimant has described what he has lost but has not specified distinctive marks, one should not give it to him.

2:8 Taking care of objects one has found, pending return to the rightful owner.

2:9 What is lost property (which must be returned)?

2:10 The limits of one's responsibility to retrieve an animal and return it to the owner.

2:11 If one has to choose between seeking what he has lost and what his father has lost, his own takes precedence.

  C. *Rules of bailment.* 3:1-12

3:1 He who deposits a beast or utensils with his fellow, and they were stolen, if the bailee made restitution and was unwilling to take an oath, and the thief was found, he pays restitution to the bailee. If not, then to the owner.

3:2 He who rents a cow from his fellow and then lent it to someone else, and it died of natural causes, the one who rented it takes an oath that it died of natural causes, and the one who borrowed it pays compensation.

3:3-5 If one said to two people, "The father of one of you deposited money with me, and I don't know which one it was," he pays a *maneh* to each of them, for he has admitted it on his own. Two further cases of bailment where there is a conflicting claim. He who deposits produce with his fellow—even if it is going to waste, the fellow should not touch it.

3:6 Produce deposited with someone should remain untouched by that person, even if it rots.

3:7-8 He who deposits produce with his fellow—the bailee when returning it may make reductions due to natural depletion or the action of mice.

3:9 He who deposits a jar with his fellow, and the owner did not specify a place for it, and it was moved and broken . . . .

3:10 He who deposits coins with his fellow, if the latter did not tend to them properly, he is responsible. He did not take care of them in the ordinary way. If he did, he is not liable to make them up.

3:11 He who deposits coins with a money changer.

3:12 He who makes use of a bailment: assessing compensation.

IV. *Commercial transactions.* 4:1-5:11

A. *Overcharge and misrepresentation.* 4:1-12

4:1-2 Coins do not acquire commodities, but commodities do acquire coins. Gold, a commodity, acquires silver coins. Thus if the buyer had made acquisition of produce but the coins were not paid over, the buyer cannot retract.

4:3 Overreaching (fraud) constitutes an overcharge of four pieces of silver out of twenty-four—one sixth of the purchase price. How long may one retract in the case of fraud?

4:4 Both buyer and seller are subject to the rules of fraud.

4:5 How much may a *sela* be defective and still not fall under the rule of fraud?

4:6 How long is it permitted to return a defective coin?

4:7-8 Defrauding involves an overcharge of four pieces of silver to a *sela*, and a claim involving a court-imposed oath, etc. Formal construction.

4:9 These are matters which are not subject to a claim of fraud on account of overcharge: slaves, bills of indebtedness, real estate, and what has been consecrated.

4:10 A claim of fraud applies to the spoken word. One may not say to a storekeeper, "How much is this object?" when he does not plan to buy it.

4:11-12 They do not commingle one sort of produce with another sort of produce (and so adulterate what is for sale).

B. *Usury.* 5:1-11

5:1 What is interest, and what is increase?

5:2 He who lends money to his fellow should not live in his courtyard for free.

5:3 If one sold him a field and the other paid part of the fee, and the vendor said to him, "Whenever you want, bring the rest of the money and then take the field"—it is forbidden. If one lent money on the security of the field and said, "If you do not pay me by this date three years hence, lo, it is mine"—it is his.

5:4 They do not set up a storekeeper for half the profit, unless one pays him an additional wage as a worker. Otherwise his free service to the partner constitutes usury.

5:5 They assess and put out for rearing a cow, an ass, or anything which works for its keep for half the profits. The rancher gets the benefit of the animal's labor, so the capitalist does not have to pay for the rancher's service in addition.

5:6 They do not accept from an Israelite a flock on 'iron terms,' that the one who tends the flock pays a fixed fee and restores the value of the flock as it was when it was handed over to him, because this is interest. There must be an equal sharing in the risks and profits.

5:7 They do not strike a bargain for the price of produce before the market-price is announced. This is 'increase' (M. 5:1).

5:8-9 A man may lend his tenant-farmers wheat to be repaid in wheat if it is for seed, but not if it is for food.

5:10 A man may say to his fellow, "Weed with me, and I'll weed with you," but not, "Weed with me, and I'll hoe with you."

5:11 Those who participate in a loan on interest violate a negative commandment.

V. *Hiring workers. Rentals and bailments.* 6:1-8:3

A. *The mutual obligations of worker and employer.* 6:1-2

6:1-2 He who hires craftsmen and one party deceived the other—one has no claim on the other except a complaint.

B. *Rentals.* 6:3-5

6:3 He who rents out an ass to drive it through hill-country but drove it through the valley, or *vice versa*, and the ass died, is liable.

6:4-5 He who hires a cow to plough in the hill-country but ploughed in the valley, if the ploughshare was broken, is exempt. If he hired the cow to plough in the valley and ploughed in the hill-country, if the ploughshare was broken, he is liable.

C. *Bailments.* 6:6-8

6:6 All craftsmen are in the status of paid bailees. But any who said, "Take what is yours and pay me," enters the status of an unpaid bailee.

6:7 If one made a loan and took a pledge, he is in the status of a paid bailee of the pledge.

6:8 The bailee who moves a jar from one place to another and broke it, whether unpaid or paid, must take an oath (that the jar was broken by accident).

D. *The mutual obligations of worker and employer.* 7:1-7

7:1 He who hires day-workers and told them to start work early or stay late—in a place in which that is not the custom, he has no right to do so.

7:2-3 And these have the right to eat the produce on which they are working, a right endowed by the Torah.

7:4 If the laborer was working on figs, he does not have the right to eat grapes.

7:5 A worker has the right to eat cucumbers, even to a *denar's* worth, or dates, even to a *denar's* worth.

7:6 A man makes a deal with the householder not to exercise his right to eat produce on which he is working, in behalf of himself or other adults, but not in behalf of dependents.

7:7 He who hires workers to work in his fourth-year plantings—lo, these do not have the right to eat. If he did not tell them in advance about the character of the crop, he has to provide food for them.

E. *Bailments.* 7:8-8:3

7:8 There are four kinds of watchmen: unpaid bailee, borrower, paid bailee, hirer. Unpaid bailee takes an oath in all cases; borrower pays in all circumstances of damages to a bailment; paid bailee and hirer take an oath.

7:9-11 A single wolf does not count as an unavoidable accident, two do (and the paid bailee and hirer do not have to pay in the latter case).

8:1 He who borrows a cow and borrowed the service of its owner with it and the cow died—the borrower is exempt.

8:2 He who borrows a cow, borrowed it for half a day and hired it for half a day, etc., and the cow died—the lender claims, "The borrowed cow died," or, "At the time it was borrowed, it died," and the borrower says, "I don't know"—the borrower is liable (as at M. B.M. 1:1).

8:3 He who borrows a cow and the one who lent it sent it along with his son, slave, or a messenger, and the cow died—the borrower is exempt, for it had not yet reached the domain of the borrower.

VI. *Real estate.* 8:4-10:6

A. *Prologue.* 8:4-5

8:4 He who exchanges a cow for an ass, and the cow produced offspring —this one says, "It was before I made the sale," and that one says, "It was after I made the purchase—let them divide the proceeds. Also: purchase of two fields, one big, one small.

8:5 He who sells olive-trees for firewood and before they were chopped down they produce a small quantity of fruit—lo, this belongs to the owner of the olive-trees (not to the landowner). Conflicting claims (as above).

B. *Landlord-tenant relationships.* 8:6-9

8:6 He who rents a house to his fellow without a lease in the rainy season has not got the right to evict him from the Festival to Passover.

8:7 He who rents out a house to his fellow is liable to provide a door, bolt, and lock, and anything made by a craftsman, but the one who rents the house can provide anything not made by a craftsman.

8:8 He who rents out a house to his fellow for a year—if the year is intercalated, it is intercalated to the advantage of the tenant. If it is rented by the month, it is intercalated to the advantage of the landlord.

8:9 He who rents out a house to his fellow, and the house fell down, is liable to provide him with another house of the same character.

C. *The landlord's relationships with a tenant-farmer and sharecropper.* 9:1-10

9:1 He who leases a field from his fellow—in a place in which it is the custom to cut the crops, he must cut them. If it is the custom to uproot them, he must uproot them.

9:2 He who leases a field from his fellow which is irrigated or an orchard —if the water-source went dry, or the trees were cut down, the tenant may not deduct the damages from the rental.

9:3 He who as a sharecropper leases a field from his fellow and then neglected the field—they make an estimate of how much the field is suitable to produce, and the tenant pays that.

9:4 He who leases a field from his fellow and did not want to weed it —they pay no attention to his claim.

9:5 He who leases a field from his fellow and it did not produce a crop still has to tend it.

9:6 He who leases a field from his fellow and locusts ate it up—if it was a disaster affecting the entire province, he may deduct the damages from his rental.

9:7 He who leases a field from his fellow in return for ten *kors* of wheat a year, and the field was smitten and produced poor quality grain—the tenant pays him off from produce grown in that field anyhow.

9:8 He who leases a field from his fellow to sow barley in it may not sow it with wheat.

9:9 He who leases a field from his fellow for a period of only a few years may not sow it with flax.

9:10 He who leases a field from his fellow "for one septannate" at the rate of seven hundred *zuz*—the Seventh Year counts in the number of years. If he leased it from him for seven years, it does not.

D. *Miscellanies: Paying laborers promptly. Taking a pledge.* 9:11-13

9:11 A day-worker collects his wage any time of the night, and a night-worker by day.

9:12 The fee owing for a worker, a beast, or a utensil must be paid promptly.

9:13 He who lends money to his fellow should exact a pledge from him only in court.

E. *Joint-holders of a common property.* 10:1-6

10:1 A house and an upper story belonging to two people which fell down—they divide the ruins.

10:2 A house and an upper story belonging to two people—if the floor of the upper room was broken and the householder does not want to repair it, lo, the owner of the upper story goes and lives downstairs.

10:3 A house and an upper story belonging to two people which fell down—if the resident of the upper story told the householder to rebuild but he does not want to rebuild, lo, the resident of the upper story rebuilds the lower story and lives there.

10:4 So too an olive-press built into a rock.

10:5 He whose wall was near the garden of his fellow and it fell down, and the owner of the garden said to him, "Clear out your stones", but the other said to him, "They're yours"—they pay no attention to him.

10:6 Two terraced gardens, one above the other, with vegetables between them—Meir: They belong to the garden on top; Judah: To the one on the bottom.

The topics of the first two units follow a simple logical sequence. Having dealt with damages done to other peoples' property (Baba Qamma II.C), with special attention to theft of what belongs to someone else, we turn to the corollary problem, avoiding theft of, or damage to, another person's possessions. This is done by restoring to the owner what one has found, on the one side, or faithfully taking care of what another person has deposited for safe-keeping, on the other. These thus are extensions of what has gone before. III.A-B treat the disposition of lost-and-found objects, and III.C the matter of bailment. It appears to me that the second treatment of bailment, V.B-C and V.E, has in mind somewhat more specific and special problems, while in the first go-around, rather general and widely applicable rules are given. But we must not lose sight of the formal unity of III.C, which we shall examine when we study Chapter Three. In any event the constituents of Unit III are well-situated. Unit IV consists of two closely related matters, overcharging and usury. These items belong together, though one could have changed places with the other without a loss in cogency.

Had Unit V come after Unit III, its curious of topics would have proven still more difficult to explain, so perhaps there was a conscious decision to keep the whole unit apart from its topical companion. In any event we have already noticed its problems. It is too long to be regarded as an appendix of some sort—e.g., to a massive construction built up from III and IV. It also is too orderly to see the alternation of the two principal topics as an error.

Finally, we notice that Unit VI starts with a rather ambitious prologue, parallel in its basic considerations—how we adjudicate conflicting claims—to the one with which we start at M. 1:1. The sequence of topics from that point—landlord to tenant, then a landlord's relationship to a tenant-farmer or a share-cropper—is not immutable. Reversing VI.C and VI.B would not have caused any confusion. But the topic of relationships in the matter of real property is so sizable and of such fundamental importance that it cannot have come prior to its present location without seriously disturbing the unfolding of the tractate as a whole.

It remains to notice that VI.D does fo unit VI what V.A and V.D do to Unit V. But I find it difficult to suppose that the same sort of redactional theory operative at Unit V accounts for the intrusion of the brief miscellany at VI.D. Mishnah's topical arrangement is simply not so orderly and uniform throughout as one might expect on the basis of the prevailing theory of redaction.

CHAPTER ONE

BABA MESIA CHAPTER ONE

The disposition of ownerless articles which one finds in the street occupies the opening chapter. It presents no significant exegetical problems. (T., by contrast, is remarkably rich and moves off in its own directions; we shall not be detained for long in explaining what is not relevant to M.) We open with a triplet of conflicting claims. If both parties have an equal claim to an object, we divide the object between them. If one claims less than the whole of the object, we divide that part which is subject to dispute and concede to the other that part which is not, so M. 1:1-2.

M. 1:3-4 deal with how one acquires a lost object. It must be through an act of taking physical possession, M. 1:3. One's domain—his inanimate property—may effect possession of an ownerless object under certain circumstances, M. 1:4. This second pair is as well balanced as the first. M. 1:5 makes the well-known point that a man's dependents effect acquisition in his behalf; his adult son or daughter do not. It seems to me this obvious point supplements M. 1:4's interest in the effective acquisition in a man's behalf on the part of his domain.

M. 1:6-8, finally, present a triplet on the disposition of documents which are found in the street. Some of these are not to be returned, since they may no longer be valid and may have been discarded. But court documents are to be restored, in the theory that the court is not going to change its mind. The theme of lost and found property is well executed and will continue.

1:1-2

I A. Two [in court] lay hold of a cloak—
    B. this one says, "I found it!"—
    C. And that one says, "I found it!"—
    D. This one says, "It's all mine!"—
    E. And that one says, "It's all mine!"—
    F. This one takes an oath he has no less a share of it than half,
    G. and that one takes an oath that he has no less a share of it than half.
    H. And they divide it up.

II I. This one says, "It's all mine!"
    J. And that one says, "Half of it is mine!"
    K. The one who says, "It's all mine" takes an oath that he has no less a share of it than three parts.

L. And the one who says, "Half of it is mine," takes an oath that he has no less a share of it than a fourth part.

M. This one then takes three shares, and that one takes the fourth.

M. 1:1

III A. Two were riding on a beast,
B. or one was riding and one was leading it—
C. This one says, "It's all mine!"—
D. and that one says, "It's all mine!"—
E. this one takes an oath that he has no less a share of it than half,
F. and that one takes an oath that he has no less a share of it than half.
G. And they divide it.
H. But when they concede [that they found it together] or have witnesses to prove it, they divide it without taking an oath.

M. 1:2

The triplet makes its points clearly and follows a rigidly precise form, as is clear. If each claims the whole thing, then it is divided. But the one who claims only half concedes to the other party the other half, in which case we divide only the half under dispute. So the claimant of the half takes a fourth, and the claimant of the whole takes the half conceded by the other as well as the quarter he gains in the compromise. H's gloss covers the whole, of course, and is obvious. The fact that each party retains physical possession of the cloak or the beast is important; if one party had control, the other would not gain his rights so easily, as T. 1:1 now tells us.

A. *Two lay hold of a cloak* [M. 1:1A]—
B. This one takes the part of the cloak which is held [by him],
C. and that one takes the part of the cloak which is held [by him].
D. Under what circumstances?
E. When both of them are holding on to it.
F. But if it was in the hand of one of them,
G. he who wishes to remove property from the hand of his fellow bears the burden of proof.

T. 1:1 Z p. 371, ls 19-21

A. This one says, "It's all mine!"
B. And that one says, "A third of it is mine!"
C. The one who says, "It's all mine" takes an oath that he has no less of a share of it than five parts.
D. And the one who says, "A third of it is mine!" takes an oath that he has no less of a share of it than a sixth [part].
E. The governing principle of the matter: One is subjected to an oath only up to one-half of his claimed share alone.

T. 1:2 Z p. 371, ls. 21-24

A. Two who were drawing a camel or pushing an ass,
B. or one of them was drawing and one was pushing [cf. M. 1:2 A-B]— [they make acquisition] by this method.

C. R. Judah says, "The one who draws the camel or pushes the ass—lo, this one has acquired possession [of the beast]."

T. 1:3 Z p. 371, ls. 25-27

T. 1:1 complements M. T. 1:2 gives another instance of M. 1:1 I-M. T. 1:3 glosses M. 1:2.

A. The confession of a party to a case is equivalent to a hundred witnesses.
B. Under what circumstances?
C. In a situation in which one has laid claim against him, and he has conceded it.
D. But if he confessed on his own, he can retract.
E. For the mouth which prohibited is the mouth which permits.
F. The confession of a party to a case is equivalent to a hundred witnesses.
G. But a depository is more credible than either one.
H. This one says, "Thus and so," and that one says, "Thus and so," and the depository says, "Thus and so."—
I. the depository is more credible than either of the others.
J. Under what circumstances?
K. When the third party produces [a document] in his possession.
L. But if the third party does not produce [a document] in his possession,
M. lo, he is equivalent to anybody else.

T. 1:10 Z p. 372, ls. 6-10

A. The seller is believed to state, "To this one did I make my sale."
B. Under what circumstances?
C. When the sale is made by him. But if the sale is not made by him,
D. lo, he is equivalent to anybody else.

T. 1:11 Z p. 372, ls. 10-12

A. A judge is believed to state, "This one did I declare innocent, and that one did I declare guilty."
B. Under what circumstances?
C. When the case is yet before him.
D. But if the case is no longer before him,
E. lo, he is equivalent to anybody else.

T. 1:12 Z p. 372, ls. 12-13

It would appear that T. 1:10 takes up the theme introduced at M. 1:2H, the notion of confession or concession of a claim. From that point, however, T. goes its own way, in a sizable, independent construction of its own.

1:3-4

I A. [If] one was riding on a beast and saw a lost object,
B. and said to his fellow, "Give it to me,"
C. [but the other] took it and said, "I take possession of it"—
D. [the latter] has acquired possession of it.

II E. If after he gave it over [to the one riding on the beast], he said, "I acquired possession of it first,"
    F. he has said nothing whatsoever.

M. 1:3

    A. [If] he saw a lost object and fell on it, and someone else came along and grabbed it,
    B. this one who grabbed it has acquired possession of it.
I C. [If] he saw [people] running after a lost object—
    D. after (1) a deer with a broken leg, (2) pigeons which could not fly,
    E. and he said, "My field has effected possession for me,"
    F. it has effected possession for him.
II G. [If] (1) the deer was running along normally, or (2) [if] the pigeons were flying,
    H. and he said, "My field has effected possession for me,"
    I. he has said nothing whatsoever.

M. 1:4

This seems to me a formal unit, despite the variation of the middle entry, M. 1:4A-B. M. 1:3 makes the obvious point that raising up an object effects possession, but a mere verbal declaration does not. If the one walking along takes possession, M. 1:3 A-C, he owns the object; if he hands it over and the other takes it, the former then cannot effect possession. The point of M. 1:4's pair is that, in the former instance, C-F, the field will contain the deer or pigeons. But in the latter, the field will not hold onto them and has no power to effect possession in behalf of its owner.

    A. He who says, "Let my house effect possession for me of any lost object which falls into it today"
    B. has said nothing whatsoever.
    C. But if any sort of lost object should turn up for him, his words are confirmed.

T. 1:4 Z p. 371, ls. 27-28

At A-B, the man speaks of what is non-existent. At C his words take effect.

    A. "Two parties to a law-suit who were stubborn with one another,
    B. "and one of them said to his fellow, 'If I do not come back between now and such and such a date, then let there be such-and-so for you in my possession'—
    C. "if the time came, let the stipulation be carried out," the words of R. Yosé.
    D. Said R. Judah, "How can this one effect possession of something which has not come into his hand?
    E. "But let him seize it."

T. 1:16 Z p. 372, ls. 20-23

A. "If one pledged a house to him, or pledged a field to him [on account of a loan],

B. "and said to him, 'If I have not given you what I owe you between now and such and such a day, then I have no claim of anything in your possession'—

C. "when that date came and he had not paid him, let his stipulation be carried out," the words of R. Yosé.

D. Said R. Judah, "How can this one effect possession of something which has not come into his hand?

E. "But let him seize it."

F. R. Judah concedes in the case of two who were quarreling about the ownership of a house or a field,

G. and one of them said to his fellow, "If I do not come back between now and such and such a date, I have no claim on you,"

H. then the specified date came and he did not come,

I. that it is certain that he has lost his claim.

J. "He who gives a pledge to his fellow for a house or a field and said to him, 'If I have not given you what I owe you between now and such and such a date, I have no claim on anything in your hand,'

K. "and the other writes for him, 'If I go back on you, lo, I shall double your pledge for you,'

L. "if the specified date came and he has not paid him, let his stipulation be carried out," the words of R. Yosé.

M. Said R. Judah, "How can this one effect possession of something which is not yet his?

N. "But let him give him back his pledge."

O. Said Rabban Simeon b. Gamaliel, "Under what circumstances?

P. "When he has written to him in a document, 'My pledge will effect possession.'

Q. "But if he took from him a house or a field for a hundred *manehs*,

R. "even though he gave him only three *manehs* of that amount,

S. "lo, the field has been acquired for him.

T. "And he pays him the rest, even after three years."

T. 1:17 Z pp. 372, ls. 23-32, 373, 1-2

A. He who gives a pledge to his fellow for his house or for his field—

B. whoever changes the conditions [of the agreement] and whoever retracts—his hand is on the bottom.

C. [If] the seller retracted, the hand of the purchaser is on top.

D. [If] he wanted to take a quarter of the payment in land, he must give him a quarter of the payment in land.

E. [If he wanted a quarter] in ready cash, he pays it,

F. and the rest he collects from land of the poorest quality.

T. 1:18 Z p. 373, ls. 2-4

It appears to me that the case of the field's not taking possession in a situation which is not now prevailing—the deer is not lame—is the reason that T. has inserted this sizable construction of essentially distinct materials.

1:5

A. (1) Things which are found by his minor son or daughter,
B. (2) things which are found by his Canaanite slave-boy or slave-girl,
C. (3) things found by his wife—
D. lo, they belong to him.
E. (1) Things found by his adult son or daughter,
F. (2) things found by his Hebrew slave-boy or slave-girl,
G. (3) things found by his wife whom he has divorced, even though he has not yet paid off her marriage-settlement—
H. lo, they belong to them.

M. 1:5

The contrast of A-D, E-H, makes the point that a man's dependents make acquisition only in his behalf. The others make acquisition in their own behalf.

1:6-8

I A. [If] one found bonds of indebtedness,
B. "if they record a lien on [the debtor's] property, he should not return them.
C. "For a court will exact payment on the strength of them.
D. "If they do not record a lien on property, he should return them,
E. "for a court will not exact payment on the strength of them," the words of R. Meir.
F. And sages say, "One way or the other, he should not return them.
G. "For a court will exact payment on the strength of them."

M. 1:6

II A. [If] he found (1) writs of divorce for women, (2) writs of emancipation for slaves, (3) wills, (4) deeds of gift, or (5) receipts for the payment of marriage-settlements,
B. lo, he should not return them.
C. For I maintain, "They were written out, but [then] the one [who is answerable] for them changed his mind and decided not to hand them over."

M. 1:7

III A. [If] one found (1) documents of evaluation, (2) letters of alimony, (3) deeds of *ḥaliṣah*-rites or (4) of the exercise of the right of refusal, (5) deeds of arbitration, or any document which is prepared in a court,
B. lo, this one should return [them].
C. [If] he found them [wrapped up] (1) in a satchel or (2) a case,
D. (3) a bundle of documents, or (4) a package of documents,
E. lo, this one should return [them].
F. How many are in a package of documents?
G. Three tied together.
H. Rabban Simeon b. Gamaliel, "[If one found a document which involved] a single individual who borrowed from three persons, he should return it to the borrower.
I. "[But if the document concerned] three borrowers from a single individual, he should return it to the lender."

J. [If] he found a document among those belonging to him, and he does not know what it is,

K. let it lie there until Elijah comes.

L. If [however] there were postscripts along with them, let him act in accord with what is written in the postscripts.

M. 1:8

The triplet goes over a new consideration: whether or not to return certain documents. The concern is that one not perpetrate injustice. If, M. 1:6, a bond of indebtedness is returned, a court will enforce it and so retrieve land sold by the borrower to a third party. The dispute is on a detail of that conception. Sages maintain that under all circumstances a court will allow the lender to seize land which the debtor has sold to third parties. If the document itself does not so specify, it is because the clause permitting the lender to do so has been omitted by the scribe's error. The contrast of the five items of M. 1:7 and of M. 1:8A-B is clearly explained by M.'s gloss, M. 1:7C. In the former case the document comes from a private party, in the latter, from a court. It follows that one might retract in the case of M. 1:7A's items, but there is no possibility of cancellation of a document listed at M. 1:8A.

The extensions of the rule are three: M. 1:8C-E+F-G, H-I and J-L. The items of C-E exhibit a particular trait permitting the owner to identify them, in line with M. 2:5. Simeon has a distinct conception. If one finds three documents of a single borrower, who has borrowed from three lenders, they go back to the borrower. The lenders cannot possibly have lost all three in one place. And the contrary is the case at I.

Since, J, we do not know whether, e.g., a lender has left the document with the man, or a borrower has done so, or whether or not part of the debt is paid, the document is not to be returned. If there are stipulations attached to it, these are to be carried out, L. J-K thus carry forward the initial conception, M. 1:6. The construction as a whole is clear and makes its points both through its formal contrasts and through its internal, substantive exegesis.

A. [If] one found bonds of indebtedness,

B. *if they do not record a lien on property* [cf. M. 1:60],

C. "when the borrower admits the debt, [the finder] should return the document to the lender.

D. "If he does not, he should not return the writ either to the borrower or to the lender," the words of R. Meir.

E. For R. Meir says, "[With] a bond of indebtedness which records a lien on property do they collect from indentured property."

T. 1:5 Z p. 371, ls. 28-30

A. [If] one found a writ of divorce of a woman [M. 1:7A1],

B. when the husband admits its validity,

C. he should return it to the wife.

D. If he does not, he should not return it either to this party or to that party.

T. 1:6 Z p. 371, ls. 30-31

A. [If one found] a receipt [in payment for the marriage-settlement] [M. 1:7A5],

B. when the woman admits its validity, he should return it to the husband.

C. And if not, he should not return it either to this party or to that party.

D. [If one found] a writ of emancipation [of a slave] [M. 1:7A2],

B. when the master admits its validity, he should return it to the [former] slave.

C. And if not, he should not return it either to this party or to that party.

D. [If he found] a writ of seizure,

E. when the borrower admits validity, he should return it to the lender.

F. And if not, he should not return it either to this party or to that party.

T. 1:7 Z p. 371, ls. 31-33, p. 372, l. 1

A. [If he found] wills [M. 1:7A3] and deeds of gift [M. 1:7A4],

B. when the donor concedes [the validity of the document], he should return it to the recipient of the gift.

C. And if not, he should not return it either to this party or to that party.

D. [If he found] writs of purchase or sale, deeds of share-cropping and receipts for a beast—

E. lo, this one should not return it either to this party or to that party.

T. 1:8 Z p. 372, ls. 1-3

A. [If one found] court decrees or *prosbols*—

B. lo, he should return them to him in whose name they are written,

C. whether he found them in the market-place or whether he found them among the documents of his father [M. 1:8A-B].

D. The governing principle of the matter is this: *If there were postscripts along with them, let him act in accord with what is written in the postscripts* [M. 1:8L].

T. 1:9 Z p. 372, ls. 3-6

T. 1:5 expands the position of Meir to include reference to other than real property. The same consideration essentially applies as has been expressed at M. The rest of T.'s points are self-evident expansions of M.

A. A postscript [to a document] which bears the names of witnesses is confirmed through the signatures of witnesses.

B. And one which does not have the names of witnesses and comes from the hand of a depository, after the validation of the signatures of documents is acceptable.

C. What is the meaning of "the validation of the signatures of documents"?

D. "I, So and so, son of So and so, accept upon myself responsibility for what is written in this document."

E. And [if] the witnesses then have signed below, it is valid.

T. 1:13 Z p. 372, ls. 13-16

A. What is a package of documents [M. 1:8D4]?
B. *Three tied together* [M. 1:8G].
C. What is a bundle of documents [M. 1:8D3]?
D. Any which is tied up around the outside with a thread or a strap or something else.
E. What is a satchel [M. 1:8C1]?
F. This is a small wallet.

T. 1:14 Z p. 372, ls. 16-18

A. Two who were laying hold of a document—
B. This one says, "It is mine, and I lost it!"
C. And that one says, "It was in my possession, and I already paid you for it!"—
D. "Let the document be confirmed through the signatures of the witnesses which it bears," the words of Rabbi.
E. And Rabban Simeon b. Gamaliel says, "Let them divide it between them."

T. 1:15 Z p. 372, ls. 18-20

T. 1:13 augments M. 1:8L. T. 1:14 glosses the specified stichs of M. T. 1:15 then introduces a secondary problem, reading the case of M. 1:1 into the conditions of M. 1:6-8, a fine piece of secondary exegesis of M. as a whole.

A. He who deposits documents with his fellow,
B. even though they are not written in his name—
C. lo, this one must return to him what is his.
D. [If] he died, [the bailment] is to be given to his estate.
E. If he said when he was dying, "Let it be given to so-and-so, to whom it belongs,"
F. let that which he has specified be done just as he has laid matters out.
G. He who lends money to his fellow on the strength of a pledge and [the debtor] said to him, "If I have not paid you between this date and such and such date, there is no possession of mine in your hand,"
H. if the specified time came and he did not pay him,
I. the pledge has entered the domain of the lender,
J. whether it is to his disadvantage or to his advantage.

T. 1:19 Z p. 373, ls. 4-8

A. "[If] one borrowed from another party a thousand *denars*, on the strength of a document of loan,
B. "and paid back to him eight hundred *zuz*—
C. "lo, this person should tear up his original writ of debt and write another one for two hundred *zuz*," the words of R. Meir.
D. And sages say, "The original writ remains valid [in its place], and this one writes to him, 'I have received from him eight hundred *zuz*.'
E. "Because otherwise he diminishes [the lender's] rights in two respects:
F. "that [the borrower] will not exert himself to pay up,
G. "and that [the lender] cannot collect from indentured property."

T. 1:20 Z p. 373, ls. 8-12

A. Two who took out a loan on a single document,
B. and one of them paid that which was his—
C. the writ remains valid,
D. and the other party writes to him, "I have received from you what was owing by you."

T. 1:21 Z p. 373, ls. 12-13

T. 1:19 completes its discourse on the general themes of M. 1:6-8, with special reference to documents and their return. T. 1:19 makes the familiar point that one carries out the instructions of the owner of the documents. T. 1:20 supplements the theme of M. 1:6. Now we have a bond of indebtedness. Sages want the original writ to remain valid, rather than issuing a new one, so as to preserve the rights of the lender. T. 1:21 then restates sages' view.

The consideration at T. 1:20 G in connection with the lender's right is to be spelled out. If the bond covers real property of the borrower, then from the date of the loan onward, the property is subject to the lender's lien. If the borrower should sell the property, then default on the debt, the lender may seize the property from the third party that has bought it. That right is valid, in particular, if the property changed hands at any point after the date of the original loan. Now if the borrower returns part of the borrowed funds, and then the lender writes up a new writ of indebtedness covering the remainder of the debt, the date of this new writ takes effect. The date of the old writ is null. If, therefore, the borrower sold off his land after the old writ's date but before the new writ's date, the lender cannot retrieve that land from the third-party-purchaser in case of default. Consequently, the lender loses substantial protection for his capital by rewriting the bond and placing on it a date later than the original transaction. Since this same consideration will recur time and again in T.'s amplification of M., it is worth spelling it out.

CHAPTER TWO

BABA MESIA CHAPTER TWO

We turn to M.'s treatment of the Scriptures which deal with returning lost objects, Deut. 22:1ff. and Ex. 23:5f., paying brief attention, as the layout of the verses requires, also to helping one's fellow's ass when it is struggling with its burden. M. has two principal concerns in its treatment of the matter: first, the sorts of objects one is required to attempt to restore to the owner; second, the sorts of objects or situations in which no such effort is required. It is this second matter which then substantively links returning lost objects to assisting an overloaded ass, since at issue will be situations in which one is under no obligation to be helpful.

M. 2:1-2 present a matched list of twenty items, ten of which one is permitted to retain, ten of which one must attempt to restore to the owner. The former are scattered at random and give no evidence of anyone's hoping to recover them. The condition of the latter clearly indicates that the owner plans to return. M. 2:3-4 go over the same matter, now with attention to the location of an object. If it is in a place in which the owner is apt to find it, one must make a good-faith effort to proclaim its discovery. If not, he does not. M. 2:5 completes this discussion with an exegesis of Deut. 22:3 to indicate that the recovery of a lost object depends upon identification of its distinguishing characteristics.

M. 2:6, 7 supplement this matter. M. 2:6 defines the length of time one is expected to make a good-faith effort to find the rightful owner ("to make proclamation"). M. 2:7 adds that the rightful owner must prove that he does own the object and must show he is not a deceiver. M. 2:7 goes on to a separate consideration. If a person has found an animal which can work for its keep, the animal does labor. If not, it is sold, so that, when the owner gets back the lost animal, he will not have pay compensation for the keep of the animal greater than its intrinsic value. Tarfon and 'Aqiba dispute about the status of the proceeds. M. 2:8, along these same general lines, asks about the finder's making use of objects he has found. He cannot wear them out, but he must keep them in good shape, e.g., by unrolling scrolls or airing out clothing. M. 2:9 concludes the discussion with a definition of what is regarded as a lost animal. It essentially says what M. 2:3-4 has told us. The other matter—helping the ass of another party—is dealt with at M. 2:10. One has to help, but need not work alone, or assist in reloading the animal. M. 2:11 concludes with a charming exercise on the priority of finding one's own lost object over finding that of his father or anyone else, then on the relative priorities of his father and his teacher, and so on. This exercise is secondary to our problem. It is an elegant effort to mark the conclusion of an M.'s treatment of this topic.

2:1-2

A. What lost items are [the finder's], and which ones is he liable to proclaim [in the lost-and-found]?
B. These lost items are his [the finder's]:
C. "[if] he found (1) pieces of fruit scattered about, (2) coins scattered about, (3) small sheaves in the public domain, (4) cakes of figs, (5) bakers' loaves, (6) strings of fish, (7) pieces of meat, (8) woolshearings [as they come] from the country [of origin], (9) stalks of flacks, or (10) tongues of purple—lo, these are his," the words of R. Meir.
D. And R. Judah says, "Anything which has an unusual trait is he liable to proclaim.
E. "How so?
F. "[If] he found a fig-cake with a potsherd inside it, a loaf with coins in it."
G. R. Simeon b. Eleazar says, "Any new merchandise [lacking an identification-mark] he is not liable to proclaim."

M. 2:1

A. And which ones is he liable to proclaim?
B. [If] he found (1) pieces of fruit in a utensil, or a utensil as is, (2) coins in a purse or a purse as is, (3) piles of fruit, (4) piles of coins, (5) three coins, one on top of the other, (6) small sheaves in private domain, (7) home-made loaves, (8) wool-shearings as they come from the craftsman's shop, (9) jars of wine, or (10) jars of oil—
C. lo, these is he liable to proclaim.

M. 2:2

There is a formal peculiarity, in that the entire construction announced at M. 2:1A-B is fully worked out and balanced by M. 2:1C and M. 2:2, while at the same time we have a dispute at M. 2:1D F, G, which should generate some sort of revision at M. 2:2 as well. To be sure, there is no reason for Judah, or Simeon b. Eleazar for the matter, to disagree with M. 2:2. Still, I should think that the entire construction was worked out before it was found necessary to attribute one of its stichs to Meir. The intrusion of M. 2:1D-G will have taken place after the rest was fully stated in its precise balance of ten items against ten. The viewpoint of all sages is that one must advertize in the lost-and-found (to resort to an anachronism) items which exhibit some evidence that an owner expects to recover them, e.g., because the items are carefully arranged. If they do not seem to be subjected to care, as at M. 2:1C, then the finder keeps them. Judah does not differ in general. He provides for the return of cakes of figs and a loaf of bread, differing from M. 2:1C4, 5. Simeon b. Eleazar states in his own way what Judah as said, assuming my interpolation is correct. In all it is a first-class piece of presenting opinions which essentially intersect with one another. M. 2:7 will further clarify the matter of M. 2:1D-G.

    A. R. Simeon b. Eleazar concedes in the case of new merchandise which has been used [that] one is liable to make a proclamation [that he has found it and will return it upon proper identification] [M. 2:1G].
    B. Now what is meant by new merchandise?
    C. Poles, needles, pins, and axes strung together.
    D. And so did R. Simeon b. Eleazar say, "All these concerning which they have said, 'Lo, these are his'—
    E. "Under what circumstances?
    F. "When he has found them one by one.
    G. "But if he found them two by two, he is liable to make proclamation."
                        T. 2:1 Z p. 373, ls. 14-17

    A. And so did R. Simeon b. Eleazar say, "He who rescues something from the mouth of a lion, a wolf, or a bear,
    B. "or from a rip-tide in the sea or a sudden surge of a river—
    C. "and he who finds something in a large plaza or parade-ground—
    D. "lo, these are deemed forthwith to be his,
    E. "for the owner despairs [of ever getting it back]."
                        T. 2:2 Z p. 373, ls. 17-19

T. qualifies and complements M. 2:1G

    A. [If] one found pieces of meat, pieces of fish, or fish which had been stuck together,
    B. he is liable to make proclamation.
    C. [If he found] strings of meat, strings of fish, jars of wine, oil, grain, figs, or olives,
    D. he is not liable to make proclamation [cf. M. 2:1C, 2:2B].
                        T. 2:3 Z p. 373, ls. 20-22

    A. [If] one has written something on a sherd and put it on the mouth of a jar,
    B. ... on paper and put it on the mouth of a circle of dried figs,
    C. [the finder] is liable to make proclamation [M. 2:1D-F].
                        T. 2:4 Z p. 373, l. 22

    A. [If] one has found small sheaves in private domain, he is liable to make proclamation.
    B. [If] he has found small sheaves in the public domain, he is not liable to make proclamation [cf. M. 2:1C].
    C. [If he found] stacks of grain, whether in private domain or in public domain,
    D. he is liable to make proclamation.
                        T. 2:5 Z p. 373, ls. 23-24

    A. [If] he found pieces of fruit arranged in piles, he is liable to make proclamation.
    B. [If he found them] scattered about, he is not liable to make proclamation [cf. M. 2:1C, 2:2B].

C. [If] part of them are arranged in piles, and part of them are scattered about,
D. he is liable to make proclamation.

T. 2:6 Z p. 373, ls. 24-25

A. [If] one has found coins arranged in little towers, he is liable to make proclamation.
B. [If] he found them scattered about, he is not liable to make proclamation.
C. [If] part of them were in little towers, and part of them were not in little towers,
D. he is liable to make proclamation.
E. And how many coins when in a pile add up to a tower?
F. Three coins one on top of the other.

T. 2:7 Z p. 373, ls. 26-27

A. [If] one found a utensil, with pieces of fruit in front of it [M. 2:2B],
B. a purse, with coins in front of it [M. 2:2B],
C. he is liable to make proclamation [cf. M. 2:4].
D. [If] part of them were in the utensil and part of them were on the ground,
E. part of them were in the purse and part of them were on the ground,
F. he is liable to make proclamation.

T. 2:8 Z p. 373, ls. 28-29

A. [If] one found something which has no distinguishing mark alongside something which does have a distinguishing mark [M. 2:1D, 2:5],
B. he is liable to make proclamation.
C. [If] the owner of the object with the distinguishing mark came along and took that which clearly belonged to him,
D. this person also has made acquisition of the [similar] object which does not have a distinguishing mark.

T. 2:9 Z p. 373, ls. 29-30

A. He who finds a *sela'*,
B. and his fellow [who claims it] says, "[The one I lost] is new,"
C. "It is of the reign of Nero,"
D. "It is of the kingdom of such and such,"
E. he has said nothing at all.
F. For a distinguishing mark does not apply to a coin.
G. And not only so, but even if the person's [own] name is written on the coin,
H. lo, it nonetheless belongs to the one who finds it.

T. 2:10 Z p. 374, ls. 1-2

T. goes over the ground of M., as indicated. There are no surprises.

2:3-4

A. [If] behind a fence or a hedge one found pigeons tied together,
B. or on paths in fields,
C. lo, this one should not touch them.

	D.	[If] he found a utensil in a dung-heap,
I	E.	if it is covered up, he should not touch it.
	F.	If it is uncovered, he takes it but must proclaim [that he has found it].

II G. [If] he found it in a pile of debris or in an old wall, lo, these belong to him.
    H. [If] he found it in a new wall,
    I. if it is located from its mid-point and outward, it is his.
    J. If it is located from its midpoint and inward, it belongs to the householder.
    K. If he had rented [the house] to others,
    L. even [if he found it] in the house,
    M. lo, these are his.

M. 2:3

III A. [If] he found [utensils] in a store, lo, these are his.
    B. [If a utensil was located] between the counter and the storekeeper, it belongs to the storekeeper.
IV C. [If he found them] in front of the money-changer, lo, they are his.
    D. [If he found them] between the stool [of the money-changer] and the money-changer, lo, these belong to the money-changer.
V E. He who purchases produce from his fellow,
    F. or sent produce to his fellow,
    G. [if] he found coins among the produce, lo, these are his.
    H. If there were bound together, he takes [the money] but proclaims [that he has found it].

M. 2:4

The definitive formal trait here appears to be the two-part apodosis, *if...*, *if....* This occurs, then, at the five units I have indicated. Then M. 2:3K-M function as a complement to their unit. M. 2:3G introduces that same unit, a somewhat more developed item than we should expect. M. 2:4A-B, 2:5C-D, and 2:5E, G-H, show us the simplest version of the form. The opening unit, M. 2:3A-C, happens to supply the point of the whole and therefore should not be seen as a prefixed interpolation. If there is locative evidence that an object belongs to someone, that evidence suffices. All the rest then serve to exemplify locations which, all by themselves, indicate that someone has put aside and expects to retrieve what is located there. But, as is clear, there are Mishnah's expected complications, and spelling these out is the purpose of the five-part set. If the object is covered in the dung-heap, someone has deliberately hidden it. If an object is in a new wall, someone may recently have put it there for safe-keeping. If an object is at a point at which a store-keeper or a money-changer can have dropped it, then it is not deemed lost. M. 2:4E-H concludes with an example explicitly tying the whole to M. 2:1-2, a truly unusual example of the work of tradents carried on in the processes of agglutination and ultimate redaction. And, in point of fact, M. 2:1-4 conclude here. The next item will now tie the whole together with an exegesis which expresses the fundamental theory.

A. [If] one found an object on a dung-heap,
B. he is liable to make proclamation.
C. For it is usual for things on the dung-heap to be cleared away.

T. 2:11 Z p. 374, l. 3

A. [*If*] *one found an object on a pile or an old wall,*
B. *lo, these things which he finds are his* [M. 2:3G],
C. For he can say to [any claimant], "They come from the time of the Amorites."

T. 2:12 Z p. 374, ls. 3-4

A. [*If*] *one found an object* in a hole or *new wall,*
B. *if* [*the object*] *was located from the midpoint and outward, it belongs to* [*the finder*].
C. [*If the object was located*] *from the midpoint and inward* [*toward the inside of the house*], *it belongs to the householder* [M. 2:3H-J].
D. [If the wall or hole] was open wholly outward, even if the object was located from the midpoint toward the inside of the house, it belongs to the finder.
E. [If the wall or hole] was open wholly inward, even if the object was located from the midpoint toward the outside of the house, it belongs to the householder.
F. [If the object was located] from the threshold and outward, it belongs to [the finder]. If it was located from the threshold and inward, it belongs to the householder.

T. 2:13 Z p. 374, ls. 4-7

A. [If] one found an object in a house,
B. if guests have left something over before him,
C. lo, they are his.
D. And if not, lo, they belong to the householder.
E. [If] he found an object in a store,
F. up to the place in which people usually enter, lo, these belong to [the finder].
G. If they are further in that that, lo, they belong to the storekeeper [M. 2:4A-B].

T. 2:14 Z p. 374, ls. 7-9

T. 2:11 differs from M. 2:3D-F in its theory of the origin of said objects. T. 2:12, 13 gloss M. T. 2:14 restates the general principle of M. in a somewhat different setting.

2:5

A. Also a garment was covered among all of these things [which one must proclaim, listed at Deut. 22:2]
B. [So] why was it singled out?
C. To use it for an analogy, to tell you:
D. Just as a garment exhibits distinctive traits, in that it has special marks of identification, and it has someone to claim it,
E. so for everything which has special marks and which has someone to claim it,
F. one is liable to make proclamation.

M. 2:5

The foregoing ends with an exegetical flourish; the important point is the requirement of identifying traits, as at M. 2:1-2.

    A. He who purchases a beast from his fellow and found on it something worth a *perutah*
    B. is liable to make proclamation.
    C. And he who finds something worth a *perutah* is liable to make proclamation.
    D. If it is worth less than a *perutah*, he is not liable to make proclamation.
    E. for it is said, [*You shall not see your brother's ox or his sheep go astray, and withhold your help from them; you shall take them back to your brother . . . And so you shall do with his ass, and so you shall do with his*] garment, [*so you shall do with any lost thing of your brother's, which he loses and you find; you may not withhold your help*] (Deut. 22:1-3).
    F. Just as a garment is distinguished in that it is worth a *perutah*, in which case one is liable to make proclamation,
    G. so for anything which is worth a *perutah* one is liable to make proclamation.
    H. But for something worth less than a *perutah*, one is not liable to make proclamation.

T. 2:15 Z p. 374, ls. 10-13

A-D add an important qualification, that one has to make an effort to find the owner only when the found item is of some material value.

2:6

    A. And for how long is one liable to make proclamation [of having found a lost object]?
    B. "Until his neighbors are informed about it," the words of R. Meir.
    C. R. Judah says, "Until three festivals [have gone by].
    D. "And for seven days after the final festival, so that one may have three days to go home and three days to come back and one day on which to proclaim [that he has lost the object]."

M. 2:6

The dispute is clear as stated. Meir's limit is not precise. Judah, D, gives someone a chance to go home and determine whether he has lost the object about which he has heard.

2:7

    A. [If a claimant] has described what he has lost but not specified its special marks, one should not give it to him.
    B. And as to a [known] deceiver, even though he has specified its special marks, one should not give it to him,
    C. as it is said, *Until your brother seeks concerning it* (Deut. 22:2)—
    D. until you will seek out your brother to find out whether or not he is a deceiver.
    E. Any sort of thing which is able to perform labor and which eats performs labor and [in exchange is allowed to] eat.

F. And something which does not perform labor but which [nonetheless has to be] fed is to be sold,
G. as it is said, *You will return it to him* (Deut. 22:2).
H. Pay attention to how to return it to him!
I. What is the rule covering the proceeds?
J. R. Ṭarfon says, "Let [the finder] make use of them. Therefore, if something happens to them, he is liable to make them up."
K. R. ʿAqiba says, "He should not make use of them. Therefore, if something happens to them, he is not liable to make them up."

M. 2:7

A-D are clear as given. E-H are then glossed by I-K. Ṭarfon regards the finder as paid bailee of the funds received for the sale of the animal.

A. At the outset, whoever came along and could give a good description of the distinguishing traits of an object would take it.
B. When deceivers became many, they made the rule that the claimant should give a good description of the distinguishing marks of the object which he claims,
C. and also bring proof that he is no deceiver.

T. 2:16 Z p. 374, ls. 13-15

A. At the outset they *would make proclamation for three successive festivals, and after the final festival for seven days* [M. 2:6C-D].
B. After the Temple was destroyed, they made the rule that one should make proclamation for an object which has been found for thirty days.
C. And from the time of danger onward, they made the rule that one should merely inform his neighbors and relatives and acquaintances and townsfolk.
D. And that is enough.

T. 2:17 Z p. 374, ls. 15-18

T. 2:16 restates in its "historical" formulary the point of M. 2:7A-D: T. 2:17 does the same for M. 2:6, which differs from M.'s conception of the prevailing rule. This version surely postdates M.'s.

A. *Any sort of thing which is able to perform labor and which eats* [M. 2:7E],
B. for example, a cow or an ass,
C. *performs labor and [in exchange is allowed to] eat* [M. 2:7E].
D. And one should not do work with them to a value greater than the cost of what they eat.
E. *And something which does not perform labor but which [nonetheless has to be] fed* [M. 2:7F],
F. for example, geese and chickens—
G. one should tend them for three days.
H. In the case of heifers or foals, one tends to them for thirty days.
I. Beyond that point, he sells them at the instance of a court.

T. 2:20 Z p. 374, ls. 22-25

T. cites and glosses M. Its important points are at D, G-I.

2:8

A. [If] he found scrolls, he reads in them once every thirty days.
B. If he does not know how to read, he [at least] unrolls them.
C. But he should not [commence to] learn [a subject] in them to begin with, nor should someone else read alongside him.
D. [If] he found a piece of clothing, he should shake it out once every thirty days,
E. and spread it out as needed—
F. but not to show off [Lit.: *for his own honor*].
G. Of utensils of silver and of copper one makes use—
H. for their own good,
I. but not to wear them out.
J. Utensils of gold and of glass—he should not touch them until Elijah comes.
K. [If] he found a sack or large basket or anything which he would not usually pick up,
L. lo, this one does not [have to lower himself and] pick it up.

M. 2:8

There are two pairs, A-B+C, D-F, and G-I, J. K-L are independent. Objects must be given appropriate care until the owner comes, A, D, G-H; but they may not be used solely for one's own benefit or allowed to wear out, B-C, F, I. One need not seek the owner of an object he himself would not usually handle. So if he finds a sack, he leaves it where it is.

A. [*If*] *one found scrolls, he reads in them once every thirty days* [M. 2:8A].
B. But one should not read the weekly lection and go over it again.
C. Nor should one read in them and translate into Aramaic.
D. And three people should not read in a single volume.
E. And one should not open in a scroll more than three columns.
F. Sumkhos says, "In the case of new ones, only once every thirty days.
G. "And in the case of old ones, once every twelve months."

T. 2:21 Z p. 374, ls. 25-28

A. As to utensils of gold, one may make use of them for cold but not for hot liquids,
B. because [hot liquids] blacken them [*vs.* M. 2:8J].
C. Utensils of copper one uses for hot liquids, but not on fire,
D. because it wears them out [cf. M. 2:8I].
E. Shovels and axes one makes use of for something soft, but not for something hard.
F. With a shovel one shovels mortar.
G. He dries it off and leaves it in its place.
H. With an ax one chops wood,
I. on condition that one not chop with it either stone-palm-wood or olive-wood.
J. And just as you specify these rules with regard to a lost object, so these rules apply with regard to a bailment.
K. He who deposits a garment with his fellow—

L. [the latter] must shake it out once in thirty days.
M. *He spreads it out for its need, not for his own honor* [M. 2:8D-F].
N. If it was abundant, one takes his wages from its value.

T. 2:22 Z pp. 374, ls. 28-32, 375, 1-2

The scrolls must not be worn out through excessive use, T. 2:21. M. has already made that point. Sumkhos qualifies M. T. 2:22A-B differ from M.'s prohibition on using gold utensils at all. The point of the rest is to clarify M.'s rule against wearing out an object awaiting the return to its rightful owner. The points are clear as T. gives them.

2:9

A. What is lost property?
B. [If] one found an ass or a cow grazing by the way,
C. this is not lost property.
D. [If he found] an ass with its trappings upset,
E. a cow running in the vineyards,
F. lo, this is lost property.
G. [If] one returned it and it ran away, returned it and it ran away,
H. even four of five times,
I. he is liable [to continue to] return it,
J. since it is said, *You shall surely bring them back* [*to your brother*] (Deut. 22:1).
K. [If] he lost [work-]time [to the value of] a *sela'*, he may not say to him, "Give me a *sela'*."
L. But he pays him a salary [for his lost time] calculated at the rate paid to an unemployed worker.
M. If there is a court there, he may stipulate before the court [for compensation for lost time] [cf. M. B.Q. 10:4].
N. If there is no court there, before whom may he make such a stipulation?
O. His own [welfare] takes precedence.

M. 2:9

The set consists of three separate items, A-F, which makes its point through the obvious contrast between B and D-E; G-J, which is similarly obvious; and K-O. Here the point is that, while one must make every effort to return an object to the owner, this is not to be at the cost of one's own benefit. K-L make one point, M-N, O, a second. The man by himself cannot claim more than what is paid to an unemployed worker. But before a court he may stipulate that that is what he is owed. If he cannot set up a court for that purpose, then he does not have to return the property at all. L-O in fact are more tightly joined to G-J than appears on the surface, since the point is that, while one must return the object, there are circumstances which allow one to refrain from doing so.

A. He who finds a lost object—
B. if it is of sufficient value for him to return it to the owner so that [the owner will enjoy the benefit of the value, at least to] a *perutah* and also to collect his fee from it,
C. he should get involved with the matter.
D. But if not, he should leave it where it is.

T. 2:18 Z p. 374, ls. 18-19

T. restates its view at T. 2:15, but complements M. 2:9G-J, O.

A. *What is lost property* [M. 2:9A]?
B. [If] one found a spade in the parade-ground or a cloak on the parade-ground,
C. or a cow feeding in a field of grain,
D. lo, this is a lost object.
E. [If one found] a cloak lying on the side of a fence, a jar lying on the side of a fence,
F. an ass feeding in high grass,
G. this is not a lost object.
H. But if he found them in such conditions for three successive days, lo, this is a lost object.

T. 2:19 Z p. 374, ls. 19-22

A-D complement M. 2:9 D-F, and E-G, M. 2:9A-C. The point is the same for both M. and T.

2:10

A. [If he found it loose] in a stable, he is not liable [to return] it.
B. [If he found it] in the public domain, he is liable to take care of it.
C. And if it was a graveyard, [and if he was a priest or a Nazirite], he should not contract corpse-uncleanness on its account.
D. If his father said to him, "Contract corpse uncleanness,"
E. or if [under normal circumstances] he said to him, "Don't return it,"
F. he should not obey him.
G. [If] he unloaded it and loaded it up again, unloaded it and loaded it up again,
H. even four or five times,
I. he is liable [to continue to do so],
J. for it is written, *You will surely help him* (Ex. 23:5).
K. [If] he went and sat down, and said, "Since the religious duty is yours, if you want to unload it, go unload it,"
L. the other is exempt [from doing a thing].
M. For it is written, *With him*.
N. If the owner was old or sick, he is liable.
O. It is a religious duty enjoined by the Torah to unload the beast, but not to load it up.
P. R. Simeon says, "Also: to load it up."
Q. R. Yosé the Galilean says, "If there was on the beast more than its proper load, he is not obligated to [the owner],
R. "since it is said, *Under its burden*—
S. "a burden which it can endure."

M. 2:10

At the end we consider the limits of one's responsibility to retrieve a lost object and return it to the owner. M. 2:10A-C express those limits. If the animal is unlikely to be lost, one need do nothing, A-B. The priest or Nazir need not contract corpse-uncleanness to retrieve the lost animal, C. D-E signal what is to follow at M. 2:11. They make no contribution here. We go on, at M. 2:10G-S, to consider the requirement specified at Ex. 23: 4-5. One must continue to help, just as he must continue to retrieve and return the animal, so M. 2:10G-J run parallel to M. 2:9G-J. K-M+N then provide one important clarification of the rule, and the dispute at O-P+ Q-S, another; both are clear as given.

    A. He who finds the beast of his fellow is liable to take care of it until he brings it into his domain.
    B. [If] he brought it into a place in which some one will see it, he is no longer liable to take care of it.
    C. [If one did not take care of it], and it was stolen or lost,
    D. he is liable to replace it.
    E. And he is under all circumstances liable to replace it until he brings it into [the owner's] domain.
    F. [If] he brought it into his garden or his ruin, and it was stolen or lost,
    G. he is exempt.

                                                  T. 2:23 Z p. 375, ls. 2-5

I have slightly revised the text at C and supplied what is needed for B. Then T.'s points to complement M. 2:10 A-B are clear.

    A. [If] he found an ass [e.g., on the Sabbath] loaded with coals,
    B. or with prohibited items,
    C. they do not require him to touch them.
    D. This is the governing principle:
    E. Whoever labors in his [own behalf]—lo, this one is obligated to help him.
    F. And whoever does not labor in his [behalf]—he is not obligated to help him [M. B.M. 2:10K-L].
    G. [If] his ass was falling down, he helps him unload it,
    H. even a hundred times [M. 2:10G-J].
    I. He is permitted to lighten the load and to collect a salary for it.

                                                  T. 2:24 Z p. 375, ls. 5-8

    A. They do not require him to stand around and put back the load, unload and load [the ass],
    B. since it is said, *if you meet [your enemy's ox or his ass going astray, you shall bring it back to him.] If you see [the ass of one who hates you lying under its burden, you shall refrain from leaving him with it, you shall help him lift it up]* (Ex. 23:4-5).
    C. One might think that he is liable to do so two or three times only.
    D. Scripture [therefore] says, *If you meet*.
    E. One might say that this is the case only within four cubits [that is, actually meeting up with him] only.
    F. Scripture says, *If you see*.

G. Sages have given as a measure for this: one seventieth of a *mil*, that is a *ris*.

T. 2:25 Z p. 375, ls. 8-11

T. systematically complements M. 2:10, as indicated. One need not help his fellow by doing what is ordinarily prohibited, T. 2:24A-C. He need not help if his fellow is not working in his own behalf, E.F. G-H go over M.'s points. T. 2:25 is clear as stated. The whole does a good job for M.

A. [If before him is the choice of helping] his friend to load up his ass, or his enemy to unload his ass,
B. his religious duty is to unload the ass with his enemy [Ex. 23:4]—
C. so as to break his heart.
D. The enemy of whom they spoke is an Israelite enemy, not an enemy from among the nations.

T. 2:26 Z p. 375, ls. 11-12

A. [If] one saw the ass of a gentile [bearing a heavy burden], he is liable to take care of it,
B. just as he is liable to take care of one belonging to an Israelite.
C. If it was bearing wine for idolatrous purposes, however, he is not permitted to touch it.

T. 2:27 Z p. 375, ls. 13-14

A. If he saw water flowing along, he is liable to dam it up.
B. This is the general rule: Any matter which is subject to a loss of material benefit also is subject to the requirement of the returning of that which is lost.
C. *It is a religious requirement of the Torah to unload an overloaded ass, but not to help load it up* [M. 2:10/O].
D. *R. Simeon says, "Even to help load it up* [M. 2:10P],
E. "since it is said, *With him*."
F. "*With him*—on his ass," the words of R. Simeon.
G. And sages say, "*With him* you share in the wages."
H. And just as the religious duty pertains to his own beast, so it pertains to the beast of his fellow.
I. His fellow who was lost—one takes him by his hand.
J. And he leads him through fields and vineyards until he reaches the town he seeks or the way he seeks.
K. And just as it is a religious duty to do so for one's fellow, so it is a religious duty to do so for oneself.
L. For if one has lost the way, one crosses fields and vineyards until he reaches the town he seeks or the way he seeks.
M. For it was on that stipulation [that people might pass across the vineyards and fields if they were lost] that Joshua caused the Israelites to inherit the land.

T. 2:28 Z p. 375, ls. 14-21

T. now turns to supplement M. Its points are clear.

2:11

I A. [If he has to choose between seeking] what he has lost and what his father has lost,
   B. his own takes precedence.
II C. ... what he has lost and what his master has lost,
   D. his own takes precedence.
III E. ... what his father has lost and what his master has lost,
   F. that of his master takes precedence.
   G. For his father brought him into this world.
   H. But his master, who taught him wisdom, will bring him into the life of the world to come.
   I. But if his father is a sage, that of his father takes precedence.
   J. [If] his father and his master were carrying heavy burdens, he removes that of his master, and afterward removes that of his father.
   K. [If] his father and his master were taken captive,
   L. he ransoms his master, and afterward he ransoms his father.
   M. But if his father is a sage, he ransoms his father, and afterward he ransoms his master.

M. 2:11

The secondary development of the triplet at A-F involves a gloss, G-H, and a qualification thereof, I; then J, K-L+M repeat the whole thing. The points are self-evident.

A. *[If he has to choose between seeking] what his master has lost, and what his father has lost,*
B. *[seeking] what his master has lost takes precedence over what his father has lost* [M. 2:11E-F].
C. If his father was equivalent to his master,
D. seeking what his father has lost takes precedence over seeking what his master has lost.

T. 2:29 Z p. 375, ls. 21-22

A. Who is one's master?
B. The one who has taught him Torah, and not the master who has taught him a trade.
C. And who is this? It is the one who started him off first.
D. R. Meir says, "It is his master who has taught him wisdom, and not his master who has taught him Scripture."
E. R. Judah says, "It is anyone from whom he has gained the greater part of his learning."
F. R. Yosé says, "It is anyone who has enlightened his eyes in his repetition of traditions."

T. 2:30 Z p. 375, ls. 22-25

A. [If one has to choose between seeking] what his father has lost and what his mother has lost,
B. seeking what his father has lost takes precedence over seeking what his mother has lost.

C. Under what circumstances?
D. When she is living with [his father and subject to his authority].
E. But when she is not living [with his father],
F. both of them are equivalent.

T. 2:31 Z p. 375, ls. 25-26

A. [If one has to choose between seeking] what the husband has lost and what the wife has lost,
B. seeking what the husband has lost takes precedence over seeking what the wife has lost.

T. 2:32 Z p. 375, l. 27

A. Gentiles and shepherds of small cattle and those who raise them do not make a difference one way or the other [in figuring out whose lost object to seek first].
B. *Minim*, apostates, and renegades are regarded as subordinate and in no way can be regarded as taking priority.

T. 2:33 Z p. 375, ls. 27-29

T.'s complement to M. is clear as given.

CHAPTER THREE

BABA MESIA CHAPTER THREE

The chapter presents rules on bailment, beginning HMPQYD at M. 3:1A, M. 3:6A, M. 3:7A, M. 3:9A, M. 3:10A, M. 3:11A—six basic units. Intruded is a sizable construction around Yosé's views, M. 3:2, 3-5, a triplet; M. 3:8 continues M. 3:7. So formally the whole has been rather carefully redacted. The main point of interest throughout is the way in which compensation is assessed and paid for damages done to a bailment. M. 3:1 makes the obvious point that if the bailee has paid the damages, then, when restitution is made by the one who actually has done the damages, it goes to the bailee. If the bailee has not taken responsibility, the owner receives the damages. M. 3:2 is relevant to this point, since it concerns the damages paid for a cow lent by a renter to a third party. Yosé's involvement in this matter explains the inclusion of an appendix, which in any case is thematically related to the interests of the chapter.

The tight redactional construction of five rules of bailment, M. 3:6-12, goes over closely related points. The first, M. 3:7-8, concerns a reduction on the volume of a bailment to be returned. We take account of the depredations of mice or of mildew, so that if one has left a bailment of a *kor* of wheat, he claims in return somewhat less than that volume. M. 3:9 makes the distinction between damages done to a bailment for which no specific location has been designated, and those done when the owner has specified where he wants his object kept. M. 3:10, dealing with a bailment of coins, states the obvious notion that when the bailee has done his duty, he is exempt from having to make restitution for the loss of the coins. M. 3:11 is equally self-evident. If a party, e.g., a money-changer, has the right to make use of coins, he also has to make them up if they are lost. If he may not make use of the money, he also does not have to make up the loss. M. 3:12 presents a Houses' dispute on compensation, e.g., in a case such as is described at M. 3:9. The House of Hillel assess damages at the value of the object when the bailee took it out of its place of storage. 'Aqiba assesses damages at the value of the object when the owner comes to claim its restoration. The House of Shammai give the owner the benefit of the best possible price. There is an appended dispute at which liability is incurred. The Shammaites say it is at the point at which the bailee expresses the intention to make use of the bailment; the Hillelites rule that only when an actual deed is done is the bailee held responsible. The issue of the interplay between deed and intent is familiar, indeed, ubiquitous.

3:1

 A. He who deposits with his fellow a beast or utensils,
 B. and they were stolen or lost,
 C. [if the bailee] made restitution and was unwilling to take an oath—
 D. (for they have said, "An unpaid bailee takes an oath and thereby carries out his obligation [without paying compensation for the loss of the bailment]"—)
 E. [if] then the thief was found,
 F. [the thief] pays twofold restitution.
 G. [If] he had slaughtered or sold the beast, he pays fourfold or fivefold restitution.
 H. To whom does he pay restitution?
 I. To him with whom the bailment was left.
 J. [If the bailee] took an oath and did not want to pay compensation,
 K. [if] the thief was found,
 L. he pays twofold restitution.
 M. [If] he slaughtered or sold the beast, he pays fourfold or fivefold restitution.
 N. To whom does he pay restitution?
 O. To the owner of the bailment.

M. 3:1

The formal complexity of this construction in no way obscures its self-evident message. The reason is the perfect contrast and balance. A-B serve the whole, then, as we see, C contrasts with J, E-H=K-M, and, at the centerpiece, I contrasts with O. The obvious point is that when the bailee makes restitution, he gains the rights accruing to the owner, and when he does not, the owner retains these rights of receiving restitution. Nothing could be more self-evident, nor, in the nature of things, more elegantly explained through the use of formal devices alone.

 A. One who borrows has no right to lend out,
 B. and one who rents has no right to rent out,
 C. and one who borrows has no right to rent out,
 D. and one who rents has no right to lend out,
 E. And the one with whom these things are left as a bailment has no right to leave them as a bailment with someone else,
 F. unless the householder [who owns the objects] has given him permission to do so.

T. 3:1 Z p. 375, ls. 30-32

 A. He who borrows a cow from someone else and it was stolen,
 B. *and the thief was found,*
 C. *the thief pays twofold restitution, or fourfold or fivefold restitution* to the first party [M. 3:1E-G].

D. [If the bailee] had paid compensation and afterward the thief was found,

E. [the thief] pays twofold restitution or fourfold or fivefold restitution to the second party.

T. 3:2 Z pp. 375, ls. 32-33, 376, 1

A. He who deposits a cow with his fellow, and it was stolen,

B. and [the bailee] said, "Lo, I shall pay you compensation for it, rather than taking an oath,"

C. and afterward the thief was found—

D. [the thief] pays twofold restitution or fourfold or fivefold restitution to the second party.

T. 3:3 Z p. 376, ls. 1-3

T. 3:1 serves as a prologue to the chapter of M., dealing as it does with bailments, but it does not relate specifically to M. 3:1. T. 3:2, 3 then restate M.'s basic point, at T. 3:2 in a different setting, and at T. 3:3 in an identical case.

3:2

A. He who rents a cow from his fellow, and then lent it to someone else,

B. and it died of natural causes—

C. let the one who rented it take an oath that it died of natural causes,

D. and the one who borrowed it then pays compensation to the one who rented it.

E. Said R. Yosé, "How should this one do business with his fellow's cow?

F. "But [the funds paid for] the cow are to return to the owner."

M. 3:2

The renter is exempt from paying compensation, but the borrower is liable (M. 7:8). Yosé's persuasive reasoning is clear as given. In fact, the pericope serves as a prologue to Yosé's set, M. 3:3-5.

3:3-5

I A. [If] one said to two people, "I stole a *maneh* [a hundred *zuz*] from one of you and I do not know from which one of you it was"—

B. "The father of one of you deposited a *maneh* with me, and I do not know the father of which one of you it was"—

C. pays off a *maneh* to this one and a *maneh* to that one,

D. for he has admitted it on his own.

M. 3:3

II A. Two who deposited something with one person, this one leaving a *maneh*, and that one leaving two hundred *zuz*—

B. this one says, "Mine is the deposit of two hundred *zuz*,"

C. and that one says, "Mine is the deposit of two hundred *zuz*"—

D. he pays off a *maneh* to this one, and a *maneh* to that one,

E. and the rest is left to set there until Elijah comes.

F. Said R. Yosé, "If so, what has the deceiver actually lost?

G. "But let the whole sum set until Elijah comes [and no one will be paid off]."

M. 3:4

III   A. And so is the rule for two utensils, one worth a *maneh*, and one worth a thousand *zuz*—

B. this one says, "The better one is mine,"

C. and that one says, "The better one is mine"—

D. he gives the smaller one to one of them.

E. And from the [funds received from the sale of] the larger one, he gives the cost of a smaller one to the other party.

F. And the rest of the money [received for the sale of the larger one] is left to set until Elijah comes.

G. Said R. Yosé, "If so, what has the deceiver actually lost?

H. "But let the whole [sum received for the sale of both utensils] set until Elijah comes."

M. 3:5

M. 3:3 sets the stage for what is to follow. The triplet formally is not effected through threefold repetition. But the framer's intention is clear at M. 3:5, which adds absolutely nothing, but serves solely to supply a third entry for the whole construction. The exegesis of M. 3:3 is supplied at M. 3:3D. Yosé's saying is so phrased as to explain the grounds of his disagreement. So, as we have observed so many times, M. supplies its own exegesis.

A. He who sells a cow to his fellow, and it was stolen—

B. this one says, "It was stolen while in your domain [and the loss is yours],"

C. and that one says, "It was stolen in your domain"—

D. let them divide [the loss].

T. 3:4 Z p. 376, ls. 3-4

A. He who says, "I owe a *maneh*, but I don't know whether it is to Mr. So-and-so that I owe it, or whether it is to Mr. Such-and-such that I owe it"—

B. *pays off a maneh to this one and a maneh to that one,*

C. *for he has admitted it on his own* that he owes a *maneh* [M. 3:3C-D].

D. And [if] he said to two people, "I stole a *maneh* from one of you, and two hundred *zuz* from one of you, and I don't know which one of you it was,"

E. he pays off two hundred *zuz* to this one, and two hundred *zuz* to that one.

F. For if not, he would have been better off to shut up.

G. This one says, "Two hundred *zuz* belong to me,"

H. and that one says, "Two hundred *zuz* belong to me,"—

I. *he pays off a maneh to this one and a maneh to that one.*

J. And the rest he should not pay out to them until they come to an agreement between themselves [cf. M. 3:4, G].

T. 3:5 Z p. 376, ls. 4-8

A. Two who left bailments with one person—
B. *this one left a* maneh,
C. *and that one left two hundred* zuz—
D. [and] when [they come to] collect,
E. this one says, "The two hundred *zuz* are mine,"
F. and that one says, "The two hundred *zuz* are mine,"
G. *[the bailee] pays off a* maneh *to this one, and a* maneh *to that one,*
H. *and the rest is left there [to set] until Elijah comes.*
I. *Said R. Yosé, "If so, what has the deceiver actually lost?*
J. *"But let the whole sum remain until Elijah comes [and no one will be paid off]"* [M. 3:4].
K. *And so is the rule for two utensils,* one large and one small.
L. *He gives the smaller one to one of them.*
M. *And from the value [received for the sale] of the larger one, he pays off the value of the smaller one to the other party.*
N. *And the rest of the money is left until Elijah comes.*
O. *Said R. Yosé, "If so, what has the deceiver actually lost?*
P. *"But the whole [sum received for the sale of both utensils] is to set until Elijah comes"* [M. 3:5].

T. 3:6 Z p. 376, ls. 8-15

What T. wants is for the parties to make a compromise between themselves. This is stated openly at T. 3:4, and, for M.'s cases, at T. 3:5. Otherwise T.'s restatements add nothing to the interpretation of M.

3:6

A. He who deposits produce with his fellow
B. even if it is going to go to waste—
C. [the fellow] should not touch it.
D. Rabban Simeon b. Gamaliel says, "He sells them in the presence of a court,
E. "for he is in the position of one who thereby restores what is lost to its rightful owner."

M. 3:6

Even if the produce is being eaten up by mice or rotting, the bailee cannot deal with it, so A-C. D-E differs, for the stated reason. The unit introduces what is to follow.

A. *He who deposits produce with his fellow—*
B. *even if it is going to go to waste,*
C. *[the fellow] should not touch it* [M. 3:6A-C].
D. Therefore the householder [who owns the produce] may designate them as heave-offering and tithes for produce located elsewhere.
E. Rabban Simeon b. Gamaliel says, "In the case of those which are rotting,

F. "he sells them in the presence of a court,
G. "for he is in the position of one who thereby restores what is lost to its rightful owner" [M. 3:6D-E].

T. 3:7 Z p. 376, ls. 15-17

A. He who deposits produce with his fellow and they rotted—
B. wine and it turned sour,
C. oil and it stank—
D. "even if they are going to go to waste,
E. "he should not touch them," the words of R. Meir.
F. And sages say, "He puts them up for sale in court.
G. "He sells them to a third party,
H. "but does not buy them for himself."

T. 3:8 Z p. 376, ls. 17-20

A. Similarly:
B. Charity-supervisors who did not find poor folk among whom to distribute beans sell [the beans] to others.
C. But they do not buy them for themselves.
D. Charity-supervisors change money for others, and do not change money for themselves.

T. 3:9 (Continued) Z p. 376, ls. 20-21

Since the owner of the produce has sole right to dispose of it, T. 3:7, he may declare it to be heave-offering or tithes for produce owned by him in some other place, T. 3:7's sole clarification of M. T. 3:8 indicates that it is Meir who takes the anonymous position in M. T. 3:8G-H, T. 3:9A-D, then make sure that there is no self-dealing in a case such as this.

3:7-8

I A. He who deposits produce with his fellow—
B. lo, this one [with whom the bailment is left, when returning it,] may exact [from the owner the following] reductions [due to natural depletion of the produce]:
C. (1) for wheat and rice, nine *qabs* and a half for a *kor*;
D. (2) for barley and durra, nine *qabs* to a *kor*;
E. (3) for spelt and linseed, three *seahs* to a *kor*.
F. All is relative to the quantity, all is relative to the time [it is left].
G. Said R. Yoḥanan b. Nuri, "But what difference does it make to the mice [as to the issue of quantity or time]? Will they not eat [plenty], whether it is from a large volume or a small volume of grain?
H. "But he may not exact from the owner the stated reductions,
I. "except from a single *kor* alone."
J. R. Judah says, "If it was a large volume of produce, he may not exact from the owner the stated reductions,
K. "for it increases [in bulk as it is stored away]."

M. 3:7

II A. He exacts [a reduction] of a sixth for wine.
B. R. Judah says, "A fifth."

III C. He extracts [reduction] of three *logs* of oil per hundred—
 D. a *log* and a half for the sediment, and a *log* and a half for absorption [into the walls of the clay jars].
 E. If it was refined oil, he may not exact a reduction for the sediment.
 F. If the jars were old, he may not exact a reduction for absorption.
 G. R. Judah says, "Also: He who sells refined oil to his fellow through the year—
 H. "lo, [the latter] must accept upon himself [agree to] a reduction of a *log* and a half per hundred because of sediment."

M. 3:8

The point is familiar from the foregoing. Since there is natural wastage due to mildew or to rats, the bailment is going to be diminished in volume. The view of the authority behind what I think is a triplet, M. 3:7A-E, M. 3:8A, M. 3:8C-D (bearing the obvious gloss at M. 3:8E-F), is that there are fixed proportions to be taken into account. These are most clearly stated in the second and third stichs of the triplet. The first opinion is somewhat complicated by F, which disagrees with the fixed proportions specified at the internal triplet of C-E. C-E clearly declare such fixed proportions. Since a *kor* = 30 *seahs* = 180 *qabs*, C allows 5.2%, D, 5%, and E, 16.6%. It is difficult to see how F will concur. It follows, I think, that, following the triplet, M. 3:7A-E, we have an interpolated dispute, F *vs.* G. The topic-sentence of F must also be A-B. This is virtually certain, since M. 3:8A and C also speak of fixed proportions.

As to the substance, it is clear from M. 3:6 that the bailee must be protected from claims for damages which lie beyond his power to prevent. The theory of the triplet is that the bailee will not have to return quite the volume of produce he has received, and on this point all parties concur. Yohanan rejects the notion of reductions covering more than a *kor*. Judah's view is clear as it is stated. Judah differs as to volume at M. 3:8B. Old jars will not absorb liquid, so M. 3:8F. Judah's last point concerns M. 3:8E. He maintains that even in the case of refined oil, there will be a deduction for sediment. If the seller supplies oil through the year, which he keeps in stock until it is drawn upon, then the buyer has to accept 1.5% of lees.

 E. *He who deposits produce with his fellow—*
 F. *lo, this one [with whom the bailment is left] may exact [from the owner of the produce] the reductions [due to the natural depletion, e.g., through mildew or consumption by rats, of the produce]* [M. 3:7A-B].
 G. Under what circumstances?
 H. When he has combined [the bailment of grain] with his own produce.
 I. But if [the deposited produce] was kept by itself, he may simply say to him, "Here is what is yours before you."
 J. It is all the same if one commingles the produce or designates second tithe in the storage-bin.

T. 3:9 (concluded) Z p. 376, ls. 22-24

A. And as to other sorts of pulse, the sages have not assigned to them a fixed measure [of depletion].

B. Said Ben 'Azzai, "On account of the strengthening of the power of R. 'Aqiba was it, [so],

C. "that he assigned fixed measures to these, but did not assign fixed measures to the others."

D. *Said R. Yoḥanan b. Nuri, "Now what difference does it make to the mice [as to the quantity of what is stored, or the time for which it is stored, that all things should be relative to the quantity and to the time]?*

E. *"Will they not eat plenty, whether it is from a large volume or a small volume of grain?*

F. *"But he may not exact from the owner the stated reductions,*

G. *"except from a single kor alone"* [M. 3:7G-I].

H. Said R. Judah, "Under what circumstances? When [the bailee] measured out [for the bailiff a quantity of grain to return on the bailment] in his house.

I. "But if he made the measurement in his threshing-floor, he may not exact the stated reductions [due to natural depletion]" [M. 3:7J-K].

J. And so did R. Judah say, "They referred to the reduction on account of sediment only in the case of oil alone.

K. "For sometimes a person may purchase from his fellow olive oil so pure as to be entirely without froth."

T. 3:10 Z p. 376, ls. 24-30

A. Said R. Yosé, "Arios asked sages, 'Lo, [if] one has set aside ten *kors* per hundred and measured out the tithe, and [the produce set aside as tithe] had diminished—

B. " 'What is the rule?'

C. " 'They said to him, 'Just as that which has been set aside as tithe has diminished in volume, so that which has been left as unconsecrated produce also has diminished in volume.

D. " 'But even though that which has been left as unconsecrated produce has not diminished in volume, it is permitted [since the part set aside as tithe is deemed valid for its purpose].'

E. "[He further asked them,] 'If he measured out the unconsecrated produce and it increased in volume, what is the rule? [Does more tithe have to be set aside?]'

G. "They said to him, 'Just as it has increased in volume as to unconsecrated produce, so it has increased in volume as to tithe.

H. " 'But even though that which has been designated as tithe has not increased in volume, it is permitted [since the part set aside as tithe is deemed valid for its purpose].'

I. "[He further asked them.] 'If one has unconsecrated produce [which is rotting] and produce in the status of second tithe and wishes to sell both kinds of produce, which sort of produce should he sell first of all?'

J. "They said to him, 'First of all he should sell the unconsecrated produce, and afterward he should sell the produce in the status of second tithe.' "

T. 3:11 Z pp. 376, ls. 30-32, 377, 1-3

T. 3:9 makes an important point at G-I. M.'s rule takes effect only when there has been a commingling of produce. Then the bailee has to take care to hand back the proper volume. But if the bailment was kept by itself, there is only the need to return untouched what the bailee has received. I do not follow J. T. 3:10 is clear as given. Judah regards the threshing-floor as not subject to natural wastage. Rather there is natural increase, as at M. 3:7J-K.

T. 3:11 presents an interesting supplement. The questions of Arios are relevant to M. because of the interest in natural decrease or increase in produce which one has in hand, e.g., as a bailment (at T. 3:11 I-J). The position of sages is that we assume there is a natural increase in the entire volume of produce, both what has been set aside as tithe—ten *kors* per hundred—and the rest, which remains as unconsecrated produce. The same thing is said a second time. I-J evidently refer us back to M. 3:7. If one is selling off deteriorating produce, he should save the unconsecrated food so that the owner will have greater benefit from the bailment.

3:9

A. He who deposits a jar with his fellow,
B. and the owner did not specify a place for it,
C. and [someone] moved it and it was broken—
D. if in the midst of his handling it, it was broken,
E. [and if he moved it to make use of it] for his own needs, he is liable.
F. [If he moved it] for its needs, he is exempt.
G. If after he had put it down it was broken,
H. whether he had moved it for his own needs or for its needs, he is exempt.
I. [If] the owner specified a place for it,
J. and [someone] moved it and it was broken—
K. whether it was in the midst of his handling it or whether it was after he had put it down—
L. [if he moved it] for his own needs, he is liable.
M. [If he moved it] for its needs, he is exempt.

M. 3:9

The operative distinction explaining the difference of D, G vs. K, is expressed at B vs. I. If the owner has designated a place for his bailment, it is to be kept there. That is why it makes no difference at all whether the object is broken while in transit or at rest, K. If it is moved, the bailee is liable, so I-K, and this without regard for the distinction of D, G.

3:10

A. He who deposits coins with his fellow—
B. [if the latter] (1) wrapped them up and threw them over his shoulder,
C. (2) gave them over to his minor son or daughter,

D. or (3) locked them up in an inadequate way,
E. he is liable [to make them up if they are lost],
F. because he did not take care of them the way people usually take care [of things].
G. But if he did take care of them the way people usually take care of things,
H. he is exempt.

M. 3:10

M. carries its own exegesis at F-G. The triplet, B-D, is hardly needed, and G-H manage nicely without a counterpart.

3:11

A. He who deposits coins with a money-changer—
B. if they are wrapped up, [the moneychanger] should not make use of them.
C. Therefore if they got lost, he is not liable to make them up [as an unpaid bailee (M. 2:7)].
D. [If they were] loose, he may make use of them.
E. Therefore if they got lost, he is liable to make them up.
F. [He who deposits coins] with a householder,
G. whether they are wrapped up or whether they are loose,—
H. [the householder] should not make use of them.
I. Therefore if they got lost, he is not liable to make them up.
J. "The storekeeper is subject to the same rule as the householder," the words of R. Meir.
K. R. Judah says, "The storekeeper is subject to the same rule as the money-changer."

M. 3:11

The contrasts, B-C, D-E, and B, D *vs.* G, tell the story. The money-changer may commingle loose change, but then makes it up if it is lost. The householder is not to use the bailment as ready cash. The dispute is a minor gloss.

3:12

I A. He who makes use of a bailment—
B. The House of Shammai say, "He suffers a disadvantage, whether the value rises or falls."
C. The House of Hillel say, "[He restores the bailment] as it was at the moment at which he took it out [to use it for his own purposes]."
D. R. 'Aqiba says, "[He restores it as it was] at the moment at which it was claimed."

II E. He who expresses the intention of making use of a bailment—
F. the House of Shammai say, "He is liable [for any damage done to the bailment, as if he had made use of it]."
G. And the House of Hillel say, "He is liable [for damages incurred] only when he will actually make use of the bailment,
H. "since it is said, *If he has not put his hand to his neighbor's property* (Ex. 22:7)."

I. [Delete:] How so?
J. [If] he tipped over the jug and took a quarter-*log* of liquid from it, and it broke—
K. he pays only the value of the quarter-*log* he has actually removed.
L. But if he raised it up [so making acquisition of it], and took a quarter-*log* of liquid from it and it broke,
M. he pays the value of the whole jug.

M. 3:12

M. continues the discourse begun at M. 3:9. The bailee has used the object for his own purposes, and it has broken. Now we have to assess compensation. The House of Hillel have the assessment made relative to the value of the object at the time that the man has misappropriated it, that is, when he took it from its assigned place. 'Aqiba has the bailee pay the value of the object at the time that the owner comes to claim it. In both instances, this may be more or less than the value of the object when it was deposited, or, as the case may be, when it was removed from its assigned location or when it was claimed. The Shammaites assign the higher of the two values. If the bailment lost value, the bailee has to pay the value at the time at which it was deposited; if the bailment gained in value, the bailee pays the gain in value, as indicated.

The second dispute is in fact unrelated to the first except in general theme. The Shammaites treat intention as tantamount to deed, so that a mere declaration of what one plans to do invokes the penalties of A-B. The House of Hillel take the view that on one is liable only for what he actually does.

I is misleading, since the illustration does not relate to the dispute, and should be dropped. The contrast of J-K, L-M points to the fact that, at J, the man has not made acquisition of the jug, so he is liable only for the contents he actually has taken. At L, he has taken up and acquired the jug, so is responsible for the whole thing. The Houses do not differ on that fact.

A. He who makes use of a bailment—
B. the House of Shammai say, "He suffers a disadvantage, whether the value rises or falls." [And the House of Hillel say, "He restores the bailment as it was at the moment at which he took it out (to use it for his own purposes)." R. 'Aqiba says, .. He restores it as it was at the moment at which it was claimed"] [M. 3: 12A-D].
C. How so?
D. [If] he deposited it [when the value was] two, and the price stood at four.
E. [or if he deposited it when the value was] four, and [the price now stood at] two,
F. [when the owner claims the bailment] he hands over to him [the value with the price at] two.

T. 3:12 Z p. 377, ls. 3-5

It appears to me that C-F illustrate the position of 'Aqiba, who is the only party to ignore a variation in the value of the object from the time of the deposit or from the time of the misappropriation of the object to the time of payment. The House of Shammai would give the price-advantage of four no matter what happens, and the House of Hillel will ignore the value at the time of the bailment, which is not alluded to. It would therefore seem that 'Aqiba is the only party who can accept the illustration.

CHAPTER FOUR

BABA MESIA CHAPTER FOUR

Another chapter which exhausts M.'s treatment of a single theme, this one turns to questions of commercial transactions, with special interest in fraud through overcharge or misrepresentation. M. has the theory, to begin with, that there is a true value, as distinct from a market value, of an object. Mishnaic law therefore maintains that, if a purchaser pays more than a sixth more than true value, or if a seller receives a sixth less than that amount, in the form of an overcharge, fraud has been committed. The sale is null. The defrauded party has the choice of getting his money back or of keeping the goods and receiving only the amount of the overcharge. This point is worked out with some care at M. 4:3-4. There is a little prologue at M. 4:1-2, having to do with the right of retraction of a sale under normal circumstances, not fraudulent ones. M. 4:1 makes the important point that a sale is regarded as final when the buyer has drawn into his own possession the commodity which is to be purchased, not merely when the seller has received the money. This point is made in a somewhat complicated way, but it is not difficult to follow. M. 4:2 then illustrates the matter of retraction along the lines of M. 4:1's theory. As indicated, M. 4:3-4 then go on to retraction in a case of overcharge.

M. 4:5 concludes this exposition with yet another important point on fraudulent coinage. A coin which diverges from the true weight of its denomination by a fixed proportion (one twenty-fourth, one twelfth, or one sixth) constitutes a fraud and may not be used. M. 4:6 specifies the time in which, on this account, the transaction is null. M. 4:7-8 conclude this discussion with a large formal exercise, of marginal relevance to what has gone before.

From discussions of cases of fraud in commercial transactions, M. proceeds to three related matters. The first, M. 4:9, is transactions not covered by a claim of fraud by reason of overcharge. These involve sales of slaves, discounted notes of indebtedness, real estate, and consecrated items. M. 4:10, second, introduces the notion of fraud through verbal misrepresentation. M. 4:11-12, finally, turn to misrepresentation through adulteration of produce for sale. In general one may not mix one kind of produce with some other. But wholesalers may gather grain from various farms and mix the whole into a single bin. Wine may be diluted only if it is customary in the province where it is sold. At the end are some miscellaneous rulings relevant to this theme.

4:1-2

A. (1) Gold acquires silver, but silver does not acquire gold.
B. (2) Copper acquires silver, but silver does not acquire copper.
C. (3) Bad coins acquire good coins, but good coins do not acquire bad coins.
D. (4) A coin lacking a mint mark acquires a minted coin, and a minted coin does not acquire a coin lacking a mint-mark.
E. (5) Movable goods acquire coins, and coins do not acquire movable goods.
F. This is the governing principle: All sorts of movable objects effect acquisition of one another.

M. 4:1

A. How so?
B. [If the buyer] had drawn produce into his possession but not yet paid over the coins,
C. he [nonetheless] cannot retract.
D. [If] he had paid over the coins but had not yet drawn the produce into his possession, he has the power to retract.
E. Truly have they said:
F. He who exacted punishment from the men of the Generation of the Flood and the Generation of the Dispersion is destined to exact punishment from him who does not keep his word.
G. R. Simeon says, "Whoever has the money in his hand—his hand is on top."

M. 4:2

What is at issue in the pericopae before us is how a purchase is effected. The datum is that transfer of funds alone does not complete a transaction. Only the transfer of the object does so. It will follow that if the buyer has transferred the money, but the seller has not yet handed over, nor the buyer received, the object of purchase, then either party may retract. Once the buyer has taken up ("lifted up") or drawn into his own possession the object or purchase, the transaction is complete. The buyer now is liable to pay off the purchase price, if it has not already been paid; the seller may no longer retract. There is here a further fundamental consideration. Since money does not effect a transaction, we have to determine that sort of specie which is deemed to constitute currency, and that which is regarded as a commodity. In general, the more precious the metal, the more likely it is to be regarded not as money or ready cash, but as a commodity, subject to purchase or sale, just as much as is grain or wine. As we shall see, this is expressed very simply: "Gold acquires silver," meaning, gold is a commodity, and when the purchaser has taken possession of the gold, the seller owns the silver paid as money for it. But if the exchange is in the reverse—someone paying in gold for silver—the transaction is effected when the seller has taken possession of the gold. In an exchange of copper and silver, copper is deemed money, silver is now the commodity. All of this is neatly worked out for us at M. 4:1, which, in the light of these remarks, should pose no special problems.

M. 4:1A-E presents five instances of the principle just now explained. M. 4:1F does not supply any sort of governing principle, but, rather, an independent entry. It cannot be regarded as a sixth item, for self-evident, formal reasons. M. 4:2A-D then satisfactorily instantiate M. 4:1's point. The sale is complete when the buyer has made acquisition of the produce, but not when the seller has received the money. I do not see much relevance of M. 4:2F, which simply would seem to add that if a person does retract at this stage in the agreement, sages do not approve.

M. 4:2G is important. Simeon rejects the theory that, once money has been paid, the commodity has not been fully purchased until it has been drawn into the buyer's possession. On the contrary, so soon as money changes hands, while the seller still has the power to retract, the purchaser does not. Since Simeon self-evidently rejects M. 4:2A-D, he must reject the theory of acquisition presented at M. 4:1 as well.

    A.   *Gold acquires silver* [M. 4:1A]—how so?
    B.   [If] one handed over a golden *denar* for twenty-five pieces of silver, lo, this one has made acquisition [of the silver], no matter where it is.
    C.   But if he handed over twenty-five pieces of silver for a single golden *denar*,
    D.   lo, this one has made acquisition only at the moment at which he actually will draw [into his own possession the golden *denar* which he is buying].
    E.   *Copper acquires silver* [M. 4:1B]—how so?
    F.   [If] one has handed over thirty *issars* [of copper] for a silver *denar*, lo, this one has made acquisition of the silver no matter where it is.
    G.   But if he handed over to him a silver *denar* for thirty *issars* of copper,
    H.   lo, this one has made acquisition only at the moment at which he actually will draw [into his own possession the pieces of copper which he is buying].

T. 3:13 Z p. 377, ls. 5-9

    A.   *A coin lacking a mint mark acquires a minted coin* [M. 4:1D],
    B.   The governing principle is this: Whatever is acquired [as a commodity] effects acquisition.
    C.   A cloak effects acquisition of a golden *denar*.
    D.   Said R. Simeon, "Also: when they said, 'A cloak effects acquisition of a golden *denar* [but not *vice versa*]—
    E.   "in any event that is the law."
    F.   *Truly they have said, He who exacted punishment from the men of the genera-*

tion of the flood and the generation of the dispersion is destined to exact punishment from him who does not keep his word [M. 4:2F].

G. But he who has give and take in words—the other party has no claim of fraud against him.

H. Nonetheless, sages have said, "Whoever nullifies his word—the spirit of sages gets no pleasure from him."

T. 3:14 Z p. 377, ls. 9-13

T. further instantiates M.'s rule, and at T. 3:14G-H introduces M. 4:10's considerations into the matter before us.

4:3

A. Fraud [overreaching] is an overcharge of four pieces of silver out of twenty four pieces of silver to the *sela*—
B. (one sixth of the purchase-price).
C. For how long is it permitted to retract [in the case of fraud]?
D. So long as it takes to show [the article] to a merchant or a relative.
E. R. Tarfon gave instructions in Lud:
F. "Fraud is an overcharge of eight pieces of silver to a *sela*—
G. "one third of the purchase price."
H. So the merchants of Lud rejoiced.
I. He said to them, "All day long it is permitted to retract."
J. They said to him, "Let R. Tarfon leave us where we were."
K. And they reverted to conduct themselves in accord with the ruling of sages.

M. 4:3

If an object has a true value of twenty-four and the seller pays twenty-eight, he has been defrauded and may retract. Tarfon gave and took, E-K.

A. *Fraud is an overcharge of four pieces of silver out of twenty four pieces of silver to the sela*—
B. *one sixth of the purchase price.*
C. *For how long is it permitted [in the case of fraud]?*
D. *For so long as it takes to show to a merchant or a relative* [M. 4:3A-D],
E. or to an expert.

T. 3:15 Z p. 377, ls. 14-15

T. lightly glosses M.

4:4

A. All the same are the buyer and the seller: both are subject to the law of fraud.
B. Just as fraud applies to an ordinary person, so it applies to a merchant.
C. R. Judah says, "Fraud does not apply to a merchant."
D. He who has been subjected [to fraud]—his hand is on top.
E. [If] he wanted, he says to him, "Return my money."
F. [Or, if he wanted, he says to him,] "Give me back the amount of the fraud."

M. 4:4

A is an important qualification. B-C in fact repeat and dispute A. D is clarified by E-F. The buyer has the power to nullify the sale or merely to collect the amount of the overcharge.

    A. *He who has been subjected to fraud—his hand is on top* [M. 4:4D].
    B. How so?
    C. [If] one sold to him a shirt worth five for six—the hand of the purchaser is on top.
    D. [If] he wants, he says to him, "Give me [my] *selas* [back]."
    E. [If] he wants, he says to him, "Here's your money, and give me back my shirt."
    F. But if he had said to him, "Sell me a shirt worth six for five,"
    G. the hand of the seller is on top.
    H. [If] he wants, he says to him, "Give me a *sela*."
    I. And if he wants, he says to him, "Here's your shirt, and give me back my money."
    J. Rabbi says, "Under all circumstances the hand of the seller is on top."
    K. And just as the seller has the right to retract, so the purchaser has the right to retract [M. 4:4A].
    L. R. Simeon says, "The seller has the right to retract,
    M. "but the purchaser does not have the right to retract.
    N. "For [the former] already has received his money" [cf. M. 4:2G].
    T. 3:16 Z p. 377, ls. 15-21

A-I go over the ground of M. 4:4D-F. M. 4:4A accords with T. 3:16K. Simeon again maintains that merely paying over the price effects acquisition.

    A. *Fraud is an overcharge of four pieces of silver* [*as an overcharge for what one has bought for a sela*];
    B. *and a claim* [*involving a court-imposed oath*] *must be for at least two silver ma'ahs* [M. 4:7A-B].
    C. Under what circumstances?
    D. In a case in which he sold without further specification.
    E. But if he made a stipulation with him,
    F. there is no further claim after a stipulation.
    T. 3:21 Z p. 378, ls. 1-2

    A. He who does business on trust,
    B. and he who says to his fellow, "[Lo, I make this sale to you] on condition that you have no claim of fraud against me,"—
    C. [the buyer] has no claim of fraud against him.
    T. 3:22 Z p. 378, ls. 2-3

    A. One should not sell him superior goods at par and an inferior goods on trust,
    B. but either both of them at par,
    C. or both of them on trust.
    D. One may reckon with him the fee for the ass and the fee for the ass-driver.
    E. But the fee for the inn he should not reckon with him [in the costs],
    F. because he receives his fee from him.
    T. 3:23 Z p. 378, ls. 3-6

Even though M. 4:7 is cited, in fact it is M. 4:4 which is complemented. T. 3:21 makes the point that the buyer may make an agreement to pay even more than the "true value" of the object. Trading on trust, in this context, involves an understanding between buyer and seller in line with T. 3:21D-F. Specifically, the seller will get back what he paid for the merchandise plus a certain fixed profit. In this case there is no possible claim for fraud, since, as at T. 3:21, a stipulation in advance governs the conditions of trade. Now there can be goods priced at par and those priced on trust, as clarified. There cannot, in a single trade, be a mixture of such arrangements, e.g., the superior merchandise at par, the inferior at cost-plus. T. 3:23D-F then go over the ground of what may be included in the costs of an item. Transportation and porterage are included, but storage is not, E.

4:5

A. How much may a *sela* be defective and [still] not fall under the rule of fraud?
B. R. Meir says, "Four *issars*, at an *issar* to a *denar*."
C. R. Judah says, "Four *pondions*, at a *pondion* to a *denar*."
D. R. Simeon says, "Eight *pondions*, at two *pondions* to a *denar*."

M. 4:5

If a *sela* is short-weight, it is not to be paid out. A *sela* = 4 *denars*; a *denar* = 12 *pondions*; a *pondion* = 2 *issars*, so Meir permits a short-weight of 1/24, Judah, 1/12, and Simeon, 1/6, in line with M. 4:3A, B.

A. *How much may a sela be defective and not fall under the rule of fraud?*
B. *"As to a sela, four issars, an issar to a denar," the words of R. Meir.*
C. *R. Judah says, "As to a sela, four pondions, a pondion to a denar."*
D. *R. Simeon says, "As to a sela, eight pondions, two pondions to a denar"* [M. 4:5A-D].
E. If it is of more [weight] than that, one [would have the right to] put it into circulation.

T. 3:17 Z p. 377, ls. 21-24

A. A *sela*—up to a *sheqel*.
B. And a *denar*—up to a quarter.
C. [If it weighs] less than this, even by an *issar*, one is not permitted to put it into circulation.

T. 3:18 Z p. 377, ls. 24-25

T. 3:18 goes on to specify acceptable deficits in the weight of other coins.

A. *One may not sell it either to a merchant* [M. 4:11J],
B. or to a highwayman or to a thug,
C. *for they deceive others thereby* [M. 4:11L].
D. But one has the right to pierce it and hang it around the neck of his little boy.
E. And just as you rule in the case of unconsecrated food,

F. so you must rule in the case of produce in the status of second tithe.
G. And this is on condition that one not intend to practice fraud in regard to second tithe [cf. M. 4:6F-H].
H. Under what circumstances [M. 4:6]?
I. In the case of *denars* and *selas* [of silver].
J. But in the case of golden *denars*, or copper coins, they would put them into circulation at their full value.

T. 3:19 Z p. 377, ls. 25-29

The defective coins may not be sold as commodities, A-C+D. E-G make the point that these coins, not suitable for purchasing ordinary food, also may not be used to purchase food in the status of second tithe. H-J qualify M. 4:6 in a fundamental way.

4:6

A. How long is it permitted to return [a defective *sela*]?
B. In large towns, for the length of time it takes to show to a money-changer.
C. And in villages, up to the eve of the Sabbath.
D. [If the one who gave it] recognizes it, even after twelve months he is to accept it from him.
E. But [if the one who gave the coin refuses to take it back], he has no valid claim against the other except resentment.
F. He may give it for produce in the status of second tithe, [for easy transportation to Jerusalem],
G. and need not scruple,
H. for it is only churlishness [to refuse a slightly depreciated coin].

M. 4:6

We go back over the issue of M. 4:3, now with reference to M. 4:5. The defective coin may be returned, within the specified time-limits, A-C. The one who handed it over has to take it back, D-E, if he recognizes the coin. But if he does not, E, the one who has been given the bad coin has no recourse. The defective coin may be exchanged for second tithe-produce and taken to Jerusalem.

A. *How long is it permitted to return [a defective sela]?*
B. *In large towns, for the length of time it takes to show it to a money-changer.*
C. *And in villages, up to the eve of the Sabbath* [M. 4:6A-C].
D. For so it is customary for the market to be held in large towns from one Friday to the next.

T. 3:20 Z pp. 377, ls. 29-30, 378, 1

T. lightly glosses M.

4:7-8

A. Defrauding involves [an overcharge of] four pieces of silver [for what one has bought for a *sela*].

B. And a claim [involving a court-imposed oath] must be [for a claim of at least] two silver *ma'ahs*.

C. An admission [as at M. 1:1] must be for at least what is worth a *perutah*.

D. There are five [kinds of rules involving] that which is worth a *perutah*:

E. (1) An admission must be for at least what is worth a *perutah*.

F. (2) A woman is betrothed for that which is worth a *perutah*.

G. (3) He who derives use to the value of a *perutah* from that which belongs to the sanctuary has committed sacrilege.

H. (4) He who finds that which is worth a *perutah* is liable to make proclamation.

I. (5) He who steals from his fellow something to the value of a *perutah* and takes [a false] oath to the contrary [and then confesses his crime] must bring it after him, even to Media [M. B.Q. 9:5].

M. 4:7

A. There are five instances in which an added fifth applies:

B. (1) He who eats (1) heave-offering, (2) heave-offering of tithe, (3) heave-offering of tithe taken from doubtfully tithed produce, (4) dough-offering, and (5) first fruits

C. adds a fifth [to the value of the principal, when he makes restitution].

D. (2) He who redeems [pays coins to bring to Jerusalem in place of] produce deriving from a fourth year planting or from his second tithe adds a fifth.

E. (3) He who redeems that which he has consecrated adds a fifth.

F. (4) He who derives benefit to the extent of a *perutah* from that which has been consecrated [when he makes restitution] adds a fifth.

G. (5) He who steals from his fellow that which is worth a *perutah* and takes a false oath to him [when he wishes to confess and effect restitution] adds a fifth.

M. 4:8

The formal plan of the unit is announced at M. 4:7D, 4:8A, and carried out with precision. This even requires the repetition of M. 4:C at E. The two sets of five entries therefore are independent of, and secondary to, the relevant entry, M. 4:7A-C. The whole is, of course, essentially external to its context. M. 4:7A restates the view of M. 4:3. M. 4:7B makes the point that a court will impose an oath upon a person who admits part, but not the whole, of a claim against him, only if he rejects a claim of a value of two silver *ma'ahs*. C holds, in like manner, that a court will impose an oath only if the person admits to owing at least a *perutah*. Thus the claimant must demand sixty-four times what the defendant admits to owing (one silver *ma'ah* = 32 *perutot*). The five rules for a *perutah* are familiar. M. 4:7F rests on M. Qid. 1:1; M. 4:7H, on M. B.M. 2:1ff.; M. 4:7I restates M. B.Q. 9:5. M. 4:8 then goes over a related formal pattern; its points are clear as given.

4:9

A. These are matters which are not subject to a claim of fraud [on account of overcharge]:

B. (1) slaves, (2) bills of indebtedness [which are discounted and sold], (3) real estate, and (4) that which has been consecrated.

C. They are not subject to twofold restitution.

D. nor [in the case of a consecrated ox or sheep] to fourfold or fivefold restitution.

E. An unpaid bailee is not required to take an oath [on their account, that he has not inflicted damage].

F. And a paid bailee does not have to pay compensation [on their account, if they are stolen or lost].

G. R. Simeon says, "Holy Things for which one is liable for replacement [should they be lost] are subject to a claim of fraud on account of overcharge.

H. "Holy Things for which one is not liable for replacement [should they be lost] are not subject to a claim of fraud on account of overcharge" [cf. M. B.Q. 7:4].

I. R. Judah says, "Also: He who sells a scroll of the Torah, a beast, or a pearl—

J. "they are not subject to a claim of fraud by reason of overcharge."

K. They said to him, "They have specified only these [of B]."

M. 4:9

The items of B are exempt from the rules governing movables which are sold, A, stolen, C-D, or subjected to negligent bailees, E-F. B2 refers to writs of indebtedness, which are sold at a discount to a bill-collector. Simeon qualifies B4. Judah's three items are explained by T.

A. R. Judah says, "Also: [He who sells] a scroll of the Torah, a beast, or a pearl—they are not subject to a claim of fraud by reason of overcharge [M. 4:9I-J].

B. "A scroll of the Torah, because it is beyond price;

C. "a beast or a pearl, because a person wants to buy them for a match with their pair [and therefore there is no limit to what he is going to be willing to pay]."

D. They said to him, "But is it not so that every sort of object a man wants to match up with its pair?"

E. R. Judah b. Petera says, "A horse, a battle-ax, and a [good] sword in time of war are not subject to a claim of fraud by reason of overcharge."

T. 3:24 Z p. 378, ls. 6-9

T. explains and complements M.

4:10

A. Just as a claim of fraud applies to buying and selling

B. so a claim of fraud applies to spoken words.

I C. One may not say to [a storekeeper], "How much is this object?" knowing that he does not want to buy it.

II D. If there was a penitent, one may not say to him, "Remember what you used to do!"

III E. If he was a child of proselytes, one may not say to him, "Remember what your folk used to do!"

F. For it is said, *And a proselyte you shall not wrong nor oppress* (Ex. 22:20).

M. 4:10

C, D, E illustrate A-B. But D, E are cases not of fraud but of mere churlishness, so it is only C which is directly relevant.

A. *Just as a claim of fraud applies to buying and selling, so a claim of fraud applies to spoken words* [M. 4:10A-B].

B. And far more abundant is fraud in spoken words than fraud in matters of property.

C. For concerning fraud in matters of property, Scripture says, [*And if you sell to your neighbor or buy from your neighbor,*] *you shall not wrong one another* (Lev. 25:14).

D. But as to matters of fraud in spoken words, Scripture says, [*If the years are many, you shall increase the price, and if the years are few, you shall diminish the price; for it is the number of the crops that he is selling to you.*] *You shall not wrong one another but you shall fear your God: for I am the Lord your God* (Lev. 25:16-17).

E. And let one fear Him who commanded concerning these things.

F. [If] there were ass-drivers seeking wine and oil, one should not say to them, "Go to So-and-so,"—who has never at any time sold wine or oil.

G. [If] ailments affected someone, or affliction came upon him, and he buried his children, one should not speak to him the way Job's friends spoke to him: "*Is not your fear of God your confidence, and the integrity of your ways your hope? Think now, who that was innocent ever perished? Or where were the upright cut off?*" (Job 4:6-7)."

H. [If] one saw a proselyte come to study Torah, he should not say to him, "Look who's coming to study Torah—this one who ate carrion and *teref*-meat, abominations and creeping things!" [M. 4:10].

I. And so it says, *And a man of the place answered, "And who is their father?"* (1 Sam. 10:12).

J. Now is there such a thing as a father, with reference to Torah?

K. And has it now been said, *What is his name, and what is his son's name? Surely you know!* (Prov. 30:4)

L. And it says, *House and wealth are inherited from fathers, but a prudent wife is from the Lord* (Prov. 19:14).

T. 3:25 Z p. 378, ls. 9-19

T. augments M.

4:11-12

A. They do not commingle one sort of produce with another sort of produce,

B. even new and new [produce, plucked in the same growing season],

C. and it goes without saying, new with old.

D. To be sure, in the case of wine they have permitted commingling strong with weak,

E. because it improves it.

F. They do not commingle the lees of wine with wine.

G. But one may hand over [to a purchaser] the lees [of the wine he is buying].
H. He whose wine got mixed with water may not sell it in a store,
I. unless he informs [the purchaser],
J. nor to a merchant,
K. even though he informs him.
L. For [the latter buys it] only to deceive others thereby.
M. In a place in which it is the custom to put water in wine,
N. one may dilute it.

M. 4:11

A. A merchant purchases grain from five threshing floors and puts it [all] into one storage-bin,
B. [wine] from five wine-presses and puts it into a single storage-jar—
C. on condition that he not intend to commingle [wine of diverse quality for the purpose of fraud].
D. R. Judah says, "A storekeeper should not hand out parched corn and nuts to little children, because in that way he makes it their habit [to buy from] him."
E. But sages permit.
F. And he should not cut the prevailing price.
G. But sages say, "[If he does so], his memory will be blessed."
H. "He should not sift crushed beans," the words of Abba Saul.
I. And sages permit.
J. But they concede that he should not sift them [solely] at the entry of the storage-bin.
K. for he would do so only to create a false picture [of the quality of what is in the bin].
L. They do not beautify [what they sell]—either man, beast, or utensils.

M. 4:12

Despite certain formal inconsistencies, I am inclined to see M. 4:11 as a triplet: A, F-G, and H-I, with rich augmentation of A at B-C, D E, and of H-I at J-N. The point is consistent with what has already been said. One may not improve the appearance of his goods [M. 4:12L]. Produce from one field should not be mixed with (better-looking) produce from some other. Certainly one who buys seasoned produce does not want new produce, or *vice versa*. D-E then qualify the foregoing. One may not sell the lees of a jug of wine with the wine. H-N simply make the point that small stores may sell diluted wine, so long as purchasers are informed. But wholesale merchants are not to be allowed to buy diluted wine. M. 4:12A-C continue this same matter. A wholesale merchant is allowed to collect merchandise from diverse sources and store it in a single bin. The triplet of disputes at the end, D-E, F-G, and H-I, J-K, is clear as given. One must not place at the top of a bin produce of a better quality than what is on the bottom, and L restates the same point in general terms.

A. *They do not commingle one sort of produce with another sort of produce* [M. 4:11A],
B. *even new with new*, or old with old,
C. *and, it goes without saying, new with old*, or old with new [M. 4:11B-C].
D. Even a *seah* of wheat for sale for a *denar* and a *seah* of wheat for sale for a *denar* and a *trissis*-coin should one not commingle and sell at the price of a *seah* for a *denar* [which would be to the buyer's advantage].
E. And they do not commingle wine,
F. not new with new, or old with old,
G. and it goes without saying, new with old, or old with new,
H. or *strong with weak.*
I. R. Judah permits *mixing strong with weak, because it improves it* [M. 4:11D-E].
J. And so did R. Judah say, "[If there is] a type which improves its fellow, it is permitted to mix them together.
K. "[If there are] two types which improve one another, it is prohibited to commingle them."

T. 3:26 Z p. 378, ls. 19-25

A. *They do not commingle the lees of wine with wine,*
B. *but one hands over* [*to a purchaser*] *the lees* [*of the wine he is buying*] [M. 4:11F-G]—how so?
C. [If] one was slowly pouring wine for ass-drivers, they give him the lees of that wine, but not the lees deriving from some other keg of wine.
D. Even when they said, "*They give him its lees*"—
E. one gives him the lees of today on this day, and those of the next day on the next day,
F. but not those of today on the morrow, or those of the morrow on the day afterward.
G. A storekeeper should not commingle them and sell them in his store,
H. unless he informed [the purchaser] [M. 4:11, H-I].
I. And a storekeeper should not sprinkle his store with wine and oil, because he thereby deceives people.
J. In a place in which it is customary to put water [into wine] for half, a third, or a quarter [of the volume of the whole],
K. they put it in,
L. and people must not vary from the established custom of the province [M. 4:11 M-N].

T. 3:27 Z p. 378, ls. 25-30

T. 3:26 contributes the striking example at D, and the attribution of M.'s rule to Judah. T. 3:27 glosses and complements M.

A. They commingle a wheat-preservative (ḤWMṬYN) in grain, at the rate of a *qab* for a *kor* of grain,
B. and one need not scruple.
C. And householders put in all they need.
D. But a storekeeper binds it up and leaves it on the mouth of the bin.

T. 3:28 Z pp. 378, l. 30, 379, 1

A. They do not curry a beast, or blow up intestines [up for sale],
B. and they do not put meat in water [to increase its weight] [cf. M. 4:12L].

T. 3:29 Z p. 379, l. 2

Since the salty dust used as a wheat-preservative increases the volume, T. 3:28, a store-keeper keeps it separate from the grain. T. 3:29 illustrate M.

CHAPTER FIVE

BABA MESIA CHAPTER FIVE

The chapter discusses the matters of interest and increase, in line with Lev. 25:35-6. It is a long and subtle discussion. I hardly claim to do full justice, in particular, to the refinements contributed by T. The chapter opens with a distinction between interest and increase. The former is defined simply as repayment of five *denars* for a loan of a *sela*, which consists of four *denars*, or repayment of three *seahs* of wheat for a loan of two. The going rate of interest appears to have been 25 percent for a loan in cash, and 50 percent for a loan in kind. We do not know the length of time of the loan. Increase is a somewhat more subtle question. It involves payment for delivery, later on, of a commodity valued at the market-price prevailing at the time of the agreement. The one who pays the money in advance thus profits, since prices are much lower at harvest-time than in advance. Trading in futures occupies much attention. The prohibition of interest is expanded with great care at M. 5:2-6. The concern not to trade in futures or to gain increase through commodities is at M. 5:7-10.

The main point of M. is to treat as prohibited interest diverse sorts of payments in kind in consideration of a loan. M. 5:2 prohibits the debtor from renting out to the creditor a courtyard at no cost or at less than the prevailing rate. It does allow a deduction for payment of rent in advance —a very different matter. M. 5:3 takes into account the possibility of a subterfuge in which, in exchange for what is in fact a loan, the creditor enjoys the usufruct of a field. This matter will require close attention. M. 5:4 goes on to prohibit interest in the form of uncompensated labor. If a capitalist assigns goods or capital to a storekeeper in exchange for half the profit, the storekeeper in addition must be paid a salary for his attention to that half of the goods, the profit of which accrues to the capitalist. But, M. 5:5, if one hands over cattle to a rancher to raise, in exchange for half the profits, the cattle are deemed to work for their keep, so that rancher need not be paid an additional fee for his labor. One may make an advance agreement on the value of the herd, when the herd yields labor for the benefit of the rancher, M. 5:6. M. 5:7, finally, prohibits the arrangement of a farmer's tending a flock on "iron terms," that is to say, on such terms that the owner of the flock is guaranteed a return of all his capital, specified at the outset, and in addition a fixed yield, while the rancher will receive the increase of the flock over and above these two fixed items. Thus the rancher, bearing the entire risk for the upkeep of the flock, shares only part of the profits thereof. Israelites may pay or exact interest from gentiles.

M. 5:7-10 go on to deal with agreements on futures and other aspects of increase. One may not agree to pay in advance a fixed sum for a certain amount of produce, if a market price is not yet available. If the produce should prove to be more expensive, then the one who receives the money will lose out and turn out to have paid interest on the advance-money. Once there is a market price, one may pay in advance for delivery later on; this no longer is speculating on futures in such a way that the creditor enjoys an unfair advantage in exchange for his payment in advance. M. 5:8-9 deal with a loan to be repaid in kind. In general if one borrows a *kor* of wheat, he cannot pledge to repay a *kor* of wheat. It may turn out that he will have to pay much more for the *kor* than it cost at the time of the loan. This is interest. One may lend his tenant-farmers a *kor* of wheat for seed, however, and receive at the end a *kor* of wheat. That is deemed an investment by the landlord in his own property. If one presently owns a *kor* of wheat but has not got access to it, on the other hand, he may agree to return a *kor* later on for one he now receives, without scruple as to violating the laws of interest. M. 5:10 has three kinds of prohibited interest for a non-material character. If one party works for another party in exchange for the other's equivalent labor, the equivalence must be exact. One may not give a gift to a lender, either before or after the loan. He also may not provide him with valuable information in consideration of the loan. M. 5:11, finally, completes the ambitious and successful essay with an appropriate homily.

5:1

A What is interest, and what is increase [which is tantamount to taking interest]?
B. What is interest (NŠK)?
C. He who lends a *sela* [which is four *denars*] for [a return of] five *denars*,
D. two *seahs* of wheat for [a return of] three—
E. because he bites [off too much (NWŠK)].
F. And what is increase (TRBYT)?
G. He who increases (HMRBH) [profits] [in commerce] in kind.
H. How so?
I. [If] one purchases from another wheat at a price of a golden *denar* [25 *denars*] for a *kor*, which [was then] the prevailing price, and [then wheat] went up to thirty *denars*.
J. [If] he said to him, "Give me my wheat, for I want to sell it and buy wine with the proceeds"—
K. [and] he said to him, "Lo, your wheat is reckoned against me for thirty *denars*, and lo, you have [a claim of] wine on me"—
L. but he has no wine.

M. 5:1

The formal structure is clear, with its prologue, A, then a systematic commentary on A at B+C-E, F+G-L. M. clearly has Lev. 25:35-6 in mind, since it alludes to the biblical word-choices, NŠK and TRBYT. But the remainder of the chapter is satisfied to refer solely to interest, or usury, as RBYT, which is translated "interest" or "usury" as the case requires. So M. 5:1 is essentially secondary to the linguistic and conceptual core of the chapter as a whole, which hardly refers to the distinction announced at the outset.

The meaning of NŠK (interest) is clear as given. It involves a repayment of 25 percent over what is lent in cash, or 50 percent over what is lent in kind. Increase is less clear. We deal with a case of trading in futures. The purchaser agrees to pay at the current price of 25 *denars* for a *kor*; delivery is postponed until the harvest. M. 5:7 permits this procedure. When the purchaser calls his contract, the vendor concurs in revising the price of the contract. But he also revises the cost of wine upward to its then-prevailing price. In point of fact, the seller has no wine for sale. This would appear, in contemporary terms, to be trading in 'naked' or uncovered futures. If that is at issue, the prohibition would be based upon the highly speculative character of the vendor's trading practices. But the "increase" is that the vendor now has to pay for the wine at a higher price than is coming to the purchaser. T. 4:23 provides a clearer case.

> A. [If] one owed [to another] money and came to buy from him in produce at the granary,
> B. and he said to him, "Go and calculate the amount for me in accord with the prevailing market price,
> C. "and I'll give it to you over the next twelve months"—
> D. lo, this is usury [cf. M. 5:1I-L].
> E. And this is not equivalent to an *issar* which just happens to come to him.
> F. But if he came to him and said to him, "Lend me a *kor* of wheat, and I'll pay you back in accord with the price prevailing at the time at which you sell it,"
> G. it is permitted [and it not deemed to smack of usury].
>
> T. 4:23 Z p. 381, ls. 6-9
>
> A. A woman rents out to her girl-friend a chick to set on eggs,
> B. for a fee of two chicks a year
> C. and she need not scruple [by reason of usury].
>
> T. 4:24 Z p. 381, ls. 9-10
>
> A. The woman who said to her girl-friend, "The chicken is mine, the eggs are yours, and we'll divide up the chicks"—
> B. R. Judah permits.
> C. And R. Simeon prohibits.
>
> T. 4:25 Z p. 381, ls. 9-12

The case of T. 4:23 involves a man to whom his neighbor owed money. He goes to the debtor's granary and asks for his money, with which he plans to buy wheat. The debtor tells him to calculate the amount owed at the current price of wheat, and over the next twelve months the debtor will furnish wheat at that price. If then the price goes up, the creditor gets more wheat than he should. If the debtor had actually received the money, it would be permitted. But since now the debtor receives no money, he may turn out to have to pay a higher price for the wheat than he presently is committed to pay. This is prohibited as "increase." The procedure of T. 4:23F-G in no way is usurious, because there is no advantage to the creditor. T. 4:24, 25, allow for the hiring of a beast.

5:2

A. He who lends money to his fellow should not live in his courtyard for free.
B. Nor should he rent [a place] from him for less [than the prevailing rate],
C. for that is [tantamount to] usury.
D. One may effect an increase in the rent-charge [not paid in advance], but not the purchase-price [not paid in advance].
E. How so?
F. [If] one rented his courtyard to him and said to him, "If you pay me now [in advance], lo, it's yours for ten *selas* a year,
G. "but if [you pay me] by the month, it's a *sela* a month"—
H. it is permitted.
I. [But if] he sold his field to him and said to him, "If you pay me the entire sum now, lo, it's yours for a thousand *zuz*.
J. "But if you pay me at the time of the harvest, it's twelve *maneh* [1, 200 *zuz*],"—
K. it is forbidden.

M. 5:2

A-C prohibit interest in kind. D is neatly explained at F-H *vs*. I-K. The rent falls due month by month, so there is no fee for "waiting" on the payment, while at I-K there is a 20 percent surcharge for postponing payment, tantamount to mortgage-interest. Since the rent falls due only month by month, it is not as if the tenant is gaining an undue advantage. The landlord is handing over two *selas* in exchange for the tenant's paying paying money which has not yet fallen due. But in the latter case, the seller of the field is owed the money as soon as the sale has been effected. By collecting 20% extra some time later, he is receiving interest on money which, in fact, already is owing to him. This is not permitted (cf. B. B.Q. 65a).

5:3

A. [If] one sold him a field, and [the other] paid him part of the price,
B. and [the vendor] said to him, "Whenever you want, bring me the rest of the money, and [then] take yours [the field]"—

C. it is forbidden.

D. [If] one lent him money on the security of his field and said to him, "If you do not pay me by this date three years hence, lo, it is mine"—

E. lo, it is his.

F. And thus did Boethus b. Zonin do, on instruction of sages.

M. 5:3

At issue here, in the contrast of A-C, D-E, is a subterfuge for the payment of interest. A-C indicate the possibility, for, as we shall see, either the vendor or the purchaser may prove to be the lender at interest, involving usufruct of the field. All depends upon whether the sale is actually consummated through the payment of the whole of the stipulated price. The case of A-C involves partial payment for a field. Transfer of ownership is postponed until full payment is made. The transfer is dated from the time of the sale. What of the usufruct? The vendor, by the terms of B, will enjoy the usufruct of the field in the meantime. If, then, the sale *is* completed, the vendor will retrospectively have made use of what in fact turns out to belong to the purchaser from the date of sale. That usufruct is a form of interest on the outstanding balance of the debt. But what if we assign the usufruct of the field to the purchaser? Then, if the sale is *not* completed, the purchaser will turn out to have enjoyed the usufruct of a field from the time of the deposit. The deposit will be returned to him. The usufruct thus will appear to be interest on it. So the terms hide a usurious loan, whether of purchaser-lender to owner-borrower or *vice versa*.

The second, and contrasting case, simply permits a loan on security, with the proviso that the security or pledge is transferred to the lender only in the event of default at the end. That is not conceived to be interest. The case at D differs from that at B because the status of the field is not left in doubt. It remains the property of the borrower, who is not represented as a purchaser, just as the lender is not a vendor. So there is no unclarity as to the status of the usufruct, which remains fully in the domain of the borrower. That is why the stated precedent, F, is acceptable.

A. He who sells produce to his fellow in the assumption that he has [produce to sell],

B. and turns out that he has none,

C. has not got the power to nullify the right of this one [who has purchased the produce, and the seller has to go into the market and buy what he has promised to deliver] [cf. M. 5:1K-L].

T. 4:1 Z p. 379, ls. 4-5

A. *They increase the rent-charge but not the purchase-prise* [M. 5:2D],

B. since it is said, *If you lend money to any of my people with you who is poor, [you shall not be to him as a creditor, and you shall not exact interest from him]* (Ex. 22:25)—

C. since a loan is distinctive, in that it is not that which you give to the other party which you take back from him,

D. so these are excluded, for that which you give to the other party is precisely that which you take back from him.

E. Rabban Simeon b. Gamaliel says, "Also: They increase the purchase-price in the case of that which has been consecrated.

F. "How so?

G. "A man rents out his coins to a money-changer to make a profit with them, to practice [learning his trade] with them, and to adorn [his table] with them.

H. "[If] they were stolen or lost, he is liable to make them up.

I. "[If] they were taken from him by force, lo, he is in the position of a paid bailee.

J. "As to receiving compensation on their account [in the case of I], it is prohibited by reason of interest.

K. "And if one has done so in the case of that which is consecrated, lo, this one has committed an act of sacrilege" [cf. TR II, pp. 111-113].

L. A year to which reference is made with regard to houses located in towns surrounded by a wall [Lev. 25:30]—lo, this is a matter of usury,

M. but the Torah itself has permitted [the arrangement].

N. [If] one had a debt of ready cash and [conditionally] wrote over his field—

O. [if] he sold it so that the seller [himself] has the right to the usufruct,

P. it is permitted

Q. But [if] the purchaser has the usufruct,

R. it is prohibited.

S. R. Judah says, "One way or the other, it is permitted."

T. Said R. Judah, "Thus was the practice of Boethus b. Zonin on the instructions of Eleazar b. 'Azariah."

U. They said to him, "How is there proof from that fact?

V. "But the seller enjoys the usufruct."

T. 4:2 Z p. 379, ls. 4-14

T. 4:1 leaves no doubt as to what is required in the case of M. 5:1J-L. Since the issue is not fraud, it has, as I indicated, to be stated in terms of unlawful increase. For a full discussion of the problems of T. 4:2E-K, cf. TR II, pp. 111-113. T. 4:2N-V bring us to M. 5:3. A man owes money and writes over his field to the creditor. Now if the seller of the field retains the right of usufruct, there is no objection. Why not? If at the end the debt is paid off and the field reverts to the debtor. the usufruct will have been his all along. So there is no objection. If the purchaser-creditor has the usufruct and the borrower-seller repays the loan, the usufruct will turn out to be usury, and so the arrangement is prohibited, Q-R. The view of Judah is that the procedure is permissible one way or the other, and he claims that Boethus did just that.

A. There are practices which are both usurious and not usurious:

B. One purchases the [right to collect the] loans of his fellow at a discount,

C. and his writs of indebtedness [owed to him by others] at a discount.

D. There are matters which are not regarded as usurious, but are nonetheless prohibited because of the possibility of deception for the practice of usury.
E. How so?
F. [If] he said to him, "Lend me a *maneh*,"
G. [and the other] said to him, "I don't have a *maneh*, but take twenty *seahs* of grain,"
H. even though the other went and purchased it back from him for twenty-four,
I. this does not constitute usury.
J. But such a practice is prohibited because of the possibility of deception for the practice of usury.

T. 4:3 Z p. 379, ls. 14-18

A-C clearly wish to prohibit factoring of any kind. The point of the second case is that the lender lends grain, in the amount of twenty *seahs*; to repay, the borrower has to pay more for the same amount of grain, because the price has gone up by 20 percent. This appears to be usury, in that the borrower has to give back more than he got, but, under the circumstances, does not constitute usury, since the lender does not receive back more than he lent.

A. He who sells his field to his fellow and said to him,
B. [that he does so] on condition that he should be a share-cropper in it,
C. or that he should be a partner in it,
D. or "... that the tithes should be mine,"
E. or "... that when you sell it, you sell it to me for this same price,"
F. or "... whenever I want, I'll pay the stipulated price and take the field back"—
G. it is permitted.

T. 4:4 Z p. 379, ls. 18-20

None of these stipulations constitutes interest.

A. [If] one owed money to another party and rented him a house for a *denar* a month, when it was worth a *sela* a month—it is prohibited.
B. [If he rented it] from him for a *denar* a month and it was worth a *sela* a month, it is permitted [cf. M. 5:2].

T. 4:5 Z p. 379, ls. 20-22

A. [If] one gave him a pledge of a house or gave him a pledge of a field,
B. and said to him, "When you will sell them, sell them to me for the value of the money you herewith lend to me,"—
C. it is prohibited.
D. But if he said to him, "You will sell it to me for its true value," it is permitted.

T. 4:6 Z p. 379, ls. 22-23

A. If one was bringing a bundle from one place to another,
B. and he said to him, "Hand it over to me, and I shall hand it over to her just as you hand it over to me in such-and-such a place,"

C. in a case in which he does this accepting responsibility to replace the bundle if it is lost,
D. the [debtor] who hands it over is permitted to do so.
E. But [if it is the debtor] who receives it from him, he is prohibited from doing so.

T. 4:7 Z p. 379, ls. 23-25

A. [If] one was bringing produce from a place in which it was expensive to a place in which it was cheap,
B, and one said to him, "Hand them over to me, and I'll put them up for you in the place in which they are expensive in accord with the lower price, out of produce which I have"—
C. if he has produce in that place, it is permitted.
D. But if he does not have, it is prohibited.
E. But ass-drivers accept produce from a householder and put it up for sale in a place in which it is expensive,
F. paying the cheaper price [to the householder],
G. and they do not have to scruple [by reason of violating the prohibiting against price-gouging].

T. 4:8 Z p. 379, ls. 25-28

A *denar* is a fourth of a *sela*. At T. 4:5 the debtor rents a house for much less than it is worth, and this obviously is interest. If he rents a house from the creditor for much less than it is worth, this is to his advantage and permitted. This illustrates M. B.M. 5:2. T. 4:6 pursues this same line of thought. If a pledge is transferred at par, it is not a matter of usury. But if the pledge is worth more than the loan and remitted in default of the loan, we have a clear case of interest. At T. 4:7 the debtor is prohibited from performing a personal service for the creditor in a situation, C, in which he is performing for free an act of labor for which the creditor would otherwise have to pay. If, D, the borrower hands it over, there is no objection, but if, E, the borrower takes on the task of transportation, there is a matter of personal service, again prohibited by M. B.M. 5:2. T. 4:8 goes over the same ground. Again, we prohibit free transportation of goods on which the creditor will further profit. If it is a mere exchange of goods, it is permitted, C.

A. If ass-drivers and workers were insistent on him in the market [awaiting payment],
B. and he said to the money-changer, "Give me copper coins for this *denar*, so that I can provide for these and I'll pay you a *denar* and a *tressis* from money which I have [at home] in my pouch"—
C. if he actually has it in the pouch, it is permitted to do so.
D. And if not, it is prohibited.

T. 4:9 Z p. 379, ls. 28-30

A. "What I am going to inherit from father is sold to you,"
B. or, "What is going to come up in my trap is sold to you"—
C. he has said nothing whatsoever.

D. "What I am going to inherit from father today is sold to you,"
E. And, "What is coming up in my trap today is sold to you"
F. his statement is confirmed.

T. 4:10 Z pp. 379, l. 30, 380, 1-2

If the man, T. 4:9A-C, has the money, the *tressis* is not interest, because the money-changer is conceived to effect possession forthwith, so the *tressis* is his fee. If not, it is not acquired and represents interest.

5:4

A. They do not set up a storekeeper for half the profit,
B. nor may one give him money to purchase merchandise [for sale] at [the return of the capital plus] half the profit,
C. unless one [in addition] pay him a wage as a worker.
D. They do not set the hens [of another person to hatch one's own eggs] in exchange for half the profit,
E. and they do not assess [and commission another person to rear calves or foals] for half the profit,
F. unless one pay him a salary for his labor and his upkeep.
G. But [without fixed assessment] they accept calves or foals [for rearing] for half the profits,
H. and they raise them until they are a third grown—
I. and as to an ass, until it can carry [a burden] [at which point profits are shared].

M. 5:4

The conception before us involves interest in the form of personal service, which also is prohibited. The case has a man commission a tradesman to sell goods in his shop and take half of the profits. But the condition is that, if the goods are lost or destroyed, the tradesman has to bear responsibility for half of the loss. Even if the stock depreciates, the tradesman makes it up at full value. Half of the commission, therefore, is in fact nothing but a loan in kind, for which the tradesman bears full responsibility. It follows that his personal service in selling the owner's half of the stock, if not compensated, in fact is a kind of interest in labor on that loan.

D, E, and G, restate this matter in the context of a factor, who commissions a farmer to raise his cattle. At D the man gives eggs to a fowl-keeper, who is to have them hatched. The keeper receives half the profits. He also bears full responsibility for half the loss. It follows that he must be paid a salary. At E, we make an assessment of the value of the calves or foals. Half of this sum becomes the fixed responsibility of the cattle-rancher. If the calves or foals die or depreciate, the rancher has to pay back that sum. So it is a loan in kind. If in addition he is not compensated for time spent taking care of the cattle-factor's share of the herd, once more his work will constitute interest. If, G-H, there is no assessment in advance of the fixed value for which the rancher bears full responsibility, however, then there is a genuine partnership. The rancher receives half the value of the profit. He acknowledges no responsibility for their loss, so there is no loan here. The conditions of the contract are such that the man's labor is amply compensated by his participation in the potential profits on half the herd.

    A. He who sets up his fellow as a storekeeper for half the profit [cf. M. 5:4A]
    B. "lo, this one pays him a wage calculated at the rate for an unemployed worker," the words of R. Meir.
    C. R. Judah says, "Even if he dipped his bread with him in brine, or even if he ate with him two dried figs, this constitutes the wage for the time lost [in the running of the shop]."
    D. R. Simeon says, "He pays him a full and proper wage.
    E. "For one who actually does work is not equivalent to one who sits and does nothing,
    F. "and one who sits in the sun is not equivalent to one who sits in the shade."
    G. But if he said to him, "For a third [of the profits] are you my partner in this enterprise [if you run it,] and that third of the profits is paid over to you in exchange for the time you spend in the project,"—that is permitted.
    T. 4:11 Z p. 380, ls. 2-7

    A. He who sets up his fellow as a storekeeper for half the profit—
    B. if [the latter] was a craftsman, he should not practice his craft.
    C. For he cannot be keeping the store when he is practicing his craft.
    D. But if he was a full partner with him in the store, it is permitted.
    T. 4:12 Z p. 380, ls. 7-9

    A. He who sets up his fellow as a storekeeper for half the profit—
    B. the latter should not buy and sell other things [than are covered by the agreement to run the store].
    C. And if he bought and sold [other things], the profit goes into the common pot.
    T. 4:13 Z p. 380, ls. 9-10

    A. He who hands over money to his fellow to buy produce with them for half the profit—
    B. lo, this one reckons with him a wage for time lost.
    C. And what is a wage for time lost?
    D. [It is to cover] the time in which he does the purchasing and the time in which he does the selling.
    E. [If] one person does the purchasing and the two [of them] do the selling, he makes a reckoning with him for the time for doing the selling.
    F. [If] one person does the selling and two do the purchasing, he makes a reckoning with him for the time spent doing the purchasing.
    G. [If] one does the purchasing and one does the selling, two do the purchasing and two do the selling,
    H. even if the time spent in the one instance is greater than that spent in the other,
    I. that is of no account.

J. But if one said to him, "The rent for the building counts, but the wage for time lost is on your account only,"

K. "... for a third of the profits you are a partner with me, and that third counts against you for the time lost,"

L. it is permitted.

T. 4:14 Z p. 380, ls. 10-16

A. He who hands over money to his fellow to buy produce with [the money] for half the profit

B. may not say to him, "Lo, this [work of yours] is counted against your account for a half, a third, or a fourth [of the profits]."

C. Lo, this one makes a reckoning with him for the cost of renting a building and for the price of time lost from that time onward.

D. If he said to him, "Let the costs of transportation [of the goods] cover the cost of the upper room," it is permitted.

T. 4:15 Z p. 380, ls. 16-18

A. He who hands over money to his fellow to buy produce for half the profits

B. and said to him, "[I shall be] near for loss and far for profit"—

C. it is permitted in regard to usury.

D. And this is the practice of truly righteous men.

E. [If he said,] "[I shall be] near for profit and far from loss"—

F. it is prohibited by reason of usury.

G. And this is the practice of truly wicked men.

H. "Near for one thing and for the other,"

I. "Far for one thing and for the other,"—

J. it is permitted in regard to usury.

K. And that is the practice of everybody.

T. 4:16 Z p. 380, ls. 19-22

A. He who hands over money to his fellow to buy produce for half the profits

B. and said to him, "Here is a *maneh* [for your share],"

C. and he is not able to give a detailed accounting—

D. it is prohibited.

E. [If] he saw that produce had gone up in price and said to him,

F. "Here is a *maneh*," and he is able to give a detailed accounting—

G. it is permitted.

T. 4:17 Z p. 380, ls. 22-24

A. He who hands over money to his fellow to buy produce for half the profits,

B. and one of them wanted to leave the profits where they are [and to continue the agreement for future commercial transactions]—

C. his fellow has the right to stop him [and to insist on keeping the terms of the original agreement alone].

D. R. Judah says, "If it was the year prior to the seventh year, it is permitted to do so,

E. "for to begin with they purchased them only for that purpose."

F. And so did R. Judah say, "At three seasons do they sell seed,

G. "on account of the planting season,

H. "and in the time of the planting,
I. "and half a month before Passover.
J. "And as to oil, they sell it from Pentecost to the Festival."

T. 4:18 Z p. 380, ls. 24-28

A. He who hands over money to his fellow to buy produce for half the profits—
B. [the purchasing agent of the partnership] should not buy with his money wheat and with his fellow's money barley,
C. but he should buy either wheat with all the money available to him, or barley with all the money available to him,
D. so that the money belonging to each of them should be treated as a single sum in partnership.

T. 4:19 Z p. 380, ls. 28-30

A. He who hands over money to his fellow to buy produce for half the profits—
B. [with instructions] to buy wheat, and he bought barley—
C. barley and he bought wheat—
D. the hand [of the one who did the buying] is underneath.
E. If the price went down, the loss is assigned to him.
F. But if the price went up, the gain is assigned to the common fund [to be divided equally].

T. 4:20 Z p. 380, ls. 30-32

A. He who hands over money to his fellow to buy produce for half the profits—
B. the one who does the purchasing has the right to buy anything he wants,
C. except that he is not to buy spelt or wood with the money.
D. He who hands over money to his fellow to buy produce for half the profits—
E. the one who does the purchasing has the right to buy that same kind [both with his own money and with the common funds],
F. and when he sells, he does not have to sell the entire amount all at once,
G. but [the grain purchased with] this fund by itself,
H. and [the grain purchased with] that fund by itself.

T. 4:21 Z pp. 380, l. 32, 381, 1-4

A. He who hands over money to his fellow to buy produce for half the profits,
B. and in the end [the latter] said to him, "I didn't buy a thing"—
C. [the former] has no stronger claim on him than a mere complaint.
D. But if there are witnesses [to the fact that] the latter had actually bought and sold,
E. they exact [the proceeds and the return of capital] from him by force.

T. 4:22 Z p. 381, ls. 4-6

T. 4:11 glosses M. 5:4C, on which point M. (as we have it) is carefully vague. G is an important qualification. One may specify that a share of the profits includes the wages. T. 4:12, 13, go on to clarify the rights of the investor. T. 4:14 goes over the matter of compensation. There are ways of paying compensation for time invested in the business apart from actual monetary transaction. This is, e.g., by specifying the compensation as a charge against profits which are to be shared. The meaning of "near" and "far" at T. 4:16 is a lesser share than half, a greater share than half. If, then, the one who puts up the capital expects the other party to bear a greater share of the profit and a lesser share of the loss, T. 4:16B-C, that is very generous. D-F prohibit the opposite. H-I note that most people give equal shares of profit or loss, respectively. T. 4:17 insists that the partner give a full account of the transaction when handing over the other party's share in the profits. T. 4:18ff, go on to other rules relevant to the partnership, but, as is clear, not to the issue of interest.

5:5

A. They assess [and put out for rearing] a cow, an ass, or anything which works for it keep,

B. for half the profits.

C. In a locale in which they are accustomed to divide up the offspring forthwith, they divide it forthwith.

D. In a place in which they are accustomed to raise the offspring, they raise it.

E. Rabban Simeon b. Gamaliel says, "They assess [and put out] a calf with its dam, a foal with its dam."

F. (And) one may pay increased rent [in exchange for a loan for the improvement of] one's field,

G. and one need not scruple by reason of interest.

M. 5:5

The one who supplies the capital, in the form of the cow or ass, benefits from the work of the rancher in raising the animal. But, unlike the case of M. 5:4D-F, since the animal works for its keep, the rancher gains the usufruct of the animal and so cannot be thought to pay "interest" to the capitalist in exchange for his share in the capital, namely, in the profits on the animals when they are sold. The rancher gets the work of the beast in return both for what he feeds it and his own work with it, so that the considerations of M. 5:4 are not invoked. C-D provide a minor qualification. Simeon even goes so far, E, as to permit the offspring of a dam to be assessed and raised, even though it is only the dam which will work.

F-G, which are separate, complete the list of permissible investments. The point of F-G is that the increased capital investment in the land may yield an increased fee fo the landowner for use of the land, without scruple as to usury.

A. [If] one has accepted [the care of] a hundred sheep worth a hundred golden [*denars*],
B. "... for a half," "... a third," "... a fourth of the profits,"
C. "And I shall take a *sela* for each one at the end,"—
D. it is prohibited.
E. [But if one has accepted the care of a hundred sheep worth a hundred golden *denars*] for half, a third, or a fourth [of the profits]—
F. half [of the payment being specified] to cover the feeding of the sheep, and half to cover the time invested in them,
G. "And I shall take a *sela* for each one at the end,"
H. it is permitted.

T. 5:1 Z p. 381, ls. 13-15

A. [If] one has accepted [the care of] a hundred calves worth a hundred golden *denars*,
B. "... for a half," "... a third," "... a fourth of the profits,"
C. "And I shall take a golden *denar* for each one at the end from your share of the profits"—
D. it is prohibited.
E. [But if one has accepted the care of a hundred calves worth a hundred golden *denars*] for a half, a third, or a fourth share of the profits—
F. half [of the payment] to cover the feeding of the sheep, and half to cover the time invested in them,
G. "And I shall take a golden *denar* from your share at the end,"—
H. it is permitted.

T. 5:2 Z p. 381, ls. 15-18

A. They do not assess [and put out for rearing] unblemished firstlings to be raised by an Israelite [since they cannot labor for him, lest they be blemished].
B. But they assess [and put out for rearing] by them blemished firstlings.
C. And they assess [and put out for rearing] by priests unblemished firstlings,
D. and, it goes without saying, blemished ones.

T. 5:3 Z p. 381, ls. 18-19

A. They do not assess and [put out for rearing] either goats or ewes or any sort of beast which does not work for its keep.
B. R. Yosé b. R. Judah says, "They assess [and put out for rearing] goats, because they give milk,
C. "and ewes, because they produce fleece,
D. "and chickens, because they work for their keep [by giving eggs]."

T. 5:4 Z p. 381, ls. 20-22

A. She who assesses [and takes over] chickens [for rearing] from her girl-friend takes care of the chicks so long as they need their mother.
B. A person takes care of an unclean beast for twelve months,
C. and in the case of a man, twenty-four months.

T. 5:5 Z p. 381, ls. 22-24

A. In a place in which it is customary to pay for the wages for carrying [the beast] in coin, they pay.
B. For a beast—they pay.

C. They pay up and they do not vary from the prevailing practice of the province.

D. *Rabban Simeon b. Gamaliel says, "They put out a calf with its dam, a foal with its dam* [M. 5:5E],

E. "and even though one pays out a fee for carrying the beast.

F. "And one does not scruple because of the possible violation of laws against taking or paying interest."

T. 5:6 Z p. 381, ls. 24-27

T. 5:1-2 introduce the considerations of M. 5:4 into the case of M. 5:5. T. wants the rancher to receive a fee for his services, and rightly so, for these are not animals which perform labor, in the way in which the cow or ass do. So T. takes very seriously the definition at M. 5:5A and consequently points out the applicability of the rule at M. 5:4, a fine piece of exegesis on completed materials. T. 5:3's concern is that the Israelite not find occasion to permit the blemishing of a firstling, to which in unblemished shape he has no right. In any event the Israelite cannot share in the unblemished firstling, so if he rears him at some pre-assessed valuation, his labor in no way will have been compensated. T. 5:4 is clear and simply goes over the ground of M. 5:5A, T. 5:1-2. T. 5:6 adds that it may be necessary to pay a wage for carrying a beast which requires that sort of careful tending. D-F then show the relevance of this point to Simeon b. Gamaliel's position. The labor of the dam is deemed sufficient compensation.

A. He who assesses [and takes over the rearing of] a beast from his fellow—how long is he liable to take care of it?

B. In the case of small cattle, for thirty days.

C. In the case of large cattle, fifty days.

D. R. Yosé says, "In the case of small cattle, three months,

E. "because they take a great deal of tending."

F. Therefore in the case of all of them, if it was the share of the householder,

G. one makes an assessment for him.

H. But they do not vary from the prevailing practice of the province.

T. 5:7 Z p. 381, ls. 27-30

A. He who assesses [and takes over the rearing of] an unclean beast from his fellow—how long is he liable to take care of it in the case of offspring?

B. Sumkhos says, "In the case of asses, eighteen months,

C. "and in the case of animals living in folds, twenty-four months."

D. And if [the rancher] laid claim upon him [for his share] during the stated time,

E. his fellow has the power to stop him.

F. But the care to be given during the first year is not equivalent to that which is to be given in the second year.

T. 5:8 Z pp. 381, l. 30-31, 382, 1-2

A. He who assesses [and takes over the care of] a beast from his fellow
B. does not tend it less than twelve months.
C. If he had worked with it throughout the dry season and wants to sell it off in the rainy season,
D. he has the power to stop him,
E. unless he has the right to work with it throughout the rainy season as well.

T. 5:9 Z p. 381, ls. 2-4

The issue of T. 5:7 is the liability to tend to the young of the beast. They are part of the profit. The rancher will be happy to make the division when the offspring is born; he gets no profit from the other half anyhow. The young of small cattle are to be tended for a month, of the large ones, somewhat longer. After that point the rancher takes his half of the young, and there is an assessment of the half which belongs to the householder. The rancher gets half of that as well. T. 5:8-9 go on to the rights of the capitalist. The rancher must tend the animal and not effect a division of the profits for a reasonable time, so that the animal may fatten and so gain in value. The rancher, after all, gets half the profits on the capital of the other party, so he has to invest some time in the improvement of the beast.

A. He who assesses [and takes over the rearing of] a beast from his fellow—
B. [if the beast] died through willful negligence,
C. he pays its entire value.
D. [If it did] not die through willful negligence,
E. he pays half.
F. For thus does he state in writing to him, "If it dies through willful negligence, I shall pay its entire value; if it dies not through willful negligence, I shall pay half."

T. 5:10 Z p. 382, ls. 4-6

A. [If] he assessed it [and took over the rearing] when it was worth a *maneh* and it increased in value so that, lo, it is now worth two hundred *zuz*
B. [if] it died through willful negligence, he pays six [*TR* II, p. 116] golden *denars*.
C. [If it died] not through willful negligence, he pays only fifty *zuz*.

T. 5:11 Z p. 382, ls. 6-7

A. [If] he assessed it [and took over the rearing] when it was worth a *maneh*, and it decreased in value so that, lo, it is now worth only fifty *zuz*,
B. if it died through willful negligence, he pays three golden *denars*.
C. [If it died] not through willful negligence, he pays fifty *zuz*.

T. 5:12 Z p. 382, ls. 8-9

A. Rabban Simeon b. Gamaliel says, "*They pay increased rent [in exchange for a loan for the improvement of] one's field*" [M. 5:5F].
B. "How so?

C. "[If] one has accepted the tenancy of a field in exchange for ten *kors* of wheat, and then said to him, 'Give me two hundred *denars*, and I shall fertilize it,

D. "and then I'll pay you twelve *kors* [of wheat] in a year's time'—

E. "it is permitted."

F. But they may not pay increased rent [in exchange for a loan for the improvement of] one's ship, shop, or anything which does not earn its keep.

T. 5:13 Z p. 382, ls. 9-12

If the beast dies through willful negligence, then the rancher has to compensate the investor. This comes out most clearly at T. 5:12, in which, if the animal died through willful negligence, the rancher has to pay the assessed value, despite the decrease in the value of the animal. T. 5:13 gives a good illustration for M. 5:5F.

5:6

A. They do not accept from an Israelite a flock on 'iron terms' [that the one who tends the flock shares the proceeds of the flock but restores the full value of the flock as it was when it was handed over to him],

B. because this is interest.

C. But they do accept a flock on 'iron terms' from gentiles.

D. And they borrow from them and lend to them on terms of interest.

E. And so is the rule for the resident alien.

F. An Israelite may lend out the capital of a gentile on the say-so of the gentile,

G. but not on the say-so of an Israelite. [If the gentile had borrowed money from an Israelite, one may not lend it out on interest with the Israelite's knowledge and consent.]

M. 5:6

We continue the interest of the foregoing. Terms of "iron flock" are such as to guarantee to the investor both full restitution of capital and a fixed return on the capital. Unlike the conditions at M. 5:4-5, the rancher undertakes to share in the profit but to bear the full burden of loss. This arrangement involves "interest" in the form of unequal risk. There must be a full participation in both profit and loss in any shared undertaking involving the investment of capital—the animals—on one party's part and of labor and grazing land on the other party's part. (It goes without saying that the perspective of M. is that of the rancher.)

C-D are linked to the foregoing in detail only, but in theme they proceed to conclude the entire discussion of interest. Their point is that the stated prohibition of M. 5:1-5 applies solely to transactions among Israelites. Gentiles may receive or pay interest. Israelites may work for gentiles in this context. G's language is obscure. It may mean that gentiles may not borrow funds from Israelites and then, through the medium of an Israelite factor, lend them to other Israelites. Or G may wish to say that on his own initiative an Israelite may not lend on interest money belonging to a gentile. The main point is clear.

    A.   A man accepts from his wife a flock on "iron terms" [that the one who tends the flock, here the husband, shares the proceeds of the flock, but restores the value of the flock as it was when it was handed over to him, thus bearing any loss but keeping any profit over a fixed per cent] [cf. M. 5:6A].
    B.   And the offspring and the shearing of the sheep belong to him.
    C.   But if they died, he is liable to make them good.
    D.   Now what is the meaning of an 'iron sheep'-contract?
    E.   [If] there were a hundred sheep, and he said to him, "Lo, they are counted against your account for a hundred golden *denars*, and the offspring and the shearing belong to you, and you must pay over to me a *sela* for each and every one at the end"—
    F.   it is prohibited.
    G.   *They accept from a gentile a flock on 'iron terms'* [M. 5:6C],
    H.   and a field on 'iron terms' even from an Israelite.
                                                       T. 5:14 Z p. 382, ls. 12-16

    A.   A man borrows money from his wife and children on usurious terms.
    B.   But thereby he teaches them to practice usury.
    C.   An Israelite is not permitted to borrow a *sheqel* and to lend out a *sela*.
    D.   But a gentile is permitted to borrow a *sheqel* and to lend out a *sela*.
                                                       T. 5:15 Z p. 382, ls. 16-18

    A.   An Israelite who borrowed money from a gentile and wants to pay it back to him—
    B.   [if] his fellow came upon him and said to him, "Give it to me, and I'll hand it over for you [on the same terms] just as you would hand it over to him"—
    C.   it is prohibited.
    D.   But if he made this request from the gentile, it is permitted.
                                                       T. 5:16 Z p. 382, ls. 18-20

    A.   A gentile who borrowed money from an Israelite and wants to pay it back to him—
    B.   [If] another Israelite came upon him and said to him, "Give them to me just as you would have given them to him"—it is permitted.
    C.   But if he made this request from the Israelite, it is prohibited.
                                                       T. 5:17 Z p. 382, ls. 20-21

    A.   An Israelite who said to a gentile, "Here's your salary. Now go and lend out my money on interest"—
    B.   it is prohibited.
    C.   And a gentile who said to an Israelite, "Here's your salary. Now go and lend out my money on interest"—
    D.   it is permitted.
    E.   But it [truly] is prohibited for appearance's sake.
                                                       T. 5:18 Z p. 382, ls. 22-23

    A.   Money belonging to an Israelite left as a bailment with a gentile—
    B.   it is permitted [for the latter] to lend the money out on interest.

C. But that of a gentile left as a bailment with an Israelite—
D. it is prohibited [for the latter] to lend the money out on interest.
E. This is the governing principle:
F. In any case in which the deposited funds fall under the responsibility of an Israelite [to be made up should they be lost], — it is prohibited.
G. In any case in which the deposited funds fall under the responsibility of a gentile [to be made up should they be lost],—it is permitted.

T. 5:19 Z p. 382, ls. 24-26

A. An Israelite who is made a guardian for the estate of a gentile, or a bailiff,
B. is permitted to lend out money of his on interest.
C. And a gentile who is made guardian of the estate of an Israelite or a bailiff
D. is prohibited from lending out money of his on interest.
E. [If] an Israelite borrows from a gentile, and a gentile borrows from an Israelite,
F. the Israelite may serve as a guarantor of the loan [of the gentile, on interest],
G. and need not scruple [as to violating the prohibition against usury].

T. 5:20 Z pp. 382, ls. 26-27, 383, 1

A. "An Israelite who borrowed money from a gentile, and a gentile who borrowed money from an Israelite—
B. "and [the gentile] converted [to Judaism], whether he encumbered him with the loan before he converted or whether he encumbered him with the loan after he converted—
C. "the gentile [convert] collects the principal, but does not collect the interest," the words of R. Meir.
D. R. Yosé says, "An Israelite who borrowed money from a gentile and [the gentile] converted,
E. "whether he encumbered him with the loan before he converted or whether he encumbered him with the loan after he converted—
F. "[the convert] collects the principal and also collects the interest."
G. [But if he made the loan] after he converted, he collects the principal but in no way has a right to collect the interest.

T. 5:21 Z p. 383, ls. 1-6

T. 5:14 provides an excellent exposition of M.'s main point. The husband takes over management of his wife's assets and enjoys the usufruct, but he also bears full responsibility for making them good in the case of loss. The entire definition is in B-C. He keeps the offspring and the fleece, B, but replaces the sheep if they die, C. E gives a more general example. The flock is estimated at a hundred golden *denars*. The rancher undertakes to pay back sheep, or equivalent, to that sum. He also undertakes in advance a return of a *sela* per golden *denar*. But he keeps the entire product of the herd. The capitalist thus has a guaranteed return of capital with a fixed return—equivalent to a U.S. Treasury bond. The return, a *sela* per golden *denar*, comes to sixteen percent. That is a golden *denar* is 25 *denars*;

2 *denars* are a *sheqel*, and 2 *sheqels* are a *sela*. So a sela is four *denars*, for a return of sixteen percent. This represents a reduction of the normal rate of interest on ready cash—twenty-five percent—by thirty-six percent, over a third, and, it goes without saying, by twice (seventy-two percent) that for the normal rate of interest on investments in kind. But the security is solid. G-H restate M. 5:6C. T. 5:16 amplifies M. 5:6F and G. If one Israelite is paying interest to a gentile, another Israelite cannot then take over the loan on the same terms, except through the gentile's intervention. T. 5:18 does not approve of the rule of M. 5:6F, but does not contradict it. T. 5:19-20 go over the same obvious conceptions about lending money belonging to gentiles, but not to Israelites. T. 5:21 takes up one of those marginal problems so beloved of the Ushans and presents the two possible positions.

    A. "He who lends money to his fellow on interest,
    B. "and [the case] came before the court—
    C. "they impose a fine on him, so that he does not collect either the principal or the interest," the words of R. Meir.
    D. For R. Meir maintained, "A writ of indebtedness which covers payments of interest—
    E. "they impose a fine on him so that he does not collect either the principal or the interest."

T. 5:22 Z p. 383, ls. 6-9

    A. He who happens to find a writ of indebtedness should tear it up.
    B. [If] it should come to a court, they tear it up.
    C. Rabban Simeon ben Gamaliel says, "All procedure follows the accepted practice of the province [in which the matter comes to court]."

T. 5:23 Z p. 383, ls. 9-10

    A. He who lends money to his fellow on interest,
    B. and the lender went and inherited documents covering interest [owing from the lender]
    C. and he said to him, "Let mine be acquitted in exchange for yours"—
    D. it is permitted.
    E. But if it came to a reckoning,
    F. it is prohibited.

T. 5:24 Z p. 383, ls. 10-12

    A. He who lends money to his fellow on interest and then repented is liable to return [to him the interest he has collected].
    B. [If] he died and left [the money] to his children, the children do not have to return [the money he collected as interest].
    C. And in such a case it is said, [*Though he heap up silver like dust and pile up clothing like clay*;] *he may pile it up, but the just will wear it, and the innocent will divide the silver* (Job 27:16-17).

T. 5:25 Z p. 383, ls. 12-13

    A. But if their father had left them a cow, a field, a cloak, or any sort of object for which he bore responsibility [for replacement, should the object be lost],

B. they are liable to return such an object,
C. for the honor of their father.

T. 5:26 Z p. 383, ls. 14-15

The remainder of T.'s materials go on to penalties for the payment or collection of interest among Israelites. The lender, in Meir's opinion, cannot even regain the principal. T. 5:24 has a situation in which two parties owe the same amount of interest to one another. They can declare it null. But if there is a need for a reckoning, T:24E, then we come perilously close to Israelites' paying interest to one another, and such a reckoning is not permitted. T. 5:25-6 are clear as stated, once more rather typical contributions of T. when T. augments and extends its own materials.

5:7

A. They do not strike a bargain for the price of produce before the market-price is announced.
B. [Once] the market-price is announced, they strike a bargain,
C. for even though this one does not have [the produce for delivery], another one will have it.
D. [If] one was the first among the reapers [of a given crop], he may strike a bargain with him
E. for (1) grain [already] stacked [on the threshing-floor],
F. or for (2) a basket of grapes,
G. or for (3) a vat of olives,
H. or for (4) the clay-balls of a potter,
I. or for (5) lime as soon as the limestone has sunk in the kiln.
J. And one strikes a bargain for the price of manure every day of the year.
K. R. Yosé says, "They do not strike a bargain for manure before the manure is on the dung-heap."
L. And sages permit.
M. And one may strike a price at the height [of the market, the cheapest rate prevailing at the time of delivery].
N. R. Judah says, "Even though one has not made a bargain at the cheapest rate [prevailing at the time of delivery], one may say to him, 'Give it to me at such-and-such a rate, or give me back my money.'"

M. 5:7

To begin with, let us see how Maimonides spells out the law just now given (*Civil Laws. Creditor and Debtor* 9:1):

No agreement may be made with respect to produce until the market price has been published; but once the market price has been published, such an agreement may be made, for even if the seller does not have the produce, another man has it. How is this to be understood? If the market price has become fixed at four seah to the sela, one may make an agreement with a vendor for the purchase of 100 *seah*, giving him 25 *sela*, and if the vendor delivers 100 *seah* of wheat after the lapse of some time, when wheat at a *sela* per *seah*, there is no usury at all in the transaction, even though the vendor had no wheat at the time when he made the agreement. This applies only if the vendor, at the time when the agreement is made, has none of the kind which he agrees to sell. But if he has some of that kind, although it has not been completely processed, it is permissible to make an agreement with respect thereto, even if the market price has not yet been published.

We take up the second general theme of M. 5:1, "increase." The case before us involves a prepayment for merchandise, e.g., produce. If the merchandise or produce is not yet on the market, one may not strike a price for delivery and accept prepayment on the contract. For this smacks of "increase," in line with M. 5:1—trading in naked contracts for futures. When a market-price is available, then prepayment may be accepted for later delivery, B-C. As we shall see, Judah, N, maintains that that price must be assumed to be the lowest available, that is to say, either the price at the time of the agreement or the price at the time of the delivery, whichever is lower. M. will spell this matter out in a principal generalization, A-C, a secondary and gray area, D-I, a special problem, J-L, and then a concluding qualification, M-N, the whole a most interesting exposition.

The main objection to trading in futures in the form of "naked calls" is that it smacks of usury. Why? First, The seller of the contract has the use of the money without clear knowledge of what his ultimate costs will be. Second, the buyer of the contract has no protection from the seller's default, should the produce not be available to the seller of the call, all in line with M. 5:1. That is why one cannot undertake to deliver a quantity of produce at a given price, unless there is some indication of the prevailing market price for the produce. B-C complete the thought of A. Even though a given farmer has not harvested his crop, he may sell what he is going to harvest, since now there is clear evidence as to what he will receive and what the purchaser should have to pay. In the case of crop-failure, the farmer can make it up, C.

D-I present a secondary qualification of foregoing rule. The prohibition of A pertains to crops which both have not been harvested, and also have not been subjected to a prevailing market price. If crops have been harvested, even though there is no prevailing market, one may strike a bargain. Why? Because the crops are now in hand and nearly ready for delivery. There is no possibility of trading in futures as naked calls. D bears five illustrations. The items are not fully manufactured. So there is an agreement to make delivery later on. The market price may go up. The prepayment, however, is not deemed to fall into the category of interest, in line with M. 5:1's conception, because it is lower. So what D-I treat is a gray area between crops which are still in the field (M. 5:1) and those which are fully harvested and ready for delivery (M. 5:7M-N). There is no market for the former. The market-price is set for the latter. There will be a lower price, when prepayment is involved, for partially completed produce, and, as we see, this is all right.

J-K go on to deal with what is always in production. J's view is that the market-price is perpetual. Yosé regards the manure as subject to a process of preparation, and L repeats the theory of J.

M-N are important. M allows striking a price at the height of the market, when the produce is cheap. The vendor then agrees to supply the produce through the year at the lowest prevailing price for each delivery. This is an important qualification of A, since the market-price is now set as a maximum, not a minimum—the theory of D-I all over again. Judah fundamentally concurs and carries the conception still further. Even though we have assumed that we speak of an advance payment at a fixed rate, Judah holds that that fact is always implied, even when it is not stipulated. The purchaser has the right to retract the sale if the lowest prevailing price is not allowed.

> A. *They do not strike a bargain for the price of produce before the market-price is announced* [M. 5:7A].
> B. Even if the produce of the past year is available for four, they do not strike a bargain for the produce of the coming year for four,
> C. until the market-price is announced for both the new and the old produce.
> D. [If] the market price is announced for other [sorts of produce], even though [the seller] does not have [that sort of produce], it is permitted to come to an agreement with him [M. 5:7C].
> E. Under what circumstances?
> F. When [the seller] is able to find produce for purchase at the price.
> G. But if they were yet being harvested and going at four,
> H. and he is able to find [produce] to purchase only [old] at three,
> I. he does not strike a bargain,
> J. until the price is announced covering both purchaser and seller.
>
> T. 6:1 Z p. 383, ls. 16-20
>
> A. *And one strikes a price with him for grain stacked [on the threshing floor], or for a basket of grapes, or for a vat of olives* [M. 5:7E-G]
> B. even though the market price has not yet been announced.
> C. But others may not make a deal relying upon him.
>
> T. 6:2 Z p. 383, ls. 20-22

The point of T. 6:1B-D, E-J is this. New produce is cheaper, since it has not dried up and is not ready for storage. If the new is at four and the old at three, no contract may be made. We wait until the price is set for new *and* old. Why? Because while the buyer pays in advance, he does not actually receive the wheat until it becomes old. If he pays in advance for the whole delivery at the price of the new, it is as if the farmer receives interest, B-C. He has to wait in making the contract until the same market price covers both types of produce. If the harvested grain is at four and ordinary stock is at three, a contract cannot be settled, F-J. There has to be a single price for the one who harvests the grain and for the merchant. T. 6:2's gloss is clear as given.

    A. *And one strikes a bargain for the price of manure every day of the year* [M. 5:7J].
    B. *For even though this one does not have it, another will have it* [M. 5:7C].
    C. They strike a price for the clay-balls of a potter only after they are manufactured [cf. M. 5:7H].
    D. Said R. Yosé, "Under what circumstances?
    E. "In the case of those which they make out of white clay.
    F. "But in the case of those which they make out of black clay,
    G. "for instance, at Kefar Hananiah and its surrounding villages, or Kefar Šihin and its surrounding villages,
    H. "it is permitted to make a deal.
    I. "For even though this one may not have any, someone else is going to have some."

                                    T. 6:3 Z p. 383, ls. 22-26

    A. They strike a price for milk and fleece only after they are produced.
    B. [If] he began to milk [the goat], it is permitted to make a deal.
    C. [If] he began to shear the sheep, it is permitted to make a deal.

                                    T. 6:4 Z p. 383, ls. 26-27

    A. They do not strike a price for chicks, young poultry, fish at Tiberias, or bundles of straw.
    B. But they strike a price for eggs, birds, fish at all other locations [but Tiberias], and bundles of wood.
    C. This is the governing principle:
    D. In the case of anything which has a 'season,' they strike a price concerning that thing in accord with its price when it is in season [M. 5:7M].
    E. And in the case of anything which has no season, they strike a price concerning that thing anytime one wants.

                                    T. 6:5 Z p. 383, ls. 27-30

    A. [If] there were before him a hundred sheep, and he said to him, "Lo, the fleece of these [sheep] are made over to you for a hundred *denars* of gold"—
    B. it is permitted.
    C. [If he said,] "For such and such per *litra* of fleece,"
    D. it is prohibited.
    E. But if he has it in hand, it is permitted to shear the sheep and to hand it over to him.
    F. If there were before him a hundred *kor* of wheat, and he said to him, "Lo, this standing grain is made over to you for a hundred golden *denars*"—
    G. it is permitted.
    H. [If he said,] "It is sold to you for such-and-such,"
    I. it is prohibited.
    J. But if he has it in hand, it is permitted to cut it and hand it over to him.

                                T. 6:6 Z pp. 383, ls. 30-31, 384, 1-3

A. A man may say to his fellow, "Here is two hundred *zuz* for what your field produces,"

B. on condition that he not say to him, "At a price of four to a *sela*," or, "two *seahs* to a *sela*."

T. 6:7 Z p. 384, ls. 3-4

T. 6:3 goes over M.'s ground, applying the reasoning of M. 5:7C to M. 5:7J. T. 6:4 applies to fleece and milk the conception that trading in futures is prohibited and then adds the qualification of M. 5:7D-I to the same sorts of produce. T. 6:5 contributes its statement of the point of M. 5:7A. We strike a price for produce in line with the going price in the 'season', that is M. 5:7M. T. 6:6-7 qualify the entire conception expressed at M. 5:7 and its accompanying amplification. While, it is true, one may not strike a price, one may nonetheless effect a purchase of an entire quantity of produce, e.g., of fleece, for a fixed fee not set in terms of a specific volume or quantity. So T. limits M. 5:7 to the notion of striking a price per a fixed measure outside of the normal market.

A. He who pays money to his fellow to hand over to him produce at harvest time—

B. [the latter] is liable to provide [the produce] to him at the intermediate price.

C. What is an intermediate price?

D. [If] the produce was going for eight, nine, and ten, he hands it over to him at the price of nine.

E. [If he specified that it would be paid] at the cheapest price,

F. he hands it over to him at the cheapest price [cf. M. 5:7M].

G. [If] at the highest price, he hands it over to him at the highest price.

H. R. Judah says, "Under all circumstances he hands it over to him at the cheapest price.

I. "Not that he should say to him, 'Give it to me at the cheapest price.'

J. "He says, 'Give me back my money and I'll buy with it produce at the cheapest price' " [cf. M. 5:7N].

K. Under what circumstances?

L. When he is able to find produce to buy purchase with all the money which he gave over to him.

M. But if he found available for purchase only a single *kor* for a *sela*,

N. the rest he gives over to him at the intermediate price.

O. R. Neḥemiah and R. Eliezer b. Jacob declare exempt in the case of a scribe [cf. M. 5:11].

P. And they declare the lender exempt from being smitten [for lending on interest],

Q. because he is subject to the requirement of effecting an affirmative action.

T. 6:16 Z p. 384, ls. 26-33

T. 6:16 goes over the case of M. 5:7 yet again. If there is an advance agreement to make a purchase, contrary to the teaching of M. 5:7A, then the produce is sold at an intermediate price, as specified. O-Q refer to M. 5:11, below.

5:8-9

A. A man may lend his tenant-farmers wheat [to be repaid in] wheat, [if] it is for seed,
B. but not [if it is] for food.
C. For Rabban Gamaliel would lend his tenant farmers wheat [to be repaid in] wheat [when it was used] for seed.
D. [If one lent the wheat when the price was] high and [wheat] became cheap,
E. [or if he lent the wheat when the price was] cheap and [wheat] became expensive,
F. he collects from them at the cheapest price,
G. not because that is what the law requires,
H. but because he wished to impose a strict rule upon himself.

M. 5:8

A. A man should not say to his fellow, "Lend me a *kor* of wheat, and I'll pay you back at [a *kor* of wheat] at threshing-time."
B. But he says to him, "Lend it to me until my son comes [bringing me wheat],"
C. or, ". . . until I find the key."
D. Hillel prohibits [even this procedure].
E. And so does Hillel say, "A woman should not lend a loaf of bread to her girl-friend unless she states its value in money.
F. "For the price of wheat may go up, and the two women will turn out to be involved in a transaction of usury."

M. 5:9

Once more our concern is to avoid setting a price so long in advance that there is the possibility of usurious profit. If someone lends a *kor* of wheat and is to be repaid a *kor* of wheat six months later, then there is the variable that the *kor* of wheat now may be much less, or more, expensive than the *kor* of wheat later on. Consequently we have to make provision for what is, and is not, permissible, in line with the basic theory of M. 5:1, 5:7. M. 5:8 and M. 5:9 go over this ground. M. 5:8A-B make a fundamental distinction between a *kor* of wheat which is invested in the land owned by the lender, and a *kor* of wheat which is consumed by the borrower. The former may be lent with the proviso that it will be returned, in like kind and quantity, at the harvest. Even though it may increase in value, the lender is deemed not to lend but to invest in his own property (= M. 5:5F-G), since, after all, he recovers a share in the profit. But if the loan of the wheat is solely for the benefit of the tenant, then it cannot be repaid in kind, for the stated reason. C-H then provide an illustration of this matter.

Gamaliel's procedure, C, is worked out at D-F and glossed at G-H. F means to speak separately to D and to E. If wheat was high when he lent it to his tenants for seed, at the harvest, when it is cheaper, he simply collects the same volume of wheat as he had lent. This then is to their advantage. So it is volume for volume. If wheat was cheap when he lent it for seed, and then, in consequence of a poor harvest, the price went up, he collects in return not the same volume of wheat, but the same value as he had lent, thus collecting less wheat than he had lent but wheat worth the same amount of money as he had handed over. This benign procedure must be in mind, even though F is rather succinct and hardly explicit, for otherwise G-H would be meaningless.

M. 5:9A-C provide for a mode by which the loan may be effected. In line with M. 5:8A-B, one cannot promise to give back the same volume of wheat. But if he owns that amount of wheat at this time, but, e.g., his son is bringing it, or he does not have the key to the granary, he may effect a loan to be repaid in the exact volume, without reference to the variation in price which may take place in the meantime. Hillel prohibits even this procedure, for the reasons stated at F.

    A. A man may lend his tenant-farmers four to a *sela* or two *seahs* to a *sela*.
    B. Under what circumstances?
    C. When [the tenant] has not gone down [to work] in his field.
    D. But if he has gone down to his field, lo, he is equivalent to any other person [who is prohibited].

                            T. 6:8 Z p. 384, ls. 4-6

    A. A man may strike a bargain with his tenant-farmers for seed [M. 5:8A].
    B. But as to expenses, lo, this is prohibited.
    C. And not only so, but even if he planted, and the field yielded two *seahs* for one,
    D. he should not pay out [the landlord's share] during the growing season in his field,
    E. unless he will convert [the produce] into money for him.

                            T. 6:9 Z p. 384, ls. 6-8

    A. [If] he made a deal with him for wheat and handed over to him barley,
    B. or for barley and handed over to him wheat,
    C. it is prohibited.
    D. [The landlord] may not say to him, "Here is a *maneh* for you, so go and buy it for yourself from the market."
    E. But [the landlord] purchases it and hands it over to him.
    F. A man may say to his fellow, "Lend me a jar of wine until my son comes," or, "... until I open the keg" [M. B.M. 5:9B-C].
    G. [If] he had a jug in his keg, and the keg was opened, and [the jug] fell and broke,
    H. even though he is liable to make it up—
    I. it is permitted.
    J. *And Hillel prohibits*[M. 5:9D].
    K. To what is the matter comparable?

L. To one who gives money to his fellow to give him produce at the threshing season,

M. and the money was stolen or lost—

N. he is liable to make them up.

O. If it proved to be too little or too much [for the required purchase], he is liable to make it up to him.

T. 6:10 Z p. 384, ls. 8-14

A. If one purchased from him *logs* and half-*logs*, quarter-, and eighth-*logs*,

B. he is permitted to say to him, "Pay now for less [at a lower rate (M. 5:2)],"

C. and he does not have to scruple that he is violating the laws against usury.

T. 6:11 Z p. 384, ls. 14-15

A. Similarly: He who makes a purchase from his fellow on condition that he pay him between that point and the next twelve months

B. has the right to say to him, "Pay me forthwith at a lower price,"

C. and does not have to scruple that he is violating the laws against usury.

T. 6:12 Z p. 384, ls. 15-17

A. He who sells wine or oil to his fellow [supplying him] all year long [and taking payment advance] is liable to provide it for him just as he would charge at retail.

B. And he should not sell the jar at three different prices.

C. And if it was going down and up, he sells the rest at whichever price he wants [cf. M. 5:7].

T. 6:13 Z p. 384, ls. 17-19

The point of T. 6:8 is that if the tenant has done no work on the field, the stated rule applies. At that point, the tenant is not necessarily going to work on the field. Since the owner provides seed, it is an indication that he plans to invest in the field and in the tenant's work therein. This is not a loan but an investment in the land, parallel in principle to M. 5:5G. In consideration, the tenant will pay the same quantity back. Even if the seed goes up in price, this is not deemed interest on a loan. But if the tenant already was established in the field, then he is equivalent, *vis à vis* the landlord, to any other person. Even a loan of seed cannot be paid back in like volume and kind. That is T.'s important qualification. T. 6:9 would appear to limit the investment to seed, but not to permit an equivalent arrangement for expenses. If the field was planted and gave its yield, moreover, during the growing season the tenant will still have to convert the grain to cash, which he pays back. So the basic arrangement holds good only for a settlement at the end of the season, as part of the final disposition of the return on the field by the tenant and the landlord together. T. 6:10 goes over the ground of Hillel's position, M. 5:9. The man does have the wine, so may make the agreement. Hillel differs, because even in this case, there is the possibility of one's having to go to the market and pay back in the purchase of produce at a higher rate than one paid for it when he originally borrowed it. T. 6:11, by contrast, permits an advance payment at a lower rate than a later payment, within conditions set by T. 6:12-13.

5:10

A. A man [may] say to his fellow, "Weed with me, and I'll weed with you,"

B. "Hoe with me, and I'll hoe with you."

C. But he [may] not say to him, "Weed with me, and I'll hoe with you,"

D. "Hoe with me, and I'll weed with you."

E. All the days of the dry season are deemed equivalent to one another.

F. All the days of the rainy season are deemed equivalent to one another.

G. One should not say to him, "Plough with me in the dry season, and I'll plough with you in the rainy season."

H. Rabban Gamaliel says, "There is usury paid in advance, and there is usury paid at the end.

I. "How so?

J. "[If] one wanted to take a loan from someone and so sent him [a present] and said, 'This is so that you'll make a loan to me,'—

K. "this is a usury paid in advance.

L. "[If] one took a loan from someone and paid him back the money and [then] sent [a gift] to him and said, 'This for your money, which was useless [to you] when it was in my hands,'—

M. "this is usury paid afterward."

N. R. Simeon says, "There is usury paid in words.

O. "One may not say to him, 'You should know that so-and-so from such-and-such a place is on his way.'"

M. 5:10

M. now covers three final matters, usury exacted through labor in excess of what one has coming, A-G, usury paid through a voluntary gift, H-M, and usury paid through inside information, N-O. The point of the first group is that an exchange of labor must be absolutely equal in all details. That of the second is that gifts either prior to the making of a loan or after the repayment of the loan are prohibited. Finally, as is clear, one must not provide inside information in exchange for a loan.

A. There was a market-supervisor in Jerusalem,

B. And they were not appointed [to supervise] prices, but [to supervise] [weights and] measures alone.

C. When a jar of wine was sold in Jerusalem, [it was sold] at three different prices, [covering the wine at] the mouth, the sides, and the middle.

D. A man may say to his fellow, "Let my ass go with you today, and yours with me tomorrow."

E. But he should not say to him, "Let my ass go with you today to the east, and yours with me tomorrow to the west."

F. "Let my cow plough with you today in the east, and yours with me tomorrow in the west."

G. But if the cost of doing so is the same, lo, this is permitted [cf. M. 5: 10A-G].

T. 6:14 Z p. 384, ls. 19-24

A. R. Judah says, "*All the days of the dry season are deemed equivalent to one another, and all the days of the rainy season are equivalent to one another*" [M. 5: 10E-F].

B. He who says to a worker, "Here's this *maneh* [in advance], and hold on to it, so you'll work with me at the harvest time at the rate of a *denar* a day," while the work is worth a *sela* [four *denars*] a day—

C. it is prohibited.

D. ". . . [charge] against it at the rate of a *denar* a day," while the work is worth a *sela* a day—

E. it is permitted.

T. 6:15 Z p. 384, ls. 24-26

T. 6:14 goes over the ground of M., as indicated. T. 6:15 speaks of a case in which a man pays a worker in advance on the condition that the worker take as his salary a *denar* a day, although the going rate is a *sela* a day, that is, four *denars*. The difference between the money paid and the wages of the laborer is usury and prohibited. If the worker starts work at once, however, and continues to work through the harvest time for a *denar* a day, although later on he will be worth four *denars* a day, that is an acceptable arrangement, and the worker gets the benefit of the advance. We more or less average out the arranged salary.

5:11

A. These [who participate in a loan on interest] violate a negative commandment:

B. (1) the lender, (2) borrower, (3) guarantor, and (4) witnesses.

C. Sages say, "Also (5) the scribe."

D. (1) They violate the negative commandment, *You will not give* [*him*] *your money upon usury* (Lev. 25:37).

E. (2) And [they violate the negative command], *You will not take usury from him* (Lev. 25:36).

F. (3) And [they violate the negative command], *You shall not be a creditor to him* (Ex. 22:25).

G. (4) And [they violate the negative command], *Nor shall you lay upon him usury* (Ex. 22:25).

H. (5) And they violate the negative command, *You shall not put a stumbling block before the blind, but you shall fear your God. I am the Lord* (Lev. 19:14).

M. 5:11

M. concludes with a striking homily, with the apodosis laid out in accord with sages' enumeration.

A. Said R. Yosé, "Come and see how blind are the eyes of those who lend at usurious rates.

B. "A man calls to his fellow to serve an idol, have unlawful sexual relations, or shed blood,

C. "[for] he wants him to fall into sin with him.

D. "Then this one brings a scribe, pen, ink, document, and witnesses,

E. "and says to them, 'Come and write concerning him that he has no share in the One who commanded concerning usury.'

F. "And he writes the document and registers it in the archives,

G. "and so denies Him who spoke and thereby brought the world into being, blessed be He.

H. "Thus you have learned that those who lend at usurious rates deny the principle [of divine authority]."

I. R. Simeon b. Eleazar says, "More than they make they lose.

J. "For they make the Torah into a fraud,

K. "and Moses into a fool,

L. "They say, 'Now if Moses knew how much we would make, he would never have written [the prohibition of usury]!'"

M. R. 'Aqiba says, "Usury is hard.

N. "For even a very greeting is a matter of usury.

O. "How so?

P. "This one never greeted the other in his entire life, until he had to borrow money from him. Now he rushes to greet him.

R. "So this is a kind of greeting which is a matter of usury" [cf. M. 5: 10N].

T. 6:17 Z pp. 384, ls. 34, 385, 1-9

A. R. Simeon says, "Whoever has money and does not put it out at usurious rates—

B. "concerning him does Scripture say, ... *who does not put out his money at interest and does not take a bribe against the innocent. He who does these things shall never be moved* (Ps. 15:5).

C. "Thus you have learned that those who lend money at usurious rates tremble and pass away from the world.

D. "Now just what this *trembling* is I do not know.

E. "But it is along the lines of that which is said, *Rescue those who are being taken away to death; hold back those who are stumbling to the slaughter* (Prov. (24:11))."

T. 6:18 Z p. 385, ls. 9-13

T. concludes with its share of homiletical materials.

CHAPTER SIX

BABA MESIA CHAPTER SIX

Laws governing relations of employer to employees express the principles that each party must abide by its commitment, and that the party which changes the terms of an agreement bears liability to the other. M. 6:1 introduces circumstances in which there is no claim for compensation, but merely a complaint, against the party which does not keep its word. This involves a case in which the employer does not pay the prevailing wage, or in which the employees do not show up for work. If there is a material loss on the latter account, however, the employer can pay to other workers more than he had stipulated and collect the difference from the ones who have disappointed him. M. 6:2 forms a bridge between M. 6:1 and M. 6:3-5. M. 6:2 simply says that whoever changes the conditions of a contract is liable. M. 6:3-5 then present two beautifully patterned triplets as examples of that principle. They bear their own exegesis, either formal and contrastive, thus implicit, or clearly expressed and explicit. M. 6:6 concludes the foregoing discussion of conditions of employment and draws in its wake M. 6:7-8, a brief unit on responsibilities of bailment. M. 6:6 makes the point that if a craftsman completes his work on a utensil, he is in the status of a paid bailee, and so has to pay the costs of damage, e.g., through fire or theft. If he announces that the work is done and asks for his fee, he is in the status of an unpaid bailee. M. 6:7 treats the lender as the paid bailee of the pledge. Judah qualifies this matter. M. 6:8 imposes an oath on a bailee who moves an object, whatever the status of the bailee. These last two pericopae have been introduced as a thematically relevant appendix to materials which, in fact, express a quite distinct principle from theirs.

6:1-2

A. He who hires craftsmen,
B. and one party deceived the other—
C. one has no claim on the other party except a complaint [which is not subject to legal recourse].
D. [If] one hired an ass-driver or wagon-driver to bring porters and pipes for a bride or a corpse,
E. or workers to take his flax out of the steep,
F. or anything which goes to waste [if there is a delay],
G. and [the workers] went back on their word—
H. in a situation in which there is no one else [available for hire],
I. he hires others at their expense,

J. or he deceives them [by promising to pay more and then not paying up more than his originally stipulated commitment].

M. 6:1

I A. He who hires craftsmen and they retracted—
   B. their hand is on the bottom.
II C. If the householder retracts,
   D. his hand is on the bottom.
I E. Whoever changes [the original terms of the agreement]—
   F. his hand is on the bottom.
II G. And whoever retracts—
   H. his hand is on the bottom.

M. 6:2

The deception, B, may be on the part of the householder, who offers less than the prevailing wage for the stated work, or of the workers, who do not agree to do the work. There is no legal recourse on either side. A-C introduce the case which follows, a triplet of possibilities, D, E, F. In this instance the workers demand more money. The employer has the right to hire others, charging to the original workers whatever additional wages he has to pay to secure help at the last minute, I, or he simply promises them whatever they want and in the end pays only the wages upon which all parties had originally agreed.

What follows at M. 6:2 is a careful construction, in which the opening entry, A-D, is repeated, stich by stich, at E-F, G-H. M. 6:2 says in general terms what M. 6:1 states through its case. A-B go over the ground, in particular, of M. 6:1D-I. If, C-D, wages go up, the householder has to pay more for the work; if wages go down, he pays at least as much as he originally stipulated, because he has changed the conditions of labor. E-F say the same, and so do G-H. M. 6:2 serves as a fine prologue to M. 6:3-5. Since M. 6:2 serves as a restatement as a generalization of the particular rules of M. 6:1, it clearly is formulated to join two completed units of material, M. 6:1 and the two triplets of M. 6:3-5, an example of tradental work for essentially redactional purposes.

A. He who hires workmen—
B. whether they deceived the householder [and did not show up for work]
C. or whether the householder deceived them [and did not pay the prevailing wage]—
D. *one has no claim on one another except a complaint* [*which is not subject to legal recourse*] [M. 6:1C].
E. Under what circumstances?
F. When the workers did not show up.
G. But [if] he hired ass-drivers [and] they came but he did not find [them],

H. or [if] hired workers and they came and found the field when it was wet [and not suitable for ploughing],.

I. he pays them wages in full.

J. But one who actually does the work is not equivalent to one who sits and does nothing.

K. And one who comes bearing a burden is not equivalent to one who comes empty-handed.

L. Under what circumstances?

M. In a case in which they did not begin [the work].

N. But if they had actually begun [the work], lo, they make an estimate for him [of how much work actually had been done].

O. How so?

P. [If] one undertook [for the householder] to cut down his standing grain for two *selas*,

Q. [and] he had cut down half of it and left half of it,

R. [or if he undertook] to weave a cloak for two *selas*,

S. and had woven half of it and had left half of it—

T. lo, these make an estimate for him.

U. How so?

V. If what he had made was worth six *denars* they hand over to him a *sela* [two *denars*] or he completes his work [and gets all six].

W. And if it was worth a *sela*, they hand over to him a *sela*.

X. R. Dosa says, "They make an estimate of the value of what is going to be made.

Y. "[If that which was going to be made] was worth five *denars*, they give him a *sheqel* or he finishes the work.

Z. "And if it was worth a *sheqel*, they give him a *sheqel*."

AA. Under what circumstances?

BB. In the case of something which does not go to waste.

CC. But in the case of *something which goes to waste* [*if there is a delay*] [M. 6:1F],

DD. *he hires others at their expense,*

EE. *or deceives them* [*by promising to pay more and then not pay up more than his originally stipulated commitment*] [M. 6:1I-J].

FF. How so?

GG. He says to [the worker] "I agreed to pay you a *sela*. Lo, I'm going to give you two."

HH. He goes and hires workers from another location then comes and takes the money from this party and hands it over to that party.

II. Under what circumstances?

JJ. In a situation in which he comes to an agreement with him while he cannot find others to hire.

KK. But if he saw ass-drivers coming along,

LL. [the worker] says to him "Go and hire one of these for yourself."

MM. And he has no claim on the other party except a complaint.

T. 7:1 Z p. 385 ls. 14-28

A. He who hires a boat,

B. and it unloaded his goods in the middle of the wharf

B. has no claim against it except a complaint.

T. 7:2 Z p. 385 ls. 28-29

A. He who hires a worker who suffers a bereavement,
B. or who suffers heat-prostration—
C. lo, they make an estimate for him [of the work already done].
D. How do they make an estimate for him?
E. If he had been hired for a month, they pay him off in accord with his salary [proportionate to the part of the month he has worked].
F. [If he had been hired by the job] as a contractor, they pay him off in proportion to the part of the job he has completed.
G. He who hires a worker to bring something from one place to another,
H. and he went but [because he did not find what he had been sent for,] he did not bring back [what he was supposed to],
I. [nonetheless] he pays off his full salary.

T. 7:3 Z p. 385 ls. 29-32

A. He who hires a worker to bring reeds and poles to a vineyard,
B. and he went but did not bring them—
C. he pays off his salary in full.
D. He who hires a worker to bring grapes, apples, and plums to a sick person,
E. and he went along but found the [sick person] dead,
F. [or he found] that he had gotten well,—
G. he may not say to him, "Take what you brought over there in lieu of your salary."
H. But he pays off his salary in full.

T. 7:4 Z pp. 385, ls. 32-34, 386, 1

A. He who hires a worker to plough may not say to him, "Come along and pull weeds."
B. [If he hired him] to pull weeds, he may not say to him, "Come along and plough."
C. [If he hired him] to plough in one field, he may not say to him, "Come and plough in the other field."
D. [If he hired him] to pull weeds in one field, he may not say to him, "Come and pull the weeds in the other field."

T. 7:5 Z p. 386, ls. 1-3

A. [If] he hired him to pull weeds and he finished the field to which he had been assigned,
B. he may not say to him, "Come along and hoe two vines."
C. [If] he hired him to hoe and he finished the field to which he had been assigned,
D. he may not say to him, "Come along and pull the weeds around two vines."
E. [If] he finished ploughing by noon-time,
F. he may not say to him, "Come and pull the weeds in another field."
G. For the worker may say to him, "Provide me with work in your property, or pay me my wage for the work I already have done."
H. [If] he finished pulling weeds by noon-time,
I. he may not say to him, "Come and pull the weeds in another field."
J. For the worker may say to him, "Provide me with work in your property, or pay me my wage for the work I already have done."

K. And so too, he who completed his ploughing by noon-time may not say to him, "Lo, I am going to plough in the field of Mr. So-and-so."

L. [If] he finished his weeding by noon-time, he may not say to him, "Lo, I'm going to pull weeds with you in such-and-such a field."

M. But if he in advance had stipulated with him in such wise,

N. lo, this is permitted.

O. The householder has the right to change the terms of work by assigning an easier form of labor,

P. but not by assigning a more exacting form of labor.

Q. How so?

R. [If] he hired him to pull weeds, and he completed the work in the field to which he was assigned,

S. he may say to him [only] with his permission, "Come and hoe around two vines."

T. [If] he hired him to hoe, and he completed the work in the field to which he had been assigned,

U. he may say to him whether he likes it or not, "Come and pull the weeds around two vines."

T. 7:6 Z p. 386, ls. 4-14

A. He who hires workers to work in his property,

B. and they made a mistake and did their work in the property of someone else—

C. he pays them their full wages and goes and collects from the householder [in whose property the work was done] the value of what he has done for him.

D. [If] he showed them his property and they went and worked in the property of his fellow,

E. he does not have to give them a thing.

F. But they go and collect from the [other] householder [in whose property the work was done] the value of what they have done for him.

T. 7:7 (continued) Z p. 386, ls. 14-17

T. provides a sizable Talmud to M. 6:1-2, as usual beginning with close attention to M. itself, then broadening the range of discussion, and at the end tacking on materials relevant in theme but not in principle, all done in an orderly way. T. 7:1A-D paraphrase M. The first clarification is important. If the workers did show up and so showed good faith, but were unable to do the work because of some circumstance not of their own devising, the workers are to be paid in full, E-K. If they started work, moreover, they are to be paid in proportion to what they have actually done, L-Z. T. then returns to exemplify M.'s rule as indicated, AA-MM. The expansion of M.'s conceptions then runs on through T. 7:2-7F. If the work is not properly done, there is nothing more than a complaint. If the worker cannot do the job because of circumstances beyond his control, he is paid proportionately, T. 7:3. If, again, the worker goes to work but cannot do the job, e.g., because he goes to bring what he is supposed to but is unable to find the merchandise, he is paid in full, T. 7:4. The terms of labor must be strictly adhered to, T. 7:5-6, which introduces into the exegesis of the theme of M. 6:1 the principles and considerations important at M. 6:3-5, and so forms a bridge between the two by its instantiation of the conceptions of M. 6:2. The final point is clear as given, T. 7:7. In all it would be difficult to improve upon this example of T. as a systematic and carefully composed exegesis of M, that is, as a Talmud.

> A. He who hires a worker,
> B. and [the worker] turned out to be taken for his service of corvée—
> C. [the employer] may not say to him, "Lo, this is yours!"
> D. but he pays his wage for what he already has done.
>
> T. 7:8 Z p. 386, ls. 23-24

> A. He who rents out a beast to his fellow should not change the beast [which he has rented out].
> B. [If] he rented him an ass, he should not seat him on a mule.
> C. [If he rented him] a mule, he should not seat him on a horse.
> D. [If he rented him] a horse, he should not seat him on a carriage.
>
> T. 7:9 Z p. 386, ls. 24-26

It is not the worker's fault, T. 7:8, and he must not be deprived of his wage. T. 7:9 brings no surprises, in line with M. 6:2 and 3-5.

6:3

I A. He who rents out an ass to drive it through hill-country but drove it through a valley,
   B. to drive it through a valley but drove it through the hill-country,
   C. even tough this route is ten *mils* and that route is ten *mils*,
   D. and [the ass] died—
   E. [the one who rented it is] liable.
II F. He who rents out an ass, and it went blind or was seized for royal service—
   G. [the one who provided it has the right to] say to [the one who rented it], "Here's yours right before you" [and he need not replace it for the stated period].
   H. [If] it died or broke a leg,
   I. [the one who provided it out] is liable to provide him with another ass.
III J. He who rents an ass to drive it through hill-country, but he drove it through a valley—
   K. if it slipped, he is exempt.
   L. But if it suffered heat-prostration, he is liable.
   M. [If he hired it out] to drive it through a valley, but he drove it through hill-country,
   N. if it slipped, he is liable.
   O. And if it suffered heat-prostration, he is exempt.
   P. But if it was on account of the elevation, he is liable.

M. 6:

The careful contrasts and balances of the triplet make M.'s points quite clearly. The one who hired the ass has changed the conditions of the contract. Even though the distance is the same, he remains liable, A-E. The lessor may claim that the ass was not suited for the work which it was made to perform. The contrast of F-G, H-I, concerns the obligations of the lessor. If the ass suffered incapacity to do the work for which it had been hired, the lessor may claim that, in any event, he has carried out the terms of his contract. But if the ass in no way could do labor, then the lessor, who rented it, has to provide another ass. The elegant balances at the third entry make M.'s points obvious, but the gloss at P clarifies matters still further.

G. *He who hires an ass and it went blind* [M. B.M. 6:3F] or grew weak—
H. [the one who rented it out] is not liable to provide him with another ass [M. 6:3G].
G. [*If*] it died or was seized *for royal service* [cf. M. 6:3F, H],
H. [*the one who rented it out*] *is liable to provide him with another ass* [M. 6:3I].
I. R. Simeon b. Eleazar says, "If it was in its normal course that it was seized, [the one who rented it out] is not liable to provide him with another ass.
J. "If it was not in its normal course that it was seized, [the one who rented it out] is liable to provide him with another ass."
K. And so did R. Simeon b. Eleazar say, "He who says to his fellow, 'Rent me your ass, and I'll ride on it from here to such-and-such a place,'
L. "and it went blind or grew weak,—[the one who rented it out] is liable to supply him with another.
M. "[If he said, 'Rent me] *this* ass of yours,' even if it died, even if it was seized for royal service,
N. "he is [not] liable to supply him with another ass."

T. 7:7 (concluded) Z p. 386, ls. 17-23

Simeon's gloss of M., at I-J, draws out M.'s principle that the renter cannot have reasonably been expected to foresee and prevent what has happened. At M-N the hirer specified a particular ass. N requires *not* (*TR* II, p. 121).

6:4-5

I A. He who hires a cow to plough in the hill-country but ploughed in the valley,
   B. if the ploughshare was broken,
   C. is exempt.
   D. [If he hired the cow to plough] in the valley and ploughed in the hill-country,
   E. if the ploughshare was broken,
   F. is liable.
II G. [If he hired a cow to] thresh pulse and he threshed grain,
   H. [if the cow slipped and fell],
   I. he is exempt.
   J. [If he hired it] to thresh grain and he threshed pulse,

104   BABA MESIA CHAPTER SIX 6:4-5

K. [if the cow slipped and fell],
L. he is liable,
M. because pulse is slippery.

M. 6:4

III A. He who hired an ass to carry wheat on it and he carried barley on it
B. is liable.
C. [If he hired it to carry] wheat and carried straw on it,
D. he is liable,
E. since the [greater] bulk is hard to carry.

IV F. [If he hired it] to carry a *letekh* of wheat and it carried a *letekh* of barley, he is exempt.
G. But if he added to its burden, he is liable.
H. And how much does he add to its burden so as to be liable?
I. Sumkhos says in the name of R. Meir, "A *seah* for a camel, and three *qabs* for an ass."

M. 6:5

M. expresses the points so carefully that no further exegesis is needed. The internal glosses, M. 6:4M, M. 6:5E, seem to me integral and valuable. The external one, M. 6:5H-I, provides useful information.

A. *He who hires an ass to carry a letekh* [fifteen *seahs*] *of wheat*, [cf. M. B.M. 6:5F],
B. *and who brought sixteen* [*seahs*] *of barley*
C. *is exempt* [from damage to the ass].
D. [*If*] *he added to its burden, he is liable.*
E. *And how much does he add to its burden so as to be liable?*
F. Sumkhos says in the name of R. Meir, "A *qab* for a porter [one that carries on his shoulder], three *seahs* for a wagon, and as to a boat, in accord with its dimensions" [M. 6:5G-I].
G. He who hires an ass to give a man a ride should not give a woman a ride.
H. [If he hired it] to give a woman a ride, it gives her a ride [without regard to] whether she is pregnant or nursing.

T. 7:10 Z p. 386, ls. 26-30

A. He who hires an ass for the householder to ride
B. loads on it his chair, provisions, and all his articles.
C. [If it was to be] more than this, the assdriver stops him.
D. An assdriver [for his part] loads on it barley, straw, and provisions until it reaches lodging.
E. [If it was to be] more than this, the householder stops him.

T. 7:11 Z p. 386, ls. 30-32

A. He who hires an ass and loaded it up with prohibited merchandise, so that the tax-collectors or excise-officers seized them from him—
B. [the one who hired the ass] is liable.
C. If he [who hired out the ass] informed [the renter] that there was a tax-collector on the road,
D. he is exempt.

T. 7:12 Z p. 386, ls. 32-34

A. A caravan which was passed through the wilderness,
B. and a band of brigands fell on it and seized [a ransom]—
C. they make a reckoning in accord with the property loss, and they do not make a reckoning in accord with the number of people.
D. But if they had sent out a pathfinder before them,
E. they also make a reckoning of the number of people.
F. But in any event they do not vary from the accepted practice governing those who travel in caravans.

T. 7:13 Z pp. 386, l. 34, 387, 1-2

A. A boat which was coming along in the sea and a storm hit it, so that they had to unload some of the cargo—
B. they make a reckoning in accord with the property loss, and they do not make a reckoning in accord with the number of people.
C. But in any event they do not vary from the accepted practice of sailors.
D. He who rents out to his fellow a boat or a wagon—
E. they reckon the cost in accord both with the burden and with the number of people to be carried.
F. But they do not reckon the cost in accord with [one's] property [capacity to pay].

T. 7:14 Z p. 387, ls. 2-5

T. 7:10 glosses M. as indicated. T. 7:11-14 proceed to supply thematically relevant materials, but along the lines of principles distinct from those at M. The point of T. 7:11 is to define the rights of both parties to the contract. T. 7:12 makes the point that if the renter accepts the conditions of the deal, the hirer need not compensate him for a predictable loss. T. 7:13, 14, make the obvious point that if there is a loss, e.g., through paying a fee to brigands to allow the caravan to pass, it is apportioned in accord with the property paid over, not in accord with the number of people involved. The same is said still more clearly at T. 7:14.

6:6

A. All craftsmen are in the status of paid bailees.
B. But any of them who said, "Take what is yours and pay me off [because the job is done]" [enters the status of] an unpaid bailee.
C. [If one person said to another], "You keep watch for me, and I'll keep watch for you," [both are] in the status of a paid bailee.
D. "Keep watch for me,"
E. and the other said to him, "Leave it down before me,"
F. [the latter] is [in the status of] unpaid bailee.

M. 6:6

The point of A-B, C-D vs. E-F, is clear. In the case of a paid bailee, if the bailment is stolen or lost, the bailee has to pay compensation. An unpaid bailee simply takes an oath that he is not responsible for the loss and pays nothing. The craftsman is deemed to include in his fee the costs of storage. But if he demands payment, then the bailment no longer is under the rule of a paid bailee. At D-E there is no exchange of services, leading to F.

    A. A weaver who left a thread on the side of a garment, and it caught fire
    B. is liable to pay compensation,
    C. because he is in the status of a paid bailee [M. 6:6A].
    D. [If] the debris [of a falling building] fell on it before it was completely manufactured,
    E. he is liable [to pay compensation].
    F. [If] it was after the work was completed,
    G. if the craftsman had informed the owner [that it was ready to be picked up], [the craftsman] is exempt.
    H. And if not, he is liable [cf. M. B.M. 6:6B].
    I. [If] he had completed making it, and it was stolen or lost,
    J. if he had informed the owner, [the craftsman] is exempt.
    K. And if not, he is liable.

                                        T. 7:15 Z p. 387, ls. 5-8

    A. [If] he said to him, "I told you [to make] a shirt,"
    B. and [the craftsman] said, "You told me [to make] a cloak,"
    C. it is the householder's job to bring proof.
    D. R. Judah says, "If the craftsman was working at the house of the householder, let the householder accept what is his.
    E. "[If he was working] at the craftsman's [own] shop, but the householder was coming and going,
    F. "let the householder accept what is his.
    G. "[But if the craftsman was working] in his own shop, and the householder was not coming and going,
    H. "then the craftsman has to bring proof."

                                        T. 7:16 Z p. 387, ls. 8-12

    A. [If the householder] said, "I told you [I would pay] a *sela*,"
    B. [and the craftsman] said, "You told me two,"
    C. so long as the goods are in the hand of the craftsman, it is the householder's job to bring proof [of the agreed price].
    D. [If the goods] are in the householder's possession,
    E. during the interval, the craftsman has to bring proof.
    F. After the interval, the weaver takes an oath [that the agreed price was as he claimed] and collects [what is owing to him].

                                        T. 7:17 Z p. 387, ls. 12-14

    A. He who hands over utensils to the craftsman to do work for him [on them],
    B. and the work was completed,
    C. before he has received his wages, lo, he is in the status of a paid bailee.
    D. Once he has received his wages, lo, he is in the status of an unpaid bailee.
    E. Under what circumstances?
    F. When [the craftsman] has laid claim upon the householder and said to him, "Come and take what's yours."

G. But if he did not lay claim on him and did not say to him, "Come and take what's yours,"

H. even though he already has received his wages, lo, he remains in the status of a paid bailee.

T. 7:18 Z p. 387, ls. 14-17

A. He who says to his fellow, "Lend to me, and I'll lend to you"—
B. "Keep watch for me, and I'll keep watch for you"—
C. "Lend to me, and I'll keep watch for you."—
D. lo, these are in the status of an unpaid bailee [cf. M. 6:6C-F].
E. And they are not in the status of a paid bailee.

T. 7:19 (continued) Z p. 387, ls. 17-19

T. 7:15 illustrates M. 6:6. T. 7:16-17 introduce a secondary case, relevant to the collection of wages mentioned at M. 6:6A-B. But the issue is distinct from M. T. 7:18, by contrast, neatly amplifies M.'s main principle and is directly relevant to the exposition of M. 6:6B. T. 7:19, as we see, simply restates the view of M. 6:6C-F.

6:7

A. [If one made] a loan and took a pledge, he is in the status [as to the pledge] of a paid bailee.
B. R. Judah says, "[If] he lent him money, he is in the status of an unpaid bailee.
C. "[If] he lent him produce, he is in the status of a paid bailee."
D. Abba Saul says, "It is permitted to a person to put out on hire a pledge left by a poor man,
E. "and so reduce [the debt] on its account little by little,
F. "for he is like one who gives back what someone has lost."

M. 6:7

The lender enjoys the security of the pledge and so is a paid bailee. Judah sees no advantage at all in a loan of cash. But the lender of produce is protected from the deterioration of his produce and so enjoys a benefit from the loan. So he has a different view of the governing principle. D-F are independent.

F. *Abba Saul says, "It is permitted to a person to put out on hire a pledge left by a poor man* [M. 6:7D]
G. "for less.
H. "But as to that of a rich man, he is not permitted to lay a hand on it."

T. 7:19 (concluded) Z p. 387, ls. 19-20

T. cites and glosses M.

6:8

A. [The bailee] who moves a jar from one place to another and broke it,
B. whether he is an unpaid bailee or a paid bailee,
C. must take an oath [that the jar was broken by accident and not through his willful negligence, and so he is exempt from having to make it up].

D. R. Eliezer says, "In either case he is to take an oath."

E. "But I wonder whether either this one or that one can in fact take a [valid] oath."

M. 6:8

This is tacked on because of the thematic relevance. Eliezer concurs. But, in line with M. 7:8, he wonders why the paid bailee has to take an oath, since in his case, even if he has not been negligent, he has to pay. The unpaid bailee likewise may be unable to take an oath in a case in which he has indeed been negligent.

CHAPTER SEVEN

BABA MESIA CHAPTER SEVEN

The chapter is in two parts, M. 7:1-7, M. 7:8-11, which are joined in a rather obvious and clumsy way at M. 7:8A. The redactional parallel to Chapter Six is very close, since both the first and the second parts of this chapter run parallel in theme and problematic to the first and second parts of the other. Both chapters treat, first, rights and obligations of workers, and, second, the status and rights of bailees.

The first topic is the right of the worker to consume part of the crop on which he is working, or of an ox to eat while he treads grain, as specified at Deut. 23:25-26, for the worker (as M. understands the datum of the verse), and, more self-evidently, Deut. 25:4, for the beast. It is mainly the former which will occupy M. But T. enriches the discussion of the latter. M. 7:1 stresses that under all circumstances workers are to be treated in accord with prevailing practice. This includes the practice of supplying them with food. M. 7:2 shifts the grounds of discourse. It now specifies that in certain instances, it is not local custom but the law of the Torah which permits the worker to eat the crop on which he is working. This then is spelled out. M. 7:3 carries forward the refinement of M. 7:2, and M. 7:4 does the same. M. 7:5 allows the worker to eat a bellyfull, though warning him of the consequences if he does. In line with this warning M. 7:6 allows a worker to give up his right to eat. M. 7:7, finally, makes it clear that the worker may assume he has the right to eat on the job until he is told otherwise. If the crop is prohibited, e.g., as a planting of the fourth year, and the worker is not so informed in advance, the householder must then provide permitted food for him. Nibbling as one works on produce is a perquisite the worker may take for granted.

M. 7:8-11 do not greatly augment our knowledge of the obligations of bailees, paid or unpaid, borrowers or hirers. M. 7:8 simply specifies the consequences of the accidental loss of the utensil or beast which is subject to bailment. M. 7:8 stresses that, if there is an unavoidable accident, the bailee need not pay compensation under certain circumstances. M. 7:9-10 then explain the meaning of an unavoidable accident, and M. 7:10 further permits a bailee to stipulate that he is not subject to the prevailing rule. For instance, if he is an unpaid bailee, he may stipulate in advance that he will not be made to take an oath if the bailment should be subject to an unavoidable accident. M. 7:11 presents a triplet on stipulations, an appendix to this brief clarification of what is, in any event, a conceptually rather flimsy construction.

7:1

A. He who hires [day-] workers and told them to start work early or to stay late—

B. in a place in which they are accustomed not to start work early or not to stay late,

C. he has no right to force them to do so.

D. In a place in which they are accustomed to provide a meal, he must provide a meal.

E. [In a place in which they are accustomed] to make do with a sweet,

F. he provides it.

G. Everything accords with the practice of the province.

H. M'SH B: R. Yohanan b. Matya said to his son, "Go, hire workers for us."

I. He went and made an agreement with them for food [without further specification].

J. Now when he came to his father, [the father] said to him, "My son, even if you should make for them a meal like one of Solomon in his day, you will not have carried out your obligation to them.

K. "For they are children of Abraham, Isaac, and Jacob.

L. "But before they begin work, go and tell them, '[Work for us] on condition that you have a claim on me [as to food] only for a piece of bread and pulse alone.'"

M. Rabban Simeon b. Gamaliel says, "He had no need to specify that in so many words.

N. "Everything [in any case] accords with the practice of the province."

M. 7:1

The point that working conditions are defined by local custom is made three times, A-C, D-F, and in Simeon b. Gamaliel's comment on the story, H-L, M-N.

7:2-3

A. And these [have the right to] eat [the produce on which they work] by [right accorded to them in] the Torah:

B. he who works on what is as yet unplucked [may eat from the produce] at the end of the time of processing;

C. [and he who works] on plucked produce [may eat from the produce] before processing is done;

D. [in both instances solely] in regard to what grows from the ground.

E. But these do not [have the right to] eat [the produce on which they labor] by [right accorded to them in] the Torah:

F. he who works on what is as yet unplucked, before the end of the time of processing;

G. [and he who works] on plucked produce after the processing is done,

H. [in both instances solely] in regard to what does not grow from the ground.

M. 7:2

A. [If] one was working with his hands but not with his feet,

B. with his feet but not with his hands,

C. even [carrying] with his shoulder,
D. lo, he [has the right to] eat [the produce on which he is working].
E. R. Yosé b. R. Judah says, "[He may eat the produce on which he is working] only if he works with both his hands and his feet."

M. 7:3

M. 7:2A-D are balanced by, and contrast with, E-H. The relevant verses in Scripture are at Deut. 23:25-26. The field-worker is allowed to eat what is not plucked from the ground only after the processing is completed, during the harvesting process. One who works on what is already plucked up has the right to nibble only before the processing is completed. Thus, one who works on pressed figs should not nibble on them, since the processing is complete and the figs are subject to tithes. Excluded from both categories are workers in cheese, milk, or meat. The balanced dispute of M. 7:3—A-B *vs.* E—is important only because of Yosé's position. Without his view that the one may eat who works with both hands and feet, I do not think the view of A-D would have required enunciation. T., cited at M. 7:7, explains Yosé's view.

A. [Referring to Deut. 25:4, *You shall not muzzle an ox when it treads out grain*], R. Yosé b. R. Judah says, "Just as treading out grain is special, as something which it does with its fore-legs, its hind-legs, and its body,
B. "so is excluded one who works with his hands but not his legs,
C. "or with his legs but not his body.
D. "Just as treading out grain is special, in that it is something, the work on which is not completed,
E. "so are excluded those engaged in kneading, cutting [the dough], and baking—
F. "things on which the work is completed [and these workers have no right to eat].
G. "Just as treading out grain is special, in that it involves something which grows from the earth,
H. "so are excluded one who milks a cow, beats milk, or makes cheese—things which do not grow from the earth [cf. M. 7:3D, H].
I. "Just as treading out grain is special, in that it involves something which is plucked up from the ground,
J. "so are excluded one who pulls weeds in the case of garlic and onions, things which are unplucked from the ground [*vs.* M. 7:2B].
K. "Just as treading out grain is special, in that it is something, work on which is not completed so far as tithes are concerned,
L. "so is excluded one who separates [clumps of] dates and figs, a matter on which work is complete so far as tithes are concerned" [cf. M. 7:7D].

T. 8:7 (continued), Z pp. 387, ls. 33-34, 388, 1-5

T. 8:7 supplies the proof-text on which Yosé b. R. Judah bases his ruling at M. 7:3E. The location of Yosé's saying where it is, further, is now clear, in T.'s exhibit of the full range of Yosé's positions. He concurs in M.'s basic principles but introduces conceptions either contrary to M.'s or unknown to M.

7:4

A. [If the laborer] was working on figs, he [has] not [got the right to] eat grapes.

B. [If he was working] on grapes, he [has] not [got the right to] eat figs.

C. But [he does have the right to] refrain [from eating] until he gets to the best produce and then [to exercise his right to] eat.

D. And in all instances they have said [that he may eat from the produce on which he is laboring] only in the time of work.

E. But on grounds of restoring lost property to the owner, they have said [in addition]:

F. Workers [have the right to] eat as they go from furrow to furrow [even though they do not then work],

G. and when they are coming back from the press [so saving time for the employer];

H. and in the case of an ass [nibbling on straw in its load], when it is being unloaded.

M. 7:4

The three rules, A-B, C, and D-H, are clear as given. The right to eat food on which one is working is specific, A-B, but unlimited, C. One may nibble while not actually engaged in an act of labor, a typical quibble.

A. He who [has the right to] eat [of the produce on which he is working] by [specification of the law of the] Torah

B. should not pare figs,

C. nor should he suck out the grapes.

D. One who works with his whole body [as a porter] has the right to eat whenever he wants.

E. And R. Judah says, "[The ass] has the right to eat only when one unloads its burden or when he loads its burden,

F. "because [eating while he is carrying the burden constitutes] robbing the householder of his labor" [cf. M. 7:4H].

T. 8:9 Z p. 388, ls. 11-14

A. He who [has muzzled cattle which] stamp on grain does not transgress the prohibition against muzzling,

B. but, because of appearance's sake, he should bring a basket and hang it on the muzzle [of the animal].

T. 8:10 Z p. 388, ls. 14-15

A. An Israelite who treads out grain with the cow of a gentile is subject to transgressing the rule against muzzling the ox.

B. And a gentile who treads out grain with the cow of an Israelite is not subject to transgressing the rule against muzzling the ox.

C. [If the ox] is treading out grain in the status of heave-offering or second tithe, [the owner] is subject to transgressing the rule against muzzling the ox.

D. What should he do?
E. He brings a basket and hangs it on the neck of the beast,
F. and puts into the basket some produce of that kind [which it is treading, so that he does not violate the law against muzzling the ox, and the ox will not consume produce in a state of consecration].

T. 8:11 Z p. 388, ls. 15-18

A. He who muzzles a cow should not give it less than six *qabs* [of fodder],
B. and in the case of an ass, three *qabs*.
C. He who actually muzzles the cow, and he who pairs different heterogeneous animals [which is not to be done in ploughing] [but does not plough]
D. is exempt [from liability].
E. You have none who is liable except the one who actually leads or drives [the muzzled ox while it is ploughing] alone.

T. 8:12 Z p. 388, ls. 18-19

M. 7:4H's reference to the right of the ass to eat while not actually working provides the occasion to make reference once more to the prohibition of muzzling an ox in its treading. That accounts for the supplements of T. 8:10-12. T. 8:10 limits the applicability of the Scriptural rule. T. 8:11 makes the obvious point that animals are subject to the rule when in the hands of Israelites, not of gentiles. One should not permit beasts to consume food in a state of consecration. T. 8:12 continuing T. 8:11D-F, makes provision for feeding a muzzled ox. It then points out that the one who merely muzzles the ox is not responsible, only the one who does work with it.

7:5

A. A worker [has the right to] eat cucumbers, even to a *denar*'s worth,
B. or dates, even to a *denar*'s worth.
C. R. Eleazar Ḥisma says, "A worker should not eat more than the value of his wages."
D. But sages permit.
E. But they instruct the man not to be a glutton and thereby slam the door in his own face [to future employment].

M. 7:5

The dispute, C-D, explains why A-B are stated. E settles the matter.

A. He who hires a worker to watch his cow for him, [or] to watch his child for him
B. does not pay him a salary for the Sabbath.
C. Therefore [the watchman] does not bear responsibility [to make up any loss which takes place] on the Sabbath.
D. But if he was hired by the week, by the month, by the year, or by the septannate, he does pay him a salary covering the Sabbath.
E. Therefore [the watchman] does bear responsibility [to make up any loss] on the Sabbath.

F. [The watchman] may not say to him, "Pay me my salary for the Sabbath."

G. But he says to him, "Pay me my salary for a ten-day period."

T. 8:1 Z p. 387, ls. 21-24

A. A worker has no right to do his own work by night and to hire himself out by day,

B. to plough with his cow by night and to hire it out in the morning.

C. Nor may he deprive himself of food and starve himself in order to give his food [supplied by the employer] to his children,

D. on account of the robbery of his labor which belongs to the householder [who hires him].

T. 8:2 Z p. 387, ls. 25-27

A. Workers have the right to eat their bread with brine,

B. so that they will [have the thirst to] eat a great many grapes.

C. And the householder has the right to make them drink wine,

D. so that they will not eat a great many grapes [cf. M. 7:5].

T. 8:3 Z p. 387, ls. 27-28

A. A householder has the right to starve and torment his cow

B. so that it will eat a great deal when it is threshing.

C. And one who hires a cow has the right to feed it a bundle of sheaves,

D. so that it will not eat a great deal when it is treshing.

T. 8:4 Z p. 387, ls. 28-30

A. An ass and a camel may eat from the burden which is on their backs as they go along,

B. on condition that [the owner] not take [the fodder in the burden, which he is paid to carry] by hand and feed it to them.

T. 8:5 Z p. 387, ls. 30-31

A. [If] one was guarding four or five cucumber-patches,

B. he should not fill his belly from one of them.

C. But he eats a bit from each and every one,

D. in proportion [M. 7:5].

T. 8:6 Z p. 387, ls. 32-33

The inclusion of T. 8:1-2 can be explained—if it should be explained at all—only as an effort to provide a prologue on the mutual obligations of worker and employer, with stress, then, at T. 8:2. There is no closer point of relevance. T. 8:3 complements M. 7:5. T. 8:4 extends the rule to cattle. The hirer will not want the cow to eat a great deal while it is at work. The owner will want the cow to eat as much as it can under the same circumstance. Either party may act to his best advantage. T. 8:5 concludes the exposition of M. 7:5, as is obvious.

7:6

A. A man makes a deal [with the householder not to exercise his right to eat produce on which he is working] in behalf of himself his adult son or daughter,

B. in behalf of his adult man-servant or woman-servant,

C. in behalf of his wife
D. because [they can exercise] sound judgment [and keep the terms of the agreement].
E. But he may not make a deal in behalf of his minor son or daughter,
F. in behalf of his minor boy-servant or girl-servant,
G. or in behalf of his beast,
H. because [they can] not [exercise] sound judgment [and keep the terms of the agreement].

M. 7:6

A-D contrast with E-H, and the point is made in the contrast. It is taken for granted that workers may decline to exercise their right to eat produce on which they labor.

7:7

A. He who hires workers to work in his fourth-year plantings [the produce of which is to be eaten not at random but only in Jerusalem or to be redeemed for money to be brought up to Jerusalem (Lev. 19-24)]
B. lo, these [do not have the right to] eat.
C. If [in advance] he did not inform them [of the character of the produce and the prohibitions affecting it], he [has to] redeem the produce and [permit them to] eat [of it].
D. [If] his fig-cakes split up,
E. his jars [of wine] burst open [while yet untithed, and workers are hired to repress the figs and rebottle the wine],
F. lo, these [do not have the right to] eat [them].
G. If he did not inform them [that the produce on which they would be working was untithed and therefore not available for their random-consumption],
H. he has to tithe [the produce] and [allow them to] eat [of it].

M. 7:7

The same point is made twice, A-C, D-H, first in regard to fourth-year produce, then to untithed produce. The right of the worker to eat may be surrendered by him, but not abridged by others, even in the stated circumstance.

M. Anything the like of which has not yet reached the time for obligation to tithing,
N. but some other sort of prohibition affects it—
O. [if the householder] hired [the worker] without making explanations [as to the prohibited status of the food in which he would be laboring], he has to redeem [the produce] and allow the worker to eat it,
P. [or] tithe [the produce] and [so] allow the worker to eat it.
Q. But if he made an agreement with him [that he would forego his right to eat while he worked in the field],
R. lo, this one is not to eat anything at all.
S. Anything the like of which has reached the time for obligation to tithing,
T. but some other sort of permitted aspect affects it—

U. [if the householder] hired [the worker] without making explanations as [to the status of the food in which he would be laboring],

V. lo, this [worker] is not to eat [at all].

W. But if [the householder] made an agreement with him [the worker] [that he would provide food], lo, this one has the right to eat.

T. 8:7 (concluded), Z p. 388, ls. 5-11

T. elegantly restates the main concern of M. 7:7. If the worker has every reason to believe he is going to have a right to eat the produce in the field, e.g., because that produce is not yet subject to tithing, but there is some factor unknown to the worker, e.g., the produce is in the status of the fourth-year-planting, which will prevent him from eating while he works, the employer must inform him or provide food for him, just as M. maintains. If the worker assumed that there would be no right of eating, e.g., because it was the season at which the crop had already fully ripened and become liable to tithes, then the householder does not have to provide for him unless he so stipulates in advance.

7:8

A. Those who keep watch over produce [have the right] to eat [it] by the laws of the province,

B. but not by [what is commanded in] the Torah.

C. There are four kinds of watchmen:

D. (1) an unpaid bailee,

E. (2) a borrower,

F. (3) a paid bailee,

G. (4) and a hirer.

H. (1) [In the case of damage to the bailment], an unpaid bailee takes an oath in all [cases of loss or damage and bears no liability whatsoever] [M. 3:1].

I. (2) The borrower pays in all circumstances [of damages to a bailment].

J. (3, 4) The paid bailee and the hirer take an oath [that they have not been negligent]

K. concerning [a beast which has suffered] a broken bone, or which has been driven away, or which has died [Ex. 22:9],

L. But they pay compensation for the one which was lost or stolen.

M. 7:8

A-B join M. 7:1-6 to M. 7:8C-G. H-L provide the exegesis of C-G. What is important at K-L is that in the former case we have an unavoidable accident. In the latter, L, there are precautions to be taken, and obviously the guardian or hirer has been negligent.

A. Under what circumstances did they rule, *An unpaid bailee takes an oath in all [cases of loss or damage and bears no liability]* [M. 7:8H] and goes forth?

B. In a case in which he carried out his duty as a bailee in the way in which people generally serve as bailees.
C. [If] he locked up as was appropriate,
D. tied up as was appropriate,
E. put [the thing] in his girdle,
F. and put it before him in his wallet, with its mouth upward,
G. or put it in a chest, box, or cupboard and locked it up,
H. and it was lost,
I. lo, this one takes an oath and goes forth.
J. And if there are witnesses that he did as he claims,
K. he is exempt even from having to take an oath.

T. 8:13 Z p. 388, ls. 20-23

A. [If] he locked up not as was appropriate,
B. tied up not as was appropriate,
C. put [the thing] in his girdle,
D. and threw it behind him in his wallet, with its mouth downward,
E. put it at the mouth of his wallet,
F. or put [an animal] up on his roof,
G. and it was stolen or lost [M. 7:8L],
H. he is liable.
I. [If] he put it into the same place in which he put his own,
J. if it is a place appropriate for safe-keeping, he is exempt.
K. And if not, he is liable.

T. 8:14 Z p. 388, ls. 23-26

T.'s interpretation of M. 7:8H is clear as extensively spelled out. Even the unpaid bailee may prove to be liable, if he has not taken requisite care, and this applies to the bailment even if he has not taken requisite care of his own possessions.

7:9-11

I A. A single wolf does not count as an unavoidable accident.
    B. Two wolves are regarded as an unavoidable accident.
    C. R. Judah says, "In a time that wolves come in packs, even a single wolf is an unavoidable accident."
II D. Two dogs do not count as an unavoidable accident.
    E. Yadu'a the Babylonian says in the name of R. Meir, "[If] they come from one direction, they do not count as an unavoidable accident.
    F. "If they come from two directions, they count as an unavoidable accident."
III G. A thug—lo, he counts as an unavoidable accident.
IV H. (1) A lion, (2) wolf, (3) leopard, (4) panther, or (5) snake—lo, these count as an unavoidable accident.
    I. Under what circumstances?
    J. When they come along on their own.
    K. But if he took [the sheep] to a place in which there were bands of wild animals or thugs,
    L. these do not constitute unavoidable accidents.

M. 7:9

I   A. [If a beast] died of natural causes, lo, this counts as an unavoidable accident.
    B. [If] one caused it distress and it died [e.g., of cold or hunger], this does not count as an unavoidable accident.
II C. [If] it went up to the top of a crag and fell down, lo, this is an unavoidable accident.
    D. [If] he brought it up to the top of a crag and it fell down and died,
    E. it is not an unavoidable accident.
    F. An unpaid bailee may stipulate that he is exempt from [having to take] an oath,
    G. and a borrower, that he is exempt from having to pay compensation,
    H. and a paid bailee and a hirer, that they are exempt from [having to take] an oath or from having to pay compensation.

M. 7:10

I   A. Whoever exacts a stipulation contrary to what is written in the Torah—his stipulation is null.
II B. And any stipulation which requires an antecedent action—that stipulation is null.
III C. But any condition which can be carried out in the end and is stipulated as a condition in the beginning—
    D. that stipulation is valid.

M. 7:11

M. 7:9-10E provide an extensive example of the distinction important at M. 7:8K/L. The bailee in the case of an unvoidable accident is exempt from having to make restitution, as specified. The six stichs, four, then two, are not closely matched, except at the apodosis. Some are heavily glossed. One may be expected to handle a single wolf, but not two, and so throughout. M. 7:9K-L are obvious, and the carefully drawn contrasts make clear what is in any case self-evident, e.g., at M. 7:10A/B, C/D.

The conclusion of the matter comes at M. 7:10F-H. It is permitted for the various sorts of bailees by stipulation to change their obligations—hence their status. M. 7:11A is important. These stipulations are valid because they do not contradict the law of the Torah. The triplet is independent of this context and pursues its own interests. M. 7:11B refers to a case in which someone arranges that another party will perform a certain deed on a given condition, but specifies the deed to be done before the condition to be met. This is not in line with the formulation of Num. 32:20-22, which speaks first of the condition to be met, then the deed to be done. If a condition may be ultimately carried out and is stated at the outset, M. 7:11C, it is a valid one. None of this advances the discussion of our chapter or tractate.

A. Who is in the status of a hirer [M. 7:8G]?
B. [If] one hired one's beast from him,
C. or hired utensils from him.
D. Who is a paid bailee [M. 7:8F]?

E. [If] one hired him to watch his beast,
F. [or] hired him to watch his utensils.
G. *And [the bailee] went to a place in which there were bands of wild animals or thugs* [M. 7:9],
H. and the wild animals ripped it up,
I. or the thugs ripped it off—
J. lo, this does not constitute an unavoidable accident.
K. *If it died of natural causes, lo, this counts as an unavoidable accident.*
L. [*If*] *one caused it distress and it died* [e.g., of cold or hunger], *this does not count as an unavoidable accident* [M. 7:10A-B].
M. [*If*] *he brought it up to the top of a crag and it fell down, this is not an unavoidable accident* [M. 7:10D-E].
N. Now what then constitute unavoidable accidents?
O. For example, such as this about which Scripture speaks: *And the Sabeans fell upon them and took them and slew the servants with the edge of the sword* (Job 1:15).

T. 8:15 Z p. 388, ls. 26-30

A. *A single wolf does not count as an unavoidable accident.*
B. *Two wolves are regarded as an unavoidable accident.*
C. *R. Judah says, "In a time that wolves come in packs, even a single wolf is an unavoidable accident"* [M. 7:9A-C].
D. A single thief is not an unavoidable accident.
E. Two thieves are an unavoidable accident.
F. R. Judah says, "If he was armed, even a single thief, lo, he is an unavoidable accident."

T. 8:16 Z pp. 388, ls. 30-32, 389, 1

A. A shepherd who was standing and keeping his sheep,
B. and a wolf came and ripped up the sheep,
C. or a lion and clawed it—
D. he is exempt.
E. [If] he has left his staff and his wallet on it[s account, and fled],
F. he is liable.

T. 8:17 Z p. 389, ls. 1-2

A. A shepherd who left his flock and went into town,
B. and thugs came and took the flock—
C. they make an assessment of the case as if he had been there.
D. If he had been able to save [the flock, had he been present], he is liable.
E. And if not, he is exempt.

T. 8:18 Z p. 389, ls. 2-3

A. An unpaid bailee may stipulate that he is in the status of a borrower [cf. M. 7:10F],
B. and a borrower may stipulate that he is in the status of an unpaid bailee [cf. M. 7:10G],
C. and a borrower may stipulate that he is in the status of a paid bailee or a hirer [cf. M. 7:10G],

D. and a paid bailee and a hirer may stipulate that they are in the status of a borrower [M. 7:10H].

T. 8:19 Z p. 389, ls. 4-5

T. 8:15 continues the glossing of M. 7:8, as indicated. Then T. comes to M. 7:9-10E, as indicated. T. 8:19 then expands the possibilities uncovered at M. 7:10F-H.

CHAPTER EIGHT

BABA MESIA CHAPTER EIGHT

We now complete the long discussion of the rights and responsibilities of those who borrow, rent, or undertake guardianship of, the animals or property of other parties. M. 8:1-5 present a series of rather complex formal structures, all of which make quite obvious points. The operative principles in general are not distinctive to the subject-matter under discussion. For instance, there is the notion that when one party makes a claim of certainty, and the other admits he does not know the fact, the former gains preference. If there is a conflict of two equally strong claims, by contrast, the disputants divide up what is under litigation. M. 1:1f. have prepared us for this idea. M. 8:1 begins this sizable unit with an exegesis of Ex. 22:12-14, making explicit what the two verses seem to wish to say. M. 8:2 develops the instantiation of the stated principle about evaluating conflicting claims. M. 8:3 makes the very obvious point that when an object has passed into the hands of the borrower, then, but only then, the borrower bears responsibility. But before that point, the lender does. M. 8:4 repeats precisely what M. 8:2 has said, now in terms of a different theme. M. 8:5 goes over the same ground.

The second half of the chapter, M. 8:6-9, introduces the topic of relationships of tenants and landlords. M. 8:6 begins the discussion with a specification of the right of the tenant not to suffer eviction at a time inconvenient to him, e.g., in the rainy season, or in circumstances detrimental to his business. M. 8:7 specifies the duties of the landlord to supply certain basic requirements of the dwelling. M. 8:8 deals with the implications of an intercalated month for rental agreements, and M. 8:9 asks about the landlord's responsibilities to restore a damaged house. There is nothing surprising in the rules stated in these units.

8:1

A. He who borrows a cow,
B. and (1) borrowed [the service] of its owner with it,
C. or (2) hired its owner with it—
D. [or] (1) borrowed [the service] of the owner,
E. or (2) hired him,
F. and afterward borrowed the cow [too],
G. and [the cow] died—
H. [the borrower] is exempt,
I. since it is said, *If the owner is with it, he shall not pay compensation* (Ex. 22:14).

J. But [if] he borrowed the cow,
K. and afterward (1) borrowed [the service] of the owner,
L. or (2) hired him,
M. and [the cow] died,
N. [the borrower] is liable,
O. since it is said, *If the owner is not with it, he shall certainly pay compensation* (Ex. 22:13).

M. 8:1

The contrast between A-I and J-O makes M.'s point, which is that if the owner is present along with the cow or beforehand, the other party is exempt, but if the cow is present before the owner, the other is liable, just as Scripture says.

A. *He who borrows a cow* [M. 8:1A],
B. and [to return it] comes along and sets it in front of the manger of its owner,
C. and [from that point] it was stolen or lost—
D. if he had informed the owner,
E. he is exempt [from making restitution].
F. And if not, he is liable.
G. *[If] he had borrowed it and borrowed [the service] of its owner* [M. 8:1B-C],
H. hired it and [at the same time] hired the service of its owner,
I. borrowed it and hired the service of its owner,
J. hired it and borrowed the service of its owner,
K. *and [the cow] died* or [suffered a] broken [leg]—
L. even though the owner is available and ploughing in some other place,
M. [the one who borrowed or hired the cow] is exempt,
N. since it is said, *If the owner is with it, he shall not pay compensation* (Ex. 22:14) [M. 8:1A-I].

T. 8:20 Z p. 389, ls. 5-9

A. [*If*] he borrowed [the cow],
B. and afterward borrowed [the service of] the owner [M. 8:1J-K],
C. hired [the cow] and afterward hired [the service of] its owner,
D. borrowed [the cow] and afterward hired the service of its owner,
E. hired [the cow] and afterward borrowed the service of its owner,
F. and [the cow] died or [suffered] a broken [leg],
G. even though the owner is available and ploughing with that animal,
H. [the borrower] is liable,
I. since it is said, *If the owner is not with it, he shall certainly pay compensation* (Ex. 22:13) [M. 8:1J-O].

T. 8:21 Z p. 389, ls. 9-12

T. restates M.'s cases, adding a rich variety of possible arrangements to make exactly the same point.

8:2

A. He who borrows a cow—
B. [If] he borrowed it for half a day and hired it for half a day,

C. [or] borrowed it for one day and hired it for the next day,
D. [or] borrowed one [cow] and hired another—
E. and [the cow] died—
I F. the lender says [D], (1) "The borrowed one died"—
G. (2) "On the day [C] on which it was borrowed, it died,"
H. (3) "At the time [B] that it was borrowed, it died,"—
I. and the [borrower] says, "I don't know"—
J. [the borrower] is liable.
II K. The hirer says, (1) "The hired one died,"
L. (2) "On the day on which it was hired, it died,"
M. (3) "at the time that it was hired, it died,"
N. and the other party says, "I don't know"—
O. [the hirer] is exempt.
III P. [If] this party claims that the borrowed one [died],
Q. and that party claims that the hired one [died],
R. the one who rents it is to take an oath that the rented one died.
S. [If] this one says, "I don't know," and that one says, "I don't know,"
T. let them divide [the loss].

M. 8:2

The one who borrows is liable for unavoidable accidents, and the one who hires is not, so M. 7:8. The case then is clear. The point does not require discussion of the theme before us, since it is that if one party claims to be certain and the other admits to doubt, the former's claim is honored, F-J. This point is then repeated, K-O. P-R conclude the construction with the vow to be taken in the case of a conflict, as is clear. The hirer, R, would be liable for an oath that the beast died of natural causes and it was an unavoidable accident, so he also is given an oath that it was the hired beast which has died. S-T provide an obvious clarification.

A. "Lo, it is on loan to you today, if you will watch it for me tomorrow,"
B. "Lo, it is on loan to you today, if you will watch its mate for me tomorrow,"
C. "Lo, its mate is on loan to you today, if you will guard it for me tomorrow,"
D. "Lo, it is on loan to you up to noon, if you will guard it for me from noon and thereafter,"
E. "Lo, it is on loan to you up to noon, if you will guard its mate for me from noon onward,"
F. "Lo, its mate is on loan to you up to noon, if you will guard it for me from noon onward,"
G. "Lo, it is on loan to you from noon onward, if you will guard its mate for me up to noon"—
H. lo, [the parties who make such agreements] are not in the status of unpaid bailees, but are only in the status of paid bailees.
I. Whether one has borrowed it today and hired it for tomorrow,
J. or hired it for today and borrowed it for tomorrow,
K. or if there were two, one which was borrowed and one which was hired—

  L. *this one says, "I don't know"*—
  M. *and that one says, "I don't know"*—
  N. *let them divide up [the loss]* [M. 8:2S-T].
  O. [If] this party claims the borrowed one [died] and that party claims the hired [one died] (M. 8:2P-Q],
  P. "lo, this one takes an oath and does not pay compensation.
  Q. "For all those who are required by the Torah to take an oath
  R. "take an oath and do not pay compensation," the words of R. Meir.
  S. And sages say, "He who lays claim against his fellow has to bring proof [in support of his claim]."

T. 8:22 Z p. 389, ls. 12-22

What is important at T. 8:22 is the specification that M.'s prescription for the solution of the conflicting claims accords with Meir as against sages. A-H set the stage for what follows, parallel to M.'s equivalent materials.

8:3

  A. He who borrowed a cow,
I B. [the one who lent it out] sent it along with his son, slave, or messenger,
  C. or with the son, slave, or messenger of the borrower—
  D. and it died—
  E. [the borrower] is exempt.
II F. If the borrower had said to him, "Send it with my son," "... my slave," "... my messenger,"
  G. or, "... with your son," "... with your slave," "... with your messenger,"
III H. or if the lender had said to him, "Lo, I'm sending it to you with my son," "my slave," "my messenger,"
  I. or, "... with your son," "... your slave," "... your messenger,"
  J. and the borrower said, "Send it along,"
  K. and he did send it along, but it died,
  L. [the borrower] is liable.
  M. And so is the rule as to returning the beast.

M. 8:3

The contrast of B-E is with both F-G and H-I, since each is served by J-L. The point is made obvious by the contrasts. As soon as the cow enters the domain of the borrower, the borrower is responsible for unavoidable accidents.

8:4

I A. He who exchanges a cow for an ass,
  B. and [the cow] produced offspring,
  C. and so too: he who sells his girl-slave and she gave birth—
  D. this one says, "It was before I made the sale,"
  E. and that one says, "It was after I made the purchase"—

	F.	let them divide the proceeds.
II	G.	[If] he had two slaves, one big and one little,
	H.	or two fields, one big and one little—
	I.	the purchaser says, "I bought the big one,"
	J.	and the other one says, "I don't know"—
	K.	[the purchaser] has acquired the big [slave].
III	L.	The seller says, "I sold the little one,"
	M.	and the other says, "I don't know"—
	N.	[the latter] has a claim only on the little one.
IV	O.	This one says, "The big one,"
	P.	and that one says, "The little one"—
	Q.	let the seller take an oath that it was the little one which he had sold.
V	R.	This one says, "I don't know,"
	S.	and that one says, "I don't know"—
	T.	let them divide up [the difference].

M. 8:4

This construction repeats the point of M. 8:2, now in a different setting.

A. He who sells a cow to his fellow and it turns out to be pregnant and gives birth—
B. this one says, "It was while in my domain that it gave birth"
C. and the other one remains silent—
D. [the former] has acquired possession [of the calf].
E. [If] the other claims, "It was while in my domain that she gave birth,"
F. and this one remains silent—
G. [the former] has acquired possession [of the calf] [M. 8:4L-N].
H. [If] this one says, "I don't know,"
I. and that one says, "I don't know,"
J. let them divide up [the proceeds] [M. 8:4H-F].
K. [If] this one says, "It was in my domain [that it gave birth],"
L. and that one says, "It was in my domain,"
M. "lo, this one takes an oath and does not pay compensation.
N. "For all those who are required by the Torah to take an oath do take an oath and do not pay compensation," the words of R. Meir [cf. M. 8:4/O-Q].
O. R. Judah says, "Under all circumstances the offspring remains in the possession of the seller."
P. And sages say, "He who lays claim against his fellow has to bring proof in support of his claim."

T. 8:23 Z p. 389, ls. 22-26

A. And so too: He who sells a girl-slave to his fellow, and she turns out to be pregnant and gave birth—
B. this one says, "It was in my domain that she gave birth,"
C. and the other remains silent—
D. [the former] has acquired possession [of the baby].
E. [If] this one claims, "It was in my domain that she gave birth,"
F. and the other remains silent,
G. he has acquired possession [of the baby].

H. [If] this one says, "I don't know,"
I. and that one says, "I don't know,"
J. let them divide [the proceeds of the sale of the slave-child].
K. [If] this one says, "It was in my domain that she gave birth,"
L. and that one says, "It was in my domain that she gave birth,"
M. "this one takes an oath and does not pay compensation,
N. "for all those who are required by the Torah to take an oath do take an oath and do not pay compensation," the words of R. Meir.
O. And sages say, "People are not required to take an oath in cases involving slaves, documents, or real estate."

T. 8:24 Z p. 389, ls. 26-31

A. A caravan which was traveling along in the wilderness,
B. and a troop of brigands attacked it,
C. and one of them went and saved [the property]—
D. what he saved, he has saved for the common fund [of all participants].
E. But if he made a stipulation with them in a court, what he has saved he has saved for his own possession.
F. Ass-drivers who were going along the way,
G. and a band of thugs attacked them.
H. and one of them went and saved [the property]—
I. what he has saved, he has saved for the common fund [of all participants].
J. But if they had given him domain, what he has saved he has saved for his own possession.
K. Partners whom tax-farmers forgave part of their taxes—
L. what they have remitted falls to the common fund shared by both parties.
M. But if [the tax-collectors] declared, "It is for Mr. So-and-so that we have remitted the taxes,"
N. then what they have remitted falls to the advantage of [Mr. So-and-so].

T. 8:25 Z pp. 389, ls. 31-33, 390, 1-3

A. As to tax-farmers and tax-collectors, doing penitence is difficult.
B. They return [what they can to those whom they] recognize.
C. And of the rest [of the taxes they propose to hand back], they make use for the public good.

T. 8:26 Z p. 390, ls. 3-4

T. 8:23-24 go over the ground of M., once more making T.'s important point about the authority behind M.'s version of the rule. But T. 8:24 adds an important fact, which allows for the differentiation among the positions taken by sages vis-à-vis Meir. T. 8:25-26 supplement the foregoing, but the principal point, the effect of a stipulation, bears no pertinence whatsoever to M.'s case or principle.

8:5

I A. He who sells olive-trees for firewood and [before they had been chopped down], they produced fruit which yielded less than a quarter-*log* of olive-oil to a *seah*—

B. lo, this belongs to the owner of the olive-trees [not to the owner of the land, who sold only the trees, not the ground].
II C. [If] they produced a quarter-*log* of oil for a *seah*,
   D. this one says, "My olive-trees made it,"
   E. and that one says, "My ground made it"—
   F. let them divide it up.
III G. [If] the river overflowed one's olive-trees and set them down in the field of his fellow [where they bore fruit],
   H. this one says, "My olive-trees made it,"
   I. and that one says, "My ground made it"—
   J. let them divide it up.

M. 8:5

The point is made twice, C-F, G-J. The only reason A is formulated is to allow for three stichs, since its point, that a paltry sum is not subject to litigation, is irrelevant to the operative issues.

8:6

I A. He who rents a house to his fellow [without a lease]—
   B. in the rainy season, he has not got the right to evict him, from the Festival to Passover.
   C. And in the dry season, [he may evict him if he gives] thirty days' [notice].
II D. And in the case of large towns,
   E. all the same are the dry season and the rainy season,
   F. [he must give notice of] twelve months.
III G. And in the case of stores,
   H. all the same are small towns and large cities,
   I. [he must give notice of] twelve months.
   J. Rabban Simeon b. Gamaliel says, "In the case of a store rented to bakers or dyers, [he must give notice of] three years."

M. 8:6

The unspecified right of the tenant is defined. When it is difficult to find housing, B, D, or to collect debts, G, the landlord must allow for the tenant's interest.

   A. He who rents a store from his fellow [has the right to remain there without eviction] for no less than twelve months [M. 8:6G-I].
   B. Under what circumstances?
   C. When the completion of the twelve months coincides with the end of the Festival [of Tabernacles].
   D. But if the completion of the twelve months coincides with the end of Passover,
   E. they give him three festivals,
   F. so that he may collect what is owing to him.
   G. *Rabban Simeon b. Gamaliel says, "In the case of a store rented to bakers or dyers, [he must give notice of] three years* [M. 8:6J],
   H. "because their accounts receivable are considerable."

I. Now when they said, "Thirty days," or when they said, "Twelve months,"

J. it is not that the tenant may dwell there for [only] thirty days, and not that the tenant may dwell there for [only] twelve months.

K. But [the landlord] has to give him notice thirty days in advance, or give him notice twelve months in advance.

L. And just as the landlord has not got the right to evict prior to notice,

M. so the tenant has not got the right to move out prior to notice.

N. So far as a wine-press is concerned, [there may not be eviction] throughout the time of the vintage.

O. So far as an olive-press is concerned, [there may not be an eviction] throughout the season of the olive-pressing.

P. And as to a pottery, there may not be a notice of less than twelve months.

Q. Said R. Nehemiah, "Under what circumstances?

R. "In the case of those who work in black clay.

S. "But as to those who work in white clay,

T. "he may gather up his store of pottery and pull out."

T. 8:27 Z p. 390, ls. 4-13

A. He who borrows a lodging from his fellow to spend the night

B. [gets] no less than a single day.

C. [If he borrowed it] for a rest, [he gets] no less than two days.

D. [If he borrowed it] for a wedding, [he gets] no less than thirty days.

E. He who borrows a cloak from his fellow to go to a house of mourning is given the garment for sufficient time to go and come home.

F. [If he borrowed it to go] to a house of rejoicing, [he has a right to keep it] that entire day.

G. [If he borrowed it to go] to a house of mourning and to a house of rejoicing, [he gets] no less than seven days.

H. R. Simeon b. Eleazar says, "[He gets] no less than two weeks,

I. "for the household of his father-in-law comes to visit him for the second Sabbath."

J. Rabban Simeon b. Gamaliel says, "He who says to his fellow, 'Lend me your cloak, so I may go and visit my father, who is sick,'

K. "and he went and found that he had died,

L. "tears the garment [as a sign of mourning] and pays compensation for the damage which he has done.

M. "But if he borrowed it without specifying his purpose, he has not got the right to touch [the cloak] at all."

T. 8:28 Z p. 390, ls. 13-20

T. glosses and explains M., with special reference to the rights of storekeepers not to be evicted so that they may collect their accounts receivable and wind up their business. Nor may a tenant be evicted at his busy season. T. 8:28 supplements the foregoing but is essentially distinct from it.

8:7

A. He who rents out a house to his fellow—

B. he who rents it out is liable [to provide] (1) a door, (2) bolt and (3) lock,

C. and anything which is made by a craftsman.
D. But as to anything which is not made by a craftsman,
E. the one who rents the house makes it [for himself].
F. Manure [left in a rented courtyard by cattle belonging to a third party] is assigned to the householder.
G. The renter has a claim only on the refuse of an oven or stove alone.

M. 8:7

The point of A-E is in the contrast of C, D. F-G are self-explanatory.

A. He who rents a store from his fellow—
B. [the lessor] has a say concerning the place in which the oven is to be located.
C. But he does not have a say concerning the place in which the stove is to be located.
D. [If] he hired a courtyard from him,
E. [the lessor] does not have a say concerning the place in which the oven is to be located or concerning the place in which the stove is to be located.
F. But [the lessee] sets up the oven in a place which is suitable for it, and the stove in a place which is suitable to it.
G. The ashes which come out of the oven—
H. whatever he collects, lo, it belongs to him [M. 8:7G].
I. That [manure] which is in the cattle-shed and in the courtyard— lo, it belongs to the owner of the courtyard [M. 8:8F].

T. 8:29 Z p. 390, ls. 20-23

A. He who rents out a house to his fellow,
B. and the house was smitten with a *nega‘*
C. says to [the tenant], "Lo, there is what is yours before you."
D. [If the landlord] consecrated [the house to the Temple], he who dwells in it has committed sacrilege.
E. The rental fee belongs to the Temple.
F. He who hires a house from his fellow—
G. [the latter] provides for him millstones turned by an ass, but not millstones turned by hand.
H. He may not make a place to store wine in it, because it lays a burden on the walls.
I. And he may not raise chickens in it,
J. because they peck at the walls.
K. And he should not prepare in it a fixed mortar, because it shakes the walls.
L. And he may not make it into a stall for cattle or into a storagehouse for grain.

T. 8:30 Z p. 390, ls. 24-28

T. complements the discussion of the rights and responsibilities of tenant and landlord. The landlord has a right to protect the value of his property, T. 8:29. The tenant may demand certain facilities, as M. indicates. But the tenant may not permanently damage the property, T. 8:30H-L.

8:8

A. He who rents out a house to his fellow for a year—
B. [if] the year was intercalated [and received an extra month of Adar],
C. it is intercalated to the advantage of the tenant.
D. [If] he rented it to him by the month,
E. [if] the year was intercalated,
F. it is intercalated to the advantage of the landlord.
G. M'SH B: In Sepphoris a person hired a bath-house from his fellow for twelve golden *denars* per year, at the rate of one *denar* per month [and the year was intercalated].
H. The case came before Rabban Simeon b. Gamaliel and before R. Yosé.
I. They ruled, "Let them divide the month added by the intercalation of the year."

M. 8:8

The contrast of A-C, D-F is illustrated in the ambiguity of the case.

A. He who rents out a house to his fellow for twelve golden *denars* a year—
B. lo, this one pays them out throughout the year.
C. [If he rented the house] up to Adar, and the year was intercalated [receiving a second Adar]—
D. this one ways, "It was up to the first Adar,"—
E. and that one says, "It was up to the second Adar inclusive of the second Adar,"—
F. they divide the difference between them [M. 8:8G-I].
G. [If he had rented the house] to the end of Adar, to the end of the second Adar,
H. and the year was intercalated [receiving a second Adar],
I. this one says, "It was up to the end of the first Adar,"
J. and that one says, "It was up to the end of the second Adar,"
K. they divide the difference between them.

T. 8:31 Z p. 390, ls. 28-32

T. restates and illustrates M.'s point.

8:9

A. He who rents out a house to his fellow,
B. and [the house] fell down,
C. is liable to provide him with [another] house.
D. [If] it was a small house, he may not make it large.
E. [If] it was a large house, he may not make it small.
F. [If] it was a single family-dwelling, he may not make it a duplex.
G. [If] it was a duplex, he may not make it a single-family dwelling.
H. He may not provide fewer windows [than had been in the house which fell down] nor more windows,
I. except with the concurrence of both parties.

M. 8:9

The point of A-C is self-evident. D-E, F-G and H-I require adherence to the unstated conditions of the original lease.

    A. *He who rents out a house to his fellow and [the house] fell down is liable to provide him with [another] house* [M. 8:9A-C].
    B.   [If] it had had a roof of cedar, he may not roof it with sycamore,
    C.   of sycamore, he may not roof it with cedar.

T. 8:32 Z pp. 390, l. 32, 391, 1

    A.   [If] it had had windows, [the householder] has not got the right not to provide windows for him [cf. M. 8:9H].
    B.   [If] it had had no windows, the householder has the right to open windows in the new house [*vs.* M. 8:9I].
    C.   Under what circumstances?
    D.   When the tenant had rented the house from him for a very long time.
    E.   But if the tenant had rented the house from him for a brief period,
    F.   [the landlord] has the right to say to him, "There is yours right in front of you!"

T. 8:33 Z p. 391, ls. 1-4

T.'s glosses and complement to M. are clear as given.

CHAPTER NINE

BABA MESIA CHAPTER NINE

Before us is a solid construction of ten entries, all beginning *he who leases a field from his fellow*, dealing with rules governing tenant-farmers, M. 9:1-10. The first principle is that lease-agreements follow local custom, M. 9:1. The language of such agreements is subject to interpretation, M. 9:2 and M. 9:10. But there are some obligations which do not require specification. If the tenant does not work the field, he has to pay in any case, M. 9:3, because this is in the lease. If he does not weed the field or tend it properly, the lessor can force him to do so, on grounds of maintaining his property, M. 9:4. If the field does not yield a meaningful crop, the lessee nonetheless has to tend it. If there is a general crop-failure, the lessee does not have to pay, M. 9:5, 6. The share-cropper shares the crop of the field with the lessor and does not have to provide him with a better grade of grain than the field has yielded, M. 9:7. The share-cropper cannot change the terms of the agreement, e.g., planting a different crop from the one he had specified, M. 9:8. If his lease is brief, he cannot sow crops which exhaust the soil for a long time, M. 9:9. There are no surprises in this fine and formally uniform set.

M. and T. make use of three different categories of lessors. The first is one who rents the field at a fixed price for the rental, SWKR. The second is the sharecropper, who takes over the field and pays a fixed proportion of the produce, MQBL. The third is one who rents the field for a fixed fee to be paid in kind, and this without regard to the actual yield of the field, ḤWKR. The distinction among these different lessors will make little difference in the laws.

The exegesis of two verses occupies the other part of the chapter. The first, dealt with at M. 9:11-12, covers not withholding the wages of an employee but paying them as soon as they come due, in line with Deut. 24:14-15: *You shall not oppress a hired servant who is poor and needy, whether he is one of your brethren or one of the sojourners who are in your land within your towns; you shall give him his hire on the day he earns it, before the sun goes down.* Relevant also is Lev. 19:13: *The wages of a hired servant shall not remain with you all night until the morning.* The other verses, M. 9:13, cover taking a pledge in exchange for a loan, with special reference to Deut. 24:6, 10-11, and 17: *No man shall take a mill or an upper millstone in pledge, for he would be taking a life in pledge; When you make your neighbor a loan of any sort, you shall not go into his house to fetch his pledge, you shall stand outside, and the man to whom you make the loan shall bring the pledge out to you*; and, *You shall not pervert the justice due to the sojourner or to the fatherless, or take a widow's garment in pledge.* M. contributes little but a restatement of what is in Scripture.

9:1

I A. He who leases a field from his fellow [as tenant-farmer or share-cropper],
    B. in a place in which they are accustomed to cut [the crops], he must cut them.
    C. [If the custom is] to uproot [the crops], he must uproot them.
    D. [If the custom is] to plough after [reaping and so to turn the soil], he must plough.
    E. All is in accord with the prevailing custom of the province.
    F. Just as they split up the grain, so they split up the straw and stubble.
    G. Just as they split up the wine, so they split up the [dead] branches and reed props.
    H. And both [parties to the agreement] must provide reed-props.
M. 9:1

The important point is the triplet, B, C, D, leading to E. F-H say the same thing without a repetition of E.

    A. He who leases a field from his fellow,
    B. and in it was grain to harvest,
    C. grapes to cut,
    D. olives to gather—
    E. lo, they make an estimate for him [of the value of what is in the field].
    F. [If in the field was] grain already harvested, grapes already cut, olives already gathered,
    G. they do not make an estimate [of their value] for him.
    H. [If] he left the field and gave up possession of it,
    I. and there was in it grain to harvest, [or] grapes to cut, [or] olives to gather,
    J. lo, they make an estimate for him [of the value of what has not yet been gathered].
    K. How do they make an estimate for him?
    L. [If] he was a hired hand, they pay him off [in the estimated value] in proportion to his salary.
    M. [If he was] a share-cropper, they pay him off in proportion to his share.
T. 9:1 Z p. 391, ls. 5-8

If the produce is fully grown and not harvested, the sharecropper is paid for his labor in harvesting it. A-E. If there is no more work to be done, he is not paid, F-G. If he left work to do, it is deducted, H-J.

    A. He who leases a field from his fellow,
    B. in a place in which people are accustomed to put beans among the barley,
    C. may put beans among the barley.

D. [In a place in which they are accustomed to plant] twice as much barley as wheat,

E. they put in twice as much barley as wheat,

F. and anything which is [suitable to be] received for storage.

G. R. Judah says, "Lentils and fenugrec—lo, they are equivalent to wheat."

T. 9:10 Z p. 301, ls. 26-28

A. He who leases a field from his fellow—

B. in a place in which they are accustomed to hire a guard for half, a third, or a fourth [of the share],

C. one hires a guard.

D. And they do not diverge from the custom prevailing in the province.

T. 9:11 Z p. 391, ls. 28-29

T. gives examples of the principle of following the local custom.

A. He who leases a field from his fellow harvests the crop, makes it into sheaves, and winnows.

B. The measurers, the diggers, the bailiffs, and the town-clerks come and collect [their fees] from the common [stack of wheat, before the division of the crop between landlord and tenant].

C. The superintendent of the well, the bath-master, the scribe, the freight-ship captain,

D. when they come as legal agents of the householder, collect their fee on the authority of the householder.

E. When they come as legal agents of the tenant, they collect their fee on the authority of the tenant.

F. And they do not vary from the accepted practice of the province.

T. 9:14 Z p. 392, ls. 4-7

T. in a general way illustrates M.'s principle.

A. He who leases a field from his fellow to plant trees in it—

B. lo, this one [the lessor] takes upon himself responsibility for ten failures out of one hundred trees planted [and has no claim on the lessee].

C. More than this they assign to the lessee all [the loss].

T. 9:17 Z p. 392, ls. 14-15

A. He who leases a field from his fellow to plant trees in it—

B. in a place in which they are accustomed to plant four [trees], he plants four [to a grove];

C. on five, [he plants] five; six, six, seven, seven.

D. And they do not vary from the accepted practice of the province.

E. He who leases a field from his fellow to plant [trees] in it—

F. how long is he liable to tend it?

G. In the case of sprouts, until they become available for secular use [after four years].

H. Rabban Simeon b. Gamaliel says, "In the case of figs, until they hold up the plough."

T. 9:18 Z p. 392, ls. 15-18

A. He who leases a vineyard from his field is liable to tend it until he produces wine [from its grapes];
B. olives—until he makes a pile of them;
C. flax—until he makes them into stalks.
D. He then splits up the crop and pays off [the landlord].
E. This party brings his share to market in the city, and that party brings his share to market in the city.

T. 9:19 Z p. 392, ls. 18-20

A. He who leases a field of figs from his fellow—
B. in a place in which they are accustomed to pack [the figs],
C. [the tenant is expected to] pack them.
D. [If they are accustomed to turn them into] dried figs, he makes them into dried figs.
E. [If they are accustomed to make them into] pressed figs, he makes them into pressed figs.
F. And they do not vary from the accepted practice of the province.

T. 9:20 Z p. 392, ls. 20-22

A. He who leases a field of vegetables from his fellow—
B. in a place in which they are accustomed to sell the vegetables in the market, he sells them in the market.
C. [In a place in which they are accustomed to sell the vegetables] in the field, he sells them in the field.
D. And they do not vary from the accepted practice of the province.

T. 9:21 Z p. 392, ls. 23-24

A. He who sharecrops a field of olives from his fellow,
B. even if he rented it from him only for the purpose of raising olives—
C. [the lessor] may not say to him, "You have no claim on what is in it except in the case of olives alone."
D. But whatever produce the field yields—
E. lo, these are his.

T. 9:22 Z p. 392, ls. 24-26

A. He who sharecrops a field of his fellow for planting has no claim on what is produced by trees therein.
B. Under what circumstances?
C. When he had said to him, "I shall plant seeds in this field." "I shall share the crop of this field."
D. But if [the landlord] had said to him, "Share the crop of this field, plant seeds in this field, and work this field,"
E. all the produce which the field yields—
F. lo, they are his [cf. M. 9:2].

T. 9:23 Z p. 392, ls. 26-28

T. presents a set of independent exercises on the principle of following established practice. T. 9:17 makes the lessor take responsibility for a normal crop failure at the rate of ten percent. Beyond this normal loss we assign the failure to the lessee. T. 9:18ff. specify what accepted procedure is, consistently alluding to the established principle.

9:2

II A. He who leases a field from his fellow,
B. which is an irrigated field,
C. or an orchard-field—
D. [if] the water-source went dry,
E. or the trees were cut down,
F. [the tenant] may not deduct [the damages] from the rental.
G. If he had said to him, "Lease me this irrigated field," or, "... this orchard-field,"
H. and the water-source went dry,
I. or the trees were cut down,
J. [the tenant] may deduct [the damages] from the rental.

M. 9:2

The difference between A-F and G-J is that in the former case the tenant did not refer to the spring or trees as a reason to pay a larger share of the yield. At G-J he expressly refers to them and shows they are important in his calculation.

A. He who rents an irrigated field from his fellow [takes it] for no less than twelve months [for a multiple harvest].
B. [If it is] a field which relies upon rainfall,
C. he gathers his [single] harvest and goes his way.

T. 9:2 Z p. 391, ls. 9-10

A. "An irrigated field I rent from you,"
B. "An orchard-field I rent from you"—
C. [if] the water-source went dry or the trees were cut down,
D. [the landlord] is liable to supply him with another water-source or another tree.
E. [If he had said to him,] "This irrigated field I rent from you," "This orchard-field I rent from you"
F. *and the water-source went dry, or the trees were cut down,*
G. [*the tenant*] *may deduct* [*the damages*] *from the rental* [M. 9:2H-J].

T. 9:3 Z p. 391, ls. 10-13

T. 9:2 supplements M. 9:2B. T. 9:3A-D complement M. 9:2A-AF, and E-G restate M., as indicated.

A. He who leases a field from his fellow,
B. and there were trees in the field—
C. in a place in which people are accustomed to rent out trees along with a field,
D. lo, they are deemed to belong to the lessee.
E. [And in a place in which people are accustomed to rent out trees] by themselves,
F. lo, they belong to the lessor.

T. 9:4 Z p. 391, ls. 13-15

A. He who purchases a field of summer fruit from his fellow,
B, and in it there were apples and pomegranates—

C. Rabban Simeon b. Gamaliel says, "Whatever fruit does not fit into the category of summer-fruit,
D. "lo, it belongs to the seller."
E. [If] it produced one shoot,
F. if this was before the summer was over, lo, it belongs to the purchaser.
G. [If it was produced] after the summer was over, lo, it belongs to the seller.

T. 9:5 Z p. 391, ls. 15-17

A. He who leases a field of vegetables from his fellow,
B. and there was in it a row of vegetables of some other sort [than the field has as a whole],
C. lo, it belongs to the purchaser.
D. If it was in a place which was separated off by itself,
E. lo, it belongs to the seller.

T. 9:6 Z p. 391, ls. 17-19

T. 9:4 is a good complement to M. 9:2, because it gives yet another example of how we interpret the language of an agreement. Here it is the accepted practice which prevails, not what is explicitly stated. At T. 9:5 we give the purchaser what he purchased, fruit normally ripening over the summer. E-G say the same thing again. T. 9:6 repeats the same conception.

9:3

III A. He who [as a sharecropper] leases a field from his fellow and then let it lie fallow—
B. they make an estimate of how much [the field] is suitable to produce,
C. [and the tenant] pays [that amount] to [the landlord].
D. For thus does he write to him [in the writ of occupancy or lease],
E. "If I let the field lie fallow and do not work it, I shall make it up to you back at its highest rate of yield."

M. 9:3

D-E explain A-C. Since it is a proportion of the crop which is coming to the lessor, the lessee has to be assessed. Had the rental been fixed, B would have been unneeded.

A. He who leases a field from his fellow should not plough one year and sew it another year.
B. But [in a given year] he ploughs half of it and sows half of it,
C. so that [the lessor] may have a source from which to collect [an income].

T. 9:7 Z p. 391, ls. 19-20

A. He who leases a field from his fellow,
B. and he would plough one year and sow another year—
C. [the landlord] should not say to him at the time of the harvest, "Give me my rent for two years."
D. But [the lessee] pays him the rent each year by itself.

T. 9:8 Z p. 391, ls. 20-22

T. 9:7 carries forward the conception of M. 9:3. T. 9:8 likewise assigns an annual rent to the lessor.

    A. He who estimated [the value] of the standing grain of his fellow at ten *kors* of wheat,
    B. and it produced more or less [than the estimate]—
    C. they pay him what he [originally] estimated [the yield of the field to be].
    D. R. Judah says, "[If] it produced less, they pay him what he had estimated.
    E. "[If it produced] more than the estimate, one hands over to him whatever his field produces."
    F. R. Yosé says, "It varies with [the yield, up or down]."
    G. And just as purchase is effected through ready cash, a document and usucaption,
    H. so a lease is effected through a transfer of ready cash, a document, and usucaption.
                                                      T. 9:9 Z p. 391, ls. 22-26

T. supplements M. 9:3B in a general way.

    A. *He who leases a field from his fellow*
    B. [and] after he had taken possession of it, *he let it lie fallow* [M. 9:3A]—
    C. *they make an estimate of how much* [*the field*] *is suitable to produce,* [*and the tenant*] *pays* [*that amount*] *to* [*the landlord*] [M. 9:3B-C].
    D. And they do not make an estimate relative to fields which are round about it.
    E. For this one is ploughed, and that one is not ploughed,
    F. this one is fertilized, and that one is not fertilized,
    G. this one has been worked, and that one has not been worked.
    H. But *they make an estimate of how much* [*the field*] *is suitable to produce,* [*and the tenant*] *pays* [*that amount*] *to* [*the landlord*].
    I. *For thus does he write to him* [*in the lease*], "*If I let the field lie fallow and do not work it, I shall pay you back at the rate of its highest yield*" [M. 9:3D-E].
                                                     T. 9:12 Z p. 391, ls. 30-33

T. cites and glosses M., as indicated.

    A. He who leases a field from his fellow and died—
    B. [the landlord] may not say to his sons, "Give me what your father has consumed."
    C. And so they may not say to him, "Give us what father has produced."
    D. But they make an estimate [of what is owing to each party] and pay it over.
                                                    T. 9:15 Z p. 392, ls. 7-9

T. supplements M. with a case in which the lease is broken through *force majeure*. Now there is a compromise-settlement.

    A. He who sharecrops a field of grain for his fellow
    B. may not say to him, "I'm not coming until the grain is gone from it" [cf. M. 9:1].
    C. And he has not got the right to sow it two times.
                                                     T. 9:27 Z p. 393, ls. 1-2

A. He who sharecrops an orchard-field of his fellow
B. may not say to him, "I'm not coming til the fruit is gone from it" [cf. M. 9:1].
C. And he has not got the right to consume the produce two times.

T. 9:28 Z p. 393, ls. 3-4

A. He who sharecrops a field of his fellow—
B. [if] he ploughed it but did not sow it, pays him his rent.
C. And even so, they make an estimate [of what he has contributed],
D. since one who leaves it for him all ploughed is not the same as one who leaves it for him with the stubble.

T. 9:29 Z p. 383, ls. 4-5

A. He who sharecropped a field of his friend for fodder, and he took the gleanings—
B. all the produce which it yields—lo, these are his.
C. [If] he hired it for planting but took the fodder,
D. he may not say to him, "Lo, I'm going to wait until all of that species has gone from it."
E. All the produce which it yields, lo, they are his.

T. 9:30 Z p. 393, ls. 5-8

The sharecropper has to take over the field as is, even though this involves clearing out the stubble of the old crop, T. 9:27, or the produce of the past year, T. 9:28. M. 9:1 surely concurs. The sharecropper, at the other end of the lease, is allowed one sowing or one harvest. The sharecropper likewise has to pay an estimated charge for the field if he does not tend it properly, T. 9:29.

9:4-5

IV A. He who leases a field from his fellow and did not want to weed it,
B. and said [to the landlord], "What difference does it make to you? I'm going to give you the rental anyhow!"—
C. they pay no attention to [his claim].
D. For the [landlord] has the right to say to him, "Tomorrow you're going to leave this field, and it's going to give me nothing but weeds!"

M. 9:4

V A. He who leases a field from his fellow,
B. and it did not produce [a crop],
C. if there was in it [nonetheless sufficient growth] to produce a heap [of grain],
D. [the lessee] is liable to tend it.
E. Said R. Judah, "What sort of measure is 'a heap'?
F. "But: if [the field yields only] so much [grain as had been] sown [there, for reseeding next year, he is liable to tend it]."

M. 9:5

In both instances the tenant must tend the field properly. At M. 9:4, the tenant must keep the field up. At M. 9:5 he has to work even a minimal crop.

A. He who leases a field from his fellow, and it did not produce [a crop],
B. if there was in it [nonetheless, sufficient growth] to produce a heap [of grain], he is liable to tend it [M. 9:5A-D].
C. For thus he writes in the lease:
D. "I shall plough, sow, weed, cut, and make a pile [of grain] before you, and you will then come and take half of the grain and straw. And for my work and expenses I shall take half."
E. And just as in the case of a field which is planted with seed, if there was in it sufficient growth to produce a heap of grain, one is liable to tend it,
F. and if not, he is not liable to tend it,
G. so in the case of an orchard-field,
H. if there was in it sufficient produce to cover his expenses,
I. he is liable to tend it.
J. And if not, he is not liable to tend it.

T. 9:13 Z pp. 391, ls. 33-34, 392, ls. 1-4

T. cites and glosses M. at A-D, and then complements M. at E-J.

A. He who leases a field from his fellow,
B. [if] he sowed it in the first year and the seed did not sprout
C. they force him to sow it a second year.
D. [If] he sowed it a second year and the seed did not sprout,
E. they do not force him to sow it a third year.
F. He who sells garden seed to his fellow,
G. in the case of seed which cannot also be consumed,
H. [if] he sowed it, and it did not sprout,
I. he is liable to make it up.
J. In the case of seed which can also be eaten,
K. if he sowed it and it did not sprout,
L. he is not liable to make it up.
M. But if he had made a stipulation with him to begin with that it was purchased for seed, he is liable to make it up.
N. What does he have to pay over to him?
O. The cost of the seed.
P. And some say, "The entire expense of the farmer's outlay in planting the seed."

T. 9:16 Z p. 392, ls. 9-13

T. supplements M. The lessee must continue to work the field for a reasonable period.

9:6

VI A. He who leases a field from his fellow,
B. and locusts ate it up,
C. or it was blighted—
D. if it is a disaster affecting the entire province,
E. he may deduct [the damages] from his rental.
F. If it is not a disaster affecting the entire province,
G. he may not deduct it from his rental.
H. R. Judah says, "If he had leased it for a [fixed] cash payment,
I. "one way or the other, he may not deduct it from his rental."

M. 9:6

The tenant has pledged a fixed volume of grain, A-E, F-G. He may pay less in the case of a general calamity (as at M. B.Q. 10:5). But if the fee was stipulated in cash, Judah holds, it must be paid as specified.

9:7

VII A. He who leases a field from his fellow
B. [in return] for ten *kors* of wheat a year,
C. [if the field was] smitten [and produced poor-quality grain],
D. [the tenant] pays him off [from produce grown] in [the field].
E. [If] the grain which it produced was of good quality,
F. he [has] not [got the right to] say to him, "Lo, I'm going to buy you grain in the marketplace."
G. But he pays him off [with produce grown] in [the field].

M. 9:7

We continue the problem of the foregoing. The lessor gets his share of the crop, whether inferior, A-D, or superior, E-G.

9:8

VIII A. He who leases a field from his fellow
B. to sow barley in it
C. may not sow it with wheat.
D. [If he leased it to sow] wheat,
E. he may sow it with barley.
F. Rabban Simeon b. Gamaliel prohibits [doing so].
G. [If he leased it to sow] grain, he may not sow it with pulse,
H. [to sow] pulse, he may sow it with grain.
I. Rabban Simeon b. Gamaliel prohibits [doing so].

M. 9:8

The triplet—A-C, D-F, G-I—presents no problems. Wheat exhausts the soil more than barley, which explains A-C. D-E then allow the lessee at a fixed fee to plant a less damaging crop without prior consultation. Simeon b. Gamaliel differs. The dispute is repeated at G-H vs. I.

A. *He who leases a field from his fellow to sow barley in it* [M. 9:8A-B]
B. may not sow it with fenugrec.
C. [If he leased it to sow] fenugrec, he may not sow it with cucumbers.
D. [If he leased it to sow] cucumbers, he may not sow it with fenugrec, nor should he sow it with barley.
E. [If he leased it to sow] woad, he should not sow it with flax.
F. [If he leased it to sow] flax, he may not sow it with woad.
G. He who leases a field from his fellow to sow it with wheat may not sow it with barley [cf. M. 9:8F].
H. [If he leased it to sow] barley, he may not sow flax.
I. [If he leased it to sow] flax, he may not sow barley.
J. [If he leased it to sow] barley, he may not sow wheat.
K. [If he leased it to sow] wheat, he may not sow flax.
L. [If he leased it to sow] flax, he may not sow wheat.

T. 9:32 Z p. 393, ls. 10-14

A. He who leased a field from his fellow and the lessee went and leased it to someone else—
B. the [lessor-householder] has the power to say to him, "I have no business with anyone else but you."
C. [If] the householder went and leased it to someone else,
D. the lessee has the right to say to him, "I have no business with anyone else but you."
E. [If] the householder went and sold the field, they make a reckoning with the householder.
F. In proportion to how the second sharecropper derived benefit from the field, so he pays to the first.
G. [If] the householder went and declared the field consecrated,
H. it is not deemed consecrated until it reverts to his domain.
I. But whatever benefit the householder derived from it [while the sharecropper was farming it]—lo, it is deemed consecrated.
J. [If] the lessee went and consecrated it,
K. lo, this is deemed consecrated until it leaves his domain.
L. And it yields [both] a rent to the owner, and it yields a rent to the sanctuary.

T. 9:33 Z p. 393, ls. 14-20

T. 9:32 goes over the ground of M. 9:8 from Simeon b. Gamaliel's viewpoint. T. 9:33 supplements M. Neither party may diverge from the original agreement. The householder cannot consecrate what is temporarily outside of his domain. The lessee may temporarily consecrate what is in his domain, with the consequence stated by L.

9:9

IX A. He who leases a field from his fellow
B. for a period of only a few years
C. may not sow it with flax.
D. And he has no [right] to [cut] beams from a sycamore.
E. [If] he leased it from him for seven years,
F. in the first year he may sow it with flax.
G. And he has [every right] to [cut] beams from a sycamore.

M. 9:9

Flax drains the soil of its fertility for seven years, hence A-C vs. E-F. Sycamore branches are cut off for beams; they too grow back in seven years, so D vs. G.

A. *He who leases a field from his fellow for a period of only a few years has no right to cut beams from a sycamore* [M. 9:9A-B, D].
B. Therefore the rods and reeds are his.
C. [*If*] *he leased it from him for seven years* [M. 9:9E],
D. in a place in which they are accustomed to plant flax,
E. even [if he leased the field] for five years,
F. in the second year he may plant flax in it.

T. 9:31 Z p. 393, ls. 8-10

T. glosses M. as indicated.

9:10

X A. He who leases a field from his fellow
B. "for one septannate"
C. at the rate of seven hundred *zuz*—
D. the Seventh Year counts [in the] number [of years].
E. [If] he leased it from him
F. "for seven years,"
G. the Seventh Year does not count [in the] number [of years].

M. 9:10

The contrast in language, B *vs.* F, explains the difference between D and G.

A. He who sharecrops a field for his fellow,
B. and he was ploughing it one year and planting it another year,
C. and [the landlord] laid claim on him [for payment] in the year of the ploughing,
D. and said to him, "Give me my share of the crop"—
E. they pay no attention to him.
F. But he is expected to wait until the harvest time comes.

T. 9:24 Z p. 392, ls. 28-30

A. He who sharecrops a field of his fellow
B. should not plough in one year after another
C. or plant seed in it one year after another.
D. [If] he sharecropped it on his behalf for a considerable period of time,
E. he may plough it one year after another and plant seed in it one year after another [cf. M. 9:9].

T. 9:25 Z p. 392, ls. 30-32

A. He who sharecrops a field for his fellow should not plough half of it and plant half of it,
B. nor should he plant two different species in it.
C. He who sharecrops two fields ploughs one of them and plants one of them and he plants two different species.
D. He who sharecrops a town for his fellow
E. ploughs half of it and plants half of it, and plants many different species in it.

T. 9:26 Z pp. 392, ls. 32-33, 383, 1

T.'s rules on sharecropping run parallel to those on leasing and present no surprises. The lessor has to wait on the crop, T. 9:24. T. 9:25 invokes the conception of M. 9:9, that we take account of the length of the lease.

9:11

A. (1) A day-worker collects his wage any time of the night.
B. (2) And a night-worker collects his wage any time of the day.
C. (3) A worker by the hour collects his wage any time of the night or day.
D. A worker hired by the week, a worker hired by the month, a worker hired by the year, a worker hired by the septannate—

E. [if] he completed [his period of labor] by day, collects all that day.
F. [If] he completed his period of labor by night,
G. he collects his wage any time during the rest of that night and the following day.

M. 9:11

The point is that if the worker is paid at any time in the following interval (A-C), the employer does not violate the law of not postponing payment. The same thing is said by the triplet, A-C, and the pair at E, F.

A. *A worker hired by the hour* by day collects his wage any time of the day.
B. *A worker hired by the hour* by day and by night collects his wage any time of the night and all the following day [cf. M. 9:11C].
C. *A worker hired by the week, a worker hired by the month, a worker hired by the year, a worker hired by the septennate, if he completed [his period of labor] by day, collects all that day.*
D. *If he completed his period of labor by night, he collects his wage any time during the rest of that night [and during the following day]* [M. 9:11D-G].
E. And in all instances [the employer] transgresses [if he does not pay forthwith] only on account of the first night alone.

T. 10:2 Z p. 393, ls. 22-25

T. 10:2A-B expand M., as is obvious.

9:12

A. All the same are a fee to be paid to a human being, a fee to be paid for use of a beast, and a fee to be paid for the rental of utensils:
B. [each is] subject to the rule, *In his day you shall give him his fee* (Deut. 24:15).
C. And [each is] subject to the rule, *The wages of a hired worker will not abide with you all night until the morning* (Lev. 19-13).
D. Under what circumstances?
E. When [the worker] has laid claim [on his wages].
F. [If] he did not lay claim [on his wages], [the employer] does not transgress [the biblical requirement].
G. [If the employer] gave him a draft on a store-keeper or money-changer,
H. [the employer] does not transgress [the biblical requirement].
I. An employee
I J. [if he claimed his salary] within the stated time
K. takes an oath [that he has not been paid] and collects his salary.
II L. [If] the stated time has passed [and he did not collect his salary],
M. he does not take an oath and collect his salary.
III N. But if there are witnesses that he had [in fact] laid claim [for his salary],
O. lo, this one takes an oath and collects his salary.
P. A resident alien is subject to the rule, *In his day you shall give him his fee* (Deut. 24:15) [since Deut. 24:14 refers to the alien].
Q. But he is not subject to the rule, *The wages of a hired worker will not abide with you all night until morning.*

M. 9:12

The conglomerate is to be divided into the following units: A-C, joined to what follows at D; E-H; I-O, and P-Q. The point of A-C is self-evident. If, E-F, the worker does not demand his salary, the employer who has not paid it does not transgress the law. G-H permit the specified procedure.

I-M deal with a case in which the employee claims his salary during the period in which the Scripture requires the salary to be paid. The employer claims that he has already paid it. The employee takes an oath that he has not been paid and collects what is coming to him. If after the stated period, the employee claims he has not been paid, then he has no oath and effects no collection. The employer now takes the oath that he has paid. The conclusion is at N-O, and the whole clearly forms a triplet, J-K, L-M, and N-O, a rather neat reconstruction. The reason for P-Q is that the latter verse does not refer to the resident alien, while the former one does.

A. He who holds back the wages of a hired hand transgresses on account of five negative commandments:

B. because of not oppressing, because of not stealing, because of the verses which say, *The wages of a hired worker will not abide with you all night until morning* (Lev. 19:13).

C. *You shall give him hire on the day he earns it before the sun goes down, because he is poor* (Deut. 24:15).

T. 10:3 Z p. 393, ls. 25-28

A. *All the same are a fee to be paid to a human being, a fee to be paid for use of a beast, and a fee to be paid for the rental of utensils* [M. 9:12A]—

B. one transgresses on these several counts.

C. R. Yosé b. R. Judah says, "[If one has held back] the wage of a human being, he transgresses on these five counts.

D. "[But if he has held back] the fee to be paid for a beast or the fee to be paid for use of utensils, he transgresses [solely on the count of] not oppressing."

E. [He who holds back the wages due to] a resident alien transgresses on the count of not oppressing and on the count of *In his day you shall give him his fee* [cf. M. 9:12P-Q].

T. 10:4 Z p. 393, ls. 28-31

T. rephrases M. and shows Yosé b. R. Judah differs from M. 9:12A.

A. *[If the employer] gave him a draft on a store-keeper of money-changer* [M. 9:12G],

B. they are subject to transgressing on his account [the rule against keeping back wages, if they do not pay up].

C. But [the employer] does not transgress [the biblical requirement].

D. And if he stipulated with him at the outset in this regard [that the wages would be deposited as specified],

E. then even they are not subject to transgressing [the biblical law] on his account.

F. And if he told someone to pay him, this one and that one are not liable to transgressing the law on his account.

T. 10:5 Z p. 393, ls. 31-33

A. *An employee [if he claimed his salary] within the stated time takes an oath [that he has not been paid] and collects his salary.*
B. *[If] the stated time had passed and he did not collect his salary, he does not take an oath and collect his salary.*
C. *[If] there are witnesses that he had in fact laid claim for his salary, lo, this one takes an oath and collects his salary* [M. 9:12I-O].
D. Under what circumstances?
E. When the employer says to him, "I've already paid you your salary," while he claims, "You never paid me."
F. But if [the worker] says, "You hired me,"
G. and the employer says," "I never employed you,"
H. the employer says, "I promised you a *sela*,"
I. and [the worker] says, "You promised me two,"
J. then he who lays claim against his fellow bears the burden of proof.

T. 10:6 Z pp. 393, l. 33, 394, 1-4

A. He who hands over utensils to a craftsman to fix for him and the work was done,
B. even if [the item] is yet with [the craftsman] for three days,
C. does not transgress on his account [for not picking up the work and paying for it when it was done].
D. But if he gave it back to him at noon,
E. once the sun has set,
F. the householder [who has not paid for the work] has transgressed on his account.

T. 10:7 Z p. 394, ls. 4-6

T. 10:5 complements M. as indicated. T. 10:6 adds the important clarification of why the oath is taken and is effective. It is not effective in the case of a claim as to the fact or conditions of employment. T. 10:7 complements M. along the lines of M. 9:12E-F.

9:13

A. He who lends money to his fellow should exact a pledge from him only in court.
B. And [the agent of the court] should not go into his house to take his pledge,
C. as it is said, *You will stand outside* (Deut. 24:11).
D. [If the borrower] had two utensils, [the lender] takes one and leaves one.
E. And he returns [his] pillow by night, and plough by day.
F. But if [the debtor] died, [the creditor] does not return [the objects] to the estate.
G. Rabban Simeon b. Gamaliel says, "Even to [the borrower] himself he returns the object only for thirty days.
H. "After thirty days [have passed], he may sell [the objects], with the permission of the court."
I. From a widow, whether poor or rich, they do not take a pledge,
J. since it is said, *You will not take a widow's garment as a pledge* (Deut. 24:17).

K. He who seizes mill-stones transgresses a negative commandment, and is liable on the count of taking two distinct utensils,

L. since it is said, *He shall not take the mill and the upper millstone as a pledge* (Deut. 24:6).

M. And not concerning a mill and the upper millstone alone did they speak,

N. but concerning any utensil with which they prepare food,

O. as it is said, *For he seizes a man's life as a pledge* (Deut. 24:6).

M. 9:13

M.'s restatement of the several cited verses presents no problems. It is in these parts: A-C, D, E-H, I-J, K-O. Simeon b. Gamaliel's view is that the loan even when unspecified is for thirty days, and thereafter the creditor recovers his money by selling the pledge.

A. He who lends money to his fellow without specification—

B. [the loan is for] no less than thirty days.

C. But in a province in which it is customary for a loan to be for less time or more time [the local custom applies].

D. Therefore they do not vary from the accepted practice of the province.

T. 10:1 Z p. 393, ls. 21-22

T. now applies the familiar principle of M. 9:1 to the distinct context of M. 9:13 and so accounts for M. 9:13G-H.

A. He who lends money to his fellow has no right [personally] to exact a pledge from him.

B. And if he has exacted a pledge from him, he has to give it back.

C. And he thereby transgresses on every count which applies.

D. An agent of a court who comes to collect a pledge stands outside, and [the residents] bring out for him the pledge [M. 9:13B-C],

E. since it says, [*When you make your neighbor a loan of any sort, you shall not go into his house to fetch his pledge,*] *you shall stand outside and the man to whom you make the loan* [*shall bring the pledge out to you*] (Deut. 24:10-11).

T. 10:8 Z p. 394, ls. 6-9

A. [If] he exacted two utensils as pledges,

B. one which the debtor needs and one which the debtor does not need,

C. this one which he needs does he take and return to him [in the evening].

D. And that one which he does not need he takes but does not return to him [night by night].

E. But if he returns it to him [one night], he continues to return it to him.

F. But if he returns it to him, why does he take it in the first place?

G. Rabbi says, "I say, lest the Sabbatical Year come and release the debt,

H. "or, lest the debtor die and the movables remain in the possession of the heirs [who then may not pay up]."

T. 10:9 Z p. 394, ls. 9-12

T.'s complement to M. 9:13A-H stresses the role of the court in taking the pledge, T. 10:8, and then expands on the return of the pledge as needed.

   A. *"From a widow, whether poor or rich*, one has no right to take a pledge [M. 9:13I],
   B. "since it is said, *You will not take a widow's garment as a pledge* (Deut. 24:17)—
   C. "all the same are a poor one and a rich one, "the words of R. Judah.
   D. R. Simeon says, "From a poor widow one has not right to exact a pledge.
   E. "But from a rich widow one takes a pledge and does not give it back [night by night],
   F. "lest this one start coming and going to her house, and give her a bad name."

T. 10:10 Z p. 394, ls. 12-15

   A. [If] one has taken as a pledge a pair of scissors belonging to a barber,
   B. or a yoke for cows,
   C. he is liable on account of this part of it by itself and on account of that part of it by itself,
   D. since it is said, *You shall not take the mill and the upper millstone as a pledge* (Deut. 24:6).
   E. Just as a mill and an uppermillstone are distinctive in that they constitute two distinct utensils which do work as one, and one is liable on account of this part by itself and on account of that part by itself,
   F. so he who exacts as a pledge two utensils which do work as one is liable on account on this part by itself and on account of that part by itself.
   G. [If] one had five millstones, he has no right to take as a pledge even one of them.
   H. But if he performs labor with only one of them,
   I. he is liable on account of taking only that one along [as a pledge].

T. 10:11 Z p. 394, ls. 15-20

T. 10:10 treats M. 9:13I-J, which accords with Judah. T. 10:11 expands upon M. 9:13K-O.

CHAPTER TEN

BABA MESIA CHAPTER TEN

This brief and rather miscellaneous chapter begins with a triplet, M. 10:1-3, on the mutual rights and responsibilities of jointholders, or of a landlord and tenant, living in the upper and lower stories of the same house. If the house collapses, they divide up the rubble, M. 10:1. If the ceiling of the lower story collapses, the landlord, living downstairs, has to repair it; if he fails to do so, the tenant above may move downstairs, M. 10:2. If the house collapses and the owner of the lower floor declines to rebuild it, the owner of the upper story has the right to rebuild and live downstairs. M. 10:4 provides an appendix to this matter and proceeds to discuss rights and responsibilities in public domain. If a wall or tree accidentally falls into the public way, the owner is not liable for damage caused by it.

M. 10:5 goes over two distinct matters. First it treats the case in which a wall falls down into someone else's garden, the owner of which tells the owner of the wall to remove it. If the former offers the latter ownership of the rubble, the latter still can insist upon removal. But if he concurs, he then acquires ownership of the rubble, and the original owner of the wall cannot then retract. M. 10:5 further limits the right of people to do their work in the public way, e.g., storing manure or building-materials. M. 10:6 concludes with an irrelevant entry on the right of owners of terraced gardens to divide what grows on the ground between their terraces. This item may be deemed a prologue to M. B.B. 1:1, though the connection is solely in theme, not in stated principle.

10:1

I A. A house and an upper story belonging to two people which fell down—
B. the two of them divide the wood, stone, and mortar.
C. And they take account of which stones are more likely to have been broken [and assign them to the likely owner of them].
D. If one of them recognized some of the stones belonging to him,
E. he takes them,
F. but they count as part of his share in the reckoning.

M. 10:1

There is the usual triplet of rules, A-B, C, D-F. The joint owners divide the rubble in proportion to their share in the house, A-B. If, C, the lower part of the house fell from a blow, the pulverized stones are assumed to belong to the owner of the ground floor. If the upper story fell in a wind, the more pulverized stones are assigned to the upper story's owner.

    A.   *A house and an upper story belonging to two people which fell down—[the two of them divide the wood, the stone, and the mortar]* [M. 10:1A-B].
    B.   Under what circumstances?
    C.   When both [the lower story and the upper story] were equivalent [in size].
    D.   But if one of them was large and the other small,
    E.   this [owner] takes a share [in the wood, stone, and mortar] in accord with his [proportion of the whole],
    F.   and that [owner] takes a share in accord with his [proportion of the whole].
    G.   And they regard [the stones of the upper story] as though they were the more likely to have been broken [M. 10:1C].

                                                         T. 11:1 Z p. 394, ls. 21-23

T. cites and glosses M.

    A.   [If] the house and the upper story belong to both of them, and the two of them decided not to rebuild,
    B.   the owner of the lower floor takes two thirds [of the rubble],
    C.   and the owner of the upper floor takes a third.
    D.   [If] the house and the upper story belong to both of them,
    E.   and lo, the owner of the upper story wants to make for himself another story,
    F.   but the householder will not let him do so,
    G.   in a place in which it is customary to build two stories, he is allowed to build himself two stories.
    H.   In a place in which it is customary to build three, he builds three.
    I.   And they do not diverge from accepted local custom.

                                                         T. 11:2 Z p. 394, ls. 23-27

A-C augment M. 10:1, as is clear. D-I make a separate point.

10:2

II   A.   A house and an upper story belonging to two people—
      B.   [if the floor of] the upper room was broken,
      C.   and the householder does not want to repair it,
      D.   lo, the owner of the upper story goes down and lives downstairs,
      E.   until [the other] will repair the upper story for him.
      F.   R. Yosé says, "The one who lives below supplies the beams, and the one who lives above supplies the plaster."

                                                                  M. 10:2

A-D hold the owner of the lower story entirely liable to build a roof on his apartment. Yosé has them share the cost.

    A.   [*If*] *the house and upper story belongs to two people, and the plaster was damaged* (M. 10:2A-B)—
    B.   *R. Yosé says,* "Menahem, my son, says, "*The one who lives below supplies the beams,*

C. "*and the one who lives above supplies the plaster* [M. 10:2F].
D. "This is by analogy to stalls which are open onto a colonade,
E. "in which case the lower one supplies the beam, and the upper one supplies the plaster."

T. 11:3 Z p. 394, ls. 27-29

T. glosses M., giving Yosé's reasoning.

10:3

III A. A house and an upper story belonging to two people which fell down—
B. [if] the resident of the upper story told the householder [of the lower story] to rebuild,
C. but he does not want to rebuild,
D. lo, the resident of the upper story rebuilds the lower story and lives there,
E. until the other party compensates him for what he has spent.
F. R. Judah says, "Also: this one is [then] living in his fellow's [housing]. [So in the end] he will have to pay him rent.
G. "But: The resident of the upper story builds both the house and the upper room,
H. "and he puts a roof on the upper story,
I. "and he lives in the lower story,
J. "until the other party compensates him for what he has spent."

M. 10:3

The position of A-E is clear as given. Each party owns part of the house. Judah is concerned that the resident of the upper story will ultimately —when he is repaid—have to pay rent. If the man builds the upper story too, then, when he is compensated, he will have no reason to pay rent, since he could have lived above, in his own house.

10:4

A. And so too: An olive-press which is built into a rock,
B. and a garden is on top of it [on its roof, above],
C. and [the roof] was broken—
D. lo, the owner of the garden [has the right to] go down and sow the area below,
E. until the other party will rebuild vaulting for his olive-press.
F. The wall or the tree which fell down into public domain and inflicted injury—
G. [the owner] is exempt from having to pay compensation.
H. [If] they gave him time to cut down the tree or to tear down the wall,
I. and they fell down during that interval,
J. [the owner] is exempt.
K. [If they fell down] after that time, [the owner] is liable.

M. 10:4

A-E repeat the view of M. 10:3A-E. F-G exempt the owner in the case of an unavoidable accident. H-K are obvious.

    A. [If] the wall [M. 10:4F] fell down because of earthquakes or because of heavy rains,
    B. if it had been properly built,
    C. [the owner] is exempt [for damage it may do].
    D. But if not, he is liable.
    E. [*If*] *they gave him time* [*to tear down the wall*], *and it fell down during that interval,* [*the owner*] *is exempt.*
    F. [*If*] *it fell down after that time,* [*the owner*] *is liable* [M. 10:4H-K].
    G. And how long an interval [is given]?
    H. Not less than thirty days.

                                                       T. 11:7 Z p. 395, ls. 10-13

A-D complement and refine M. 10:4F-G, and E-H gloss M. as indicated.

10:5

I   A. He whose wall was near the garden of his fellow, and it fell down—
    B. and [the owner of the garden] said to him, "Clear out your stones,"
    C. but the other said to him, "They're yours!"—
    D. they pay no attention to [the latter].
    E. [But if] after the other party had accepted [the ownership of the stones] upon himself,
    F. [the original owner of the wall] said to him, "Here's what you laid out! Now I'll take mine!"
    G. they do not pay attention to [the former].
II H. He who hires a worker to work with him in chopped straw and stubble,
    I. and [the worker] said to him, "Pay me my wage,"
    J. and [the employer] said to him, "Take what you've made for your wage!"—
    K. they do not pay attention to [the employer].
    L. But [if,] after [the worker] had accepted [the proposition],
    M. [the employer] said to him, "Here's your salary, and now I'll take mine!"—
    N. they do not pay attention to [the employer].
    O. He who brings out his manure to the public domain—
    P. while one party pitches it out, the other party must be bringing it in to manure his field.
    Q. They do not soak clay in the public domain,
    R. and they do not make bricks.
    S. And they knead clay in the public way,
    T. but not bricks.
    U. He who builds in the public way—
    V. while one party brings stones, the builder must make use of them in building.
    W. And if one has inflicted injury, he must pay for the damages he has caused.

X. Rabban Simeon b. Gamaliel says, "Also: He may prepare for doing his work [on site in the public way] for thirty days [before the actual work of building]."

M. 10:5

A-G, H-N make the same obvious point twice. Once the agreement is made, it stands. O-P, Q-T, and U-W and X constitute a triplet of rules, prohibiting extended interference with public passage on the roads. If one puts manure or building materials out, O-P, U-W, he must leave them there only briefly. The doublet of Q-R, S-T, express the same principle. Simeon b. Gamaliel allows a slight interval of preparation for building.

A. A person may bring along his stones and unload them in the public way at the door of his house,
B. in order to bring them up to the top layer [of the wall].
C. But if it is to leave them there, lo, this is prohibited.
D. And if someone else came along and was injured on them,
E. lo, this one is liable.
F. [If] he had handed them over to a camel-driver,
G. the camel-driver is liable.
H. [If he had handed them over to] a stone-cutter, the stone-cutter is liable.
I. [If] the stone-cutter [had handed them over] to a porter, the porter is liable.
J. [If] he had brought them up to the top layer [of the wall] and they fell down,
K. all of them are liable.
L. [If] the camel-driver handed them over to a stone-cutter, and someone was injured by them,
M. whether by a stone or by a chip of the stone,
N. the stone-cutter is liable.
O. [If] the stone-cutter [had handed them over] to the porter, and one was injured by a chip of a stone,
P. the stone-cutter is liable.
Q. [If one was injured] by a stone,
R. the porter [is liable].
S. [If the load of stones] was set down on the top layer [of the wall],
T. or if one was testing [its foundations],
U. and it fell down,
V. the architect is liable.

T. 11:5, Z p. 395, ls. 2-8

A. A person may bring dirt and pile it up at the door of his house in the public way to knead it into mortar.
B. [But if it is] to keep it there, lo, this is prohibited.
C. And if another party came along and was injured by it,
D. lo, this person is liable.
E. And he should not knead the mortar on one side and build on the other side.
F. But he should knead on the side at which he builds.

T. 11:6 Z p. 395, ls. 8-10

A. A person may take out his manure and pile it up at the door of his house in the public way—
B. [if this is] to take it out to manure with it.
C. [But if it was] to keep it there, lo, this is prohibited.
D. If another party came along and was injured by it, [the owner] is liable.
E. R. Judah says, "At the time of fertilizing [the fields], a man may take out his manure and pile it up at the door of his house in the public way,
F. "so that it will be pulverized by the feet of man and beast,
G. "for thirty days.
H. "For it was on that very stipulation that Joshua caused the Israelites to inherit the land."

T. 11:8 Z p. 395, ls. 13-16

A-E complement M. 10:5Uff. The rest of T. 11:5 assigns liability in the case of various damages caused in the process of building or testing a wall. T. 11:6 expresses M.'s principle once again. T. 11:8 is important only because of Judah's familiar qualification.

A. This one has a courtyard nearby on this side, and that one has a courtyard nearby on that side—
B. this pile [of manure] is near his courtyard, and that pile is near his courtyard—
C. R. Judah says, "They have been given permission [to pile up their manure at the gate of the courtyard] for only thirty days.
D. "[If] one was injured during thirty days, [the owner] is exempt.
E. "[If one was injured] after the thirty days, he is liable."
F. R. Simeon says, "They have been given permission [to leave the manure where it is] for only three days.
G. "[If the manure-heap] caused damage during the three days, [the owner is exempt].
H. "[If the manure-heap caused damage] after the three days, he is liable" [cf. M. 10:5].

T. 11:9 (continued) Z p. 395, ls. 17-20

T. amplifies the issues of M. Note that the other and concluding part of this pericope serves and explicitly cites M. B.B. 1:6C and is given *ad loc.*

10:6

A. Two [terraced] gardens, one above the other—
B. and vegetables [grow] between them—
C. R. Meir says, "[They belong to the garden] on top."
D. R. Judah says, "[They belong to the garden] below."
E. Said R. Meir, "If the one on top wants to take away his dirt, there will not be any vegetables there."
F. Said R. Judah, "If the one on the bottom wants to fill up his garden with dirt, there won't be any vegetables there."
G. Said R. Meir, "Since each party can stop the other, they consider from whence the vegetables derive sustenance [which is from the dirt (E)]."

H. Said R. Simeon, "Any [vegetables] which the one on top can reach out and pick—lo, these are his.
I. "And the rest belong to the one down below."

M. 10:6

The dispute, A-D, concerns vegetables growing out of the bank between the two gardens. The positions of C, D, are supplied with an exegesis at E, F, leaving G to repeat E's point. Simeon's compromise is clear.[1]

---

[1] The rest of T. B.M. Chapter Eleven serves M. B.B. Chapter One.

INDEX TO BIBLICAL AND TALMUDIC REFERENCES

BIBLE

Deuteronomy
- 22:1ff 26
- 22:1-3 32
- 22:1-4 2
- 22:2 10, 31-33
- 22:3 26
- 23:20-21 2
- 23:24-25 3
- 23:25-26 109, 111
- 23:6 4, 132, 147-148
- 24:10-11 132, 147
- 24:10-13 4
- 24:11 146
- 24:14 144
- 24:14-15 3, 132
- 24:15 144-145
- 24:17 132, 146, 148
- 24:17-18 4
- 25:4 109, 111

Exodus
- 7:15 3
- 21:26-27 6
- 21:35 6
- 22:7 50
- 22:9 116
- 22:12-14 121
- 22:13 122
- 22:14 8, 121
- 22:20 2, 162
- 22:23-24 2
- 22:25 70, 95
- 22:25-27 3
- 23:4 38
- 23:4-5 37
- 23:5 36
- 23:5f 26

Job
- 1:15 119
- 4:6-7 62
- 27:16-17 85

Leviticus
- 19:13 3, 132, 144-145
- 19:14 95
- 19:24 115
- 19:33 2
- 25:14 2, 62
- 25:16-17 62
- 25:17 2
- 25:30 71
- 25:35-36 66-67
- 25:35-37 2
- 25:36 95
- 25:37 95

Numbers
- 5:8 9
- 5:10 9
- 32:20-22 118

Proverbs
- 30:4 62
- 19:14 62
- 24:11 96

Psalms
- 15:5 96

I Samuel
- 10:12 62

MISHNAH

Baba Batra
- 1:1 149
- 1:6 154

Baba Mesia
- 1:1 13, 15, 17-18, 24, 60, 121
- 1:1-2 10, 16
- 1:1-4 10
- 1:1-3:12 10-11

- 1:2 17-18
- 1:3 16, 19
- 1:3-4 10, 16, 18-20
- 1:4 16, 19
- 1:5 10, 16, 21
- 1:5-2:11 10
- 1:6 21-22, 25
- 1:6-8 10, 16, 21-22, 24-25
- 1:7 21-23

INDEX TO BIBLICAL AND TALMUDIC REFERENCES 157

1:8 22-24
2:1 27-29
2:1-2 10, 26-30, 32
2:1-4 30
2:2 27, 29
2:3 30-31
2:3-4 10, 26, 29-31
2:4 29-31
2:5 10, 22, 26, 29-32
2:6 10, 26, 32-33
2:7 10, 26, 28, 32-33, 50
2:8 10, 26, 34-35
2:9 10, 26, 35-37
2:10 10, 26, 36-38
2:11 10, 26, 37, 39-40
3:1 10, 41-43
3:1-12 10-11
3:2 10, 41, 43
3:3 43-44
3:3-5 11, 43-45
3:4 44-45
3:5 41, 44-45
3:6 41, 45-47
3:6-12 41
3:7 41, 46-49
3:7-8 11, 41, 46-49
3:8 41, 47
3:9 11, 41, 49, 51
3:10 11, 41, 49-50
3:11 11, 41, 50
3:12 11, 41, 50-52
4:1 11, 53-55
4:1-2 11, 53-56
4:1-12 11
4:1-5:11 11-12
4:2 11, 53-57
4:3 11, 56, 59-60
4:3-4 53
4:4 11, 56-58
4:5 11, 53, 58-59
4:6 11, 53, 59
4:7 57-58, 60
4:7-8 11, 53, 59-60
4:8 60
4:9 11, 53, 61
4:10 11, 53, 56, 61-62
4:11 58, 63-64
4:11-12 11, 53, 62-65
4:12 63, 65
5:1 11-12, 67-71, 87, 91
5:1-5 82
5:1-11 11-12
5:2 11, 66, 69-70, 72-73, 93
5:2-6 66
5:3 11, 66, 69-74
5:4 12, 66, 74-78, 80

5:4-5 82
5:5 12, 66, 78-82, 91, 93
5:6 12, 66, 82-86
5:7 12, 66, 68, 89-93
5:7-10 66-67
5:8 91-92
5:8-9 12, 67, 91-94
5:9 91-93
5:10 12, 67, 94-96
5:11 12, 67, 91, 95-96
6:1 12, 97-99, 102
6:1-2 12, 97-102
6:1-8:3 12-13
6:2 97-98, 102
6:3 12, 102-103
6:3-5 12, 97-98, 102
6:4 104
6:4-5 12, 103-105
6:5 104
6:6 12, 97, 105-107
6:6-8 12
6:7 12, 97, 107
6:7-8 97
6:8 12, 97, 107-108
7:1 12, 109-110
7:1-6 116
7:1-7 12-13, 109
7:2 109-111
7:2-3 13, 110-112
7:3 109, 111
7:4 13, 109, 112-113
7:5 13, 109, 113-114
7:6 13, 109, 114-115
7:7 13, 109, 111, 115-116
7:8 13, 109, 116-118, 120, 123
7:8-11 109
7:8-8:3 13
7:9 109, 118-119
7:9-10 118, 122
7:9-11 13, 117-120
7:10 109, 118-120
7:11 109, 118
8:1 13, 121-122
8:1-5 121
8:2 13, 121-125
8:3 13, 121, 124
8:4 121, 124-126
8:4-5 13
8:4-10:6 13-15
8:5 121, 126-127
8:6 13, 121, 127-128
8:6-7 13, 121
8:7 13, 121, 128-130
8:8 13, 121, 129-130
8:9 121, 130-131
9:1 14, 132-135, 138-139, 147

9:1-10   14, 132
9:2   14, 132, 135-137
9:3   14, 132, 137-139
9:4   14, 132, 139
9:4-5   139-140
9:5   14, 132, 139-140
9:6   14, 132, 140
9:7   14, 132, 141
9:8   14, 43, 132, 141-142
9:9   14, 132, 142-143
9:10   14, 132, 143
9:11   14, 143-144
9:11-12   132
9:12   14, 144-146
9:13   14, 132, 146-148
10:1   14, 149-150
10:1-3   149
10:1-6   14-15
10:2   14, 149-151
10:3   14, 151-152
10:4   14, 149, 151-152
10:5   14, 149, 152-154
10:6   15, 149, 154-155

Baba Qamma
  1:1   5, 7-8
  1:1-2:6   5-6
  1:1-6:6   5-8
  1:2   5
  1:3   5
  1:4   5
  2:1   5
  2:2   5
  2:3   5
  2:4   5
  2:5   5
  2:6   6
  3:1   6
  3:1-7   6
  3:2-3   6
  3:4   6
  3:5   6
  3:6   6
  3:7   6
  3:8   6
  3:8-4:4   6-7
  3:9   6
  3:10   6
  3:11   6
  4:1   6
  4:2   6
  4:3   6
  4:4   7
  4:5   7
  4:5-5:4   7
  4:6   7

4:7   7
4:8   7
4:9   7
5:1   7
5:2   7
5:2-3   7
5:4   7
5:5   7
5:5-7   7
5:6   7
5:7   7
6:1-2   7
6:1-3   7
6:3   7
6:4-6   8
6:5   8
6:6   8
7:1   8
7:1-10:10   8-10
7:2   8
7:3   8
7:4   8, 61
7:5   8
7:6   8
7:7   8
8:1   8
8:1-7   8
8:2   8
8:3   8
8:4   8
8:5   8
8:6   8
8:7   8
9:1   9
9:1-10:10   9-10
9:2   9
9:3   9
9:4   9
9:5   9, 60
9:6   9
9:7   9
9:8   9
9:9-10   9
9:11
9:12   9
10:1   9
10:2   9
10:3   9
10:4   9, 35
10:5   9
10:6   9
10:7   9
10:8   10

Qiddushin
  1:1   60

TOSEFTA

Baba Mesia

1:1	17-18
1:2	17-18
1:3	18
1:4	19
1:5	22-23
1:6	23
1:7	23
1:8	23
1:9	23
1:10	18
1:11	18
1:12	18
1:13	23-24
1:14	24
1:15	24
1:16	19
1:17	20
1:18	20
1:19	24-25
1:20	24-25
1:21	25
2:1	28
2:2	28
2:3	28
2:4	28
2:5	28
2:6	29
2:7	29
2:8	29
2:9	29
2:10	29
2:11	31
2:12	31
2:13	31
2:14	31
2:15	32, 36
2:16	33
2:17	33
2:18	36
2:19	36
2:20	33
2:21	34-35
2:22	35
2:23	37
2:24	37-38
2:25	38
2:26	38
2:27	38
2:28	38
2:29	39
2:30	39
2:31	40
2:32	40
2:33	40
3:1	42-43
3:2	43
3:3	43
3:4	44-45
3:5	45
3:6	45
3:7	46
3:8	46
3:9	46-47, 49
3:10	48-49
3:11	48-49
3:12	51
3:13	55
3:14	56
3:15	56
3:16	57
3:17	58
3:18	58
3:19	59
3:20	59
3:21	57-58
3:22	57
3:23	57-58
3:24	61
3:25	62
3:26	64
3:27	64
3:28	64-65
3:29	65
4:1	70-71
4:2	71
4:3	72
4:4	72
4:5	72-73
4:6	72-73
4:7	73
4:8	73
4:9	73
4:10	74
4:11	75, 77
4:12	75, 78
4:13	75, 78
4:14	76, 78
4:15	76
4:16	76, 78
4:17	76, 78
4:18	77-78
4:19	77
4:20	77
4:21	77
4:22	77
4:23	68-69
4:24	68-69

4:25   68-69
5:1   79
5:1-2   80
5:2   79
5:3   79-80
5:4   79-80
5:5   79
5:6   80
5:7   80-81
5:8   80
5:8-9   81
5:9   81
5:10   81
5:11   81
5:12   81
5:13   82
5:14   83-84
5:15   83
5:16   83-85
5:17   83
5:18   83-85
5:19   84
5:19-20   85
5:20   84
5:21   84-85
5:22   85
5:23   85
5:24   85-86
5:25   85-86
5:26   86
6:1   88
6:2   88-89
6:3   89-90
6:4   89-90
6:5   89-90
6:6   89
6:6-7   90
6:8   92-93
6:9   92-93
6:10   93
6:11   93-94
6:12   93
6:12-13   94
6:13   93
6:14   95
6:15   95
6:16   90
6:17   96
6:18   96
7:1   99, 101
7:2   99, 101
7:3   100, 101
7:4   100, 102
7:5   100
7:5-6   102
7:6   101

7:7   101, 103
7:8   102
7:9   102
7:10   104-105
7:11   104-105
7:11-14   105
7:12   104-105
7:13   105
7:14   105
7:15   106-107
7:16   106
7:16-17   107
7:17   106
7:18   107
7:19   107
8:1   114
8:2   114
8:3   114
8:4   114
8:5   114
8:6   114
8:7   111, 116
8:9   112
8:10   112-113
8:10-2   113
8:11   113
8:12   113
8:13   117
8:14   117
8:15   119-120
8:16   119
8:17   119
8:18   119
8:19   120
8:20   122
8:21   122
8:22   124
8:23   125
8:23-24   126
8:24   126
8:25   126
8:26   126
8:27   128
8:28   128
8:29   129
8:30   129
8:31   130
8:32   131
8:33   131
9:1   133
9:2   136
9:3   136
9:4   136-137
9:5   137
9:6   137
9:7   137-138

INDEX TO BIBLICAL AND TALMUDIC REFERENCES

9:8	137-138	9:31	142
9:9	138	9:32	141-142
9:10	134	9:33	142
9:11	134	10:1	147
9:12	138	10:2	144
9:13	140	10:3	145
9:14	134	10:4	145
9:15	138	10:5	145-146
9:16	140	10:6	146
9:17	134-135	10:7	146
9:18	135	10:8	147
9:19	135	10:9	147
9:20	135	10:10	148
9:21	135	10:11	148
9:22	135	11:1	150
9:23	135	11:2	150
9:24	143	11:3	151
9:25	143	11:5	153-154
9:26	143	11:6	153
9:27	138-139	11:7	152
9:28	139	11:8	154
9:29	139	11:9	154
9:30	139		

GENERAL INDEX

Abba Saul, bailment, liability for, 107
ʿAqiba, bailment, liability for, 41, 50-52; rightful owner, returned possession, 26, 33; usury, 96
Assessing damages, 5-6

Bailment, liability for, 10-13, 41-52, 105-108, 116-124
Ben ʿAzzai, bailment, liability for, 48

Chattels causing damage, 5-8
Crop-destroying beast, 7

Dosa, employer-employee obligations, 12-13, 97-124

Eleazar b. ʿAzariah, usury, 71
Eleazar Ḥisma, employer-employee obligations, 113
Eliezer, bailment, liability for, 108
Eliezer b. Jacob, usury, 90
Employer-employee obligations, 12-13, 97-124

Fire causing damage, 8
Fraudulent overcharges, 11, 53-65

Gamaliel, usury, 91, 94

Hillel, House of, bailment, liability for, 41, 50-52; usury, 91, 93
Joint ownership of property, mutual rights, 14-15, 149-155
Judah, bailment, liability for, 46-50, 106-107, 117, 119; employer-employee obligations, 97, 112, 117, 119; fraudulent overcharges, 56, 58, 61, 63-64; joint ownership of property, mutual rights, 151, 154; landlord and tenant, 134, 139-141; lost objects, claims for, 18, 20; real estate, responsibilities of parties, 123, 134, 138-141, 148, 151, 154; rightful owner, returned property, 27, 32, 39; usury, 68, 71, 75-76, 86-88, 90, 95; wages, time for payment, 148
Judah the Patriarch, fraudulent overcharges, 57; real estate, responsibilities of parties, 147; wages, time for payment, 147
Judah b. Petera, fraudulent overcharges, 61

Landlord and tenant, 13-14, 127-143
Lost objects, claims for, 10, 16-20

Meir, bailment, liability for, 46, 50, 117, 124; employer-employee obligations, 104, 117, 124; fraudulent overcharges, 58; joint ownership of property, mutual rights, 154; real estate, responsibilities of parties, 125-126, 154; usury, 75, 84-85; rightful owner, returned property, 21-24, 27
Misrepresenting goods or services, 11, 53-65

Neḥemiah, landlord and tenant, 128; real estate, responsibilities of parties, 128; usury, 90
Open pit, responsibility for, 7
Oxen, liability for, 6-7

Property damaged during theft, 9-10
Public domain, damages in, 6

Real estate, responsibilities of parties, 13, 124
Rightful owner, returned possessions, 10, 21-40

Shammai, House of, bailment, liability for, 41, 50-52
Simeon, fraudulent overcharges, 54-55, 57-58, 61; joint ownership of property, mutual rights, 154; real estate, responsibilities of parties, 148, 154; rightful owner, returned property, 22, 36, 38; usury, 65, 75, 78, 94, 96; wages, time for payment, 148
Simeon b. Eleazar, employer-employee obligations, 103; landlord and tenant, 128; rightful owner, returned property, 27-28; usury, 96
Simeon b. Gamaliel, bailment, liability for, 45; employer-employee obligations, 110; joint ownership of property, mutual rights, 153; landlord and tenant, 127-128, 130, 134, 137, 141-142; lost objects, claims for, 20; real estate, responsibilities of parties, 127-128, 130, 134, 137, 141-142, 146-147, 153; rightful owner, returned property, 21, 24; usury, 71, 78, 80-81, 85; wages, time for payment, 146-147
Sumkhos, employer-employee obligations, 104; usury, 80; rightful owner, returned property, 34

Ṭarfon, fraudulent overcharges, 56; returned property rightful owner, 26, 33
Theft and restitution, 8-10

Usury, 11, 66-96

Wages, time for payment, 14, 143-148

Yaduʿa the Babylonian, bailment, responsibility for, 117; employer-employee obligations, 117
Yoḥanna b. Matya, employer-employee obligations, 110
Yoḥanna b. Nuri, bailment, liability for, 46-48

Yosé, bailment, liability for, 41, 43-45, 48; joint ownership of property, mutual rights, 150-151; landlord and tenant, 130, 138; lost objects, claims for, 20; real estate, responsibilities of parties, 130, 138, 150-151; returned property, rightful owner, 39; usury, 80, 84, 86, 88-89, 95
Yosé b. R. Judah, employer-employee obligations, 111; real estate, responsibilities of parties, 145; usury, 79; wages, time for payment, 145

www.ingramcontent.com/pod-product-compliance
Lightning Source LLC
Chambersburg PA
CBHW071446150426
43191CB00008B/1257